A HISTORY OF
THE ARGENTINE REPUBLIC

JOSÉ DE SAN MARTÍN

From the engraving published by the
Archivo General de la Nación Argentina

A HISTORY OF THE
ARGENTINE REPUBLIC

BY

F. A. KIRKPATRICK, M.A.

Reader in Spanish in the University of Cambridge
Corresponding Member of the Junta de
Historia y Numismática Americana

With an Introduction by

HAROLD TEMPERLEY, Litt.D., F.B.A.

Professor of Modern History in the University of Cambridge

CAMBRIDGE
AT THE UNIVERSITY PRESS
1931

CAMBRIDGE
UNIVERSITY PRESS

University Printing House, Cambridge CB2 8BS, United Kingdom

Cambridge University Press is part of the University of Cambridge.

It furthers the University's mission by disseminating knowledge in the pursuit of
education, learning and research at the highest international levels of excellence.

www.cambridge.org
Information on this title: www.cambridge.org/9781107455610

© Cambridge University Press 1931

First published 1931
First paperback edition 2014

A catalogue record for this publication is available from the British Library

ISBN 978-1-107-45561-0 Paperback

DEDICATED

by permission

WITH GREAT RESPECT

TO

H.R.H.

THE PRINCE OF WALES

CONTENTS

ILLUSTRATIONS

PORTRAITS

José de San Martín   *frontispiece*
From the engraving published by the Archivo General
de la Nación Argentina

George Canning   *facing page* xvii
*From a miniature by E. Scotney, by kind permission of the
Earl of Harewood*

MAPS

PREFACE

THIS book is, in the first place, intended as an attempt to interpret to English readers the history of the Argentine people, and in some degree to interpret the character of that people as illustrated by their history: with a view to a better understanding, an endeavour is made throughout to present the Argentine rather than the European point of view, to examine matters from within rather than from an external standpoint. A second object is, by means of a Spanish version, to make known to Argentine readers the sympathetic interest with which the astonishing advance of their nation from its first small beginnings is viewed in England.

Englishmen have made a notable contribution to that advance. The material side of their contribution is fairly familiar: English capital invested in Argentina exceeds five hundred millions sterling; three-fourths of the railways are British; and Englishmen have played their part in the development of the land; 'Hereford', 'Shorthorn', 'Durham', 'Lincoln', 'Romney Marsh', are everyday names on the lips of Argentines. This tangible and material work of the British has had an influence which is much more than material. The services rendered to the country by the Royal Mail Steampacket Company during its century of active life are such as cannot be measured by statistics. The railways have furthered political union, peace and order; the English estanciero has brought with him a long tradition of cultured country life. Dr Alejandro Bunge, the distinguished Argentine economist, bears emphatic testimony to the influence exercised upon Argentine life by the high standard of integrity which has prevailed in commercial intercourse with the British.

But there is another and a wider aspect of intercourse with Great Britain. The connexion between the two countries has been singularly intimate ever since the British invasions of 1806–7. Those invasions, which were attacks upon Spain as the ally of Napoleon, left no resentment behind them. On the contrary, the combatants learned to know and esteem one another. Three years after the close of that episode, when an independent Government was set up in Buenos Aires, the British merchant-ships anchored in the river were dressed with flags; British war-ships, similarly flag-dressed, fired a salute, and British naval officers landed to take a prominent part in the official celebrations. One of the first acts of the new Government was to send an emissary to England, and the amity of Great Britain both during and after the struggle for emancipation was the leading factor in the relations between Argentina and Europe. The generous policy of Canning has never been forgotten in the River Plate; and the Treaty concluded with Great Britain in 1825 is a notable landmark in the early history of the Republic. Individual Englishmen also played their part as volunteers in the struggle for independence; and the many books written by English travellers in the River Plate in the early days bear witness to much intelligent intercourse.

Relations of this kind have continued and developed throughout the hundred and twenty years of Argentine independence. A visible and picturesque example of the fact is furnished by the prevalence of English games and sports. 'You English', remarked an official of the Pan-American Union to the present writer, 'have done a wonderful work in introducing football into Argentina.' And he went on to emphasise the value of the game in the formation of character and in the education of youth.

But Englishmen, in characteristic fashion, have not talked much about themselves. They have made little deliberate effort to make known to the Argentines the literature, the art and the culture of Great Britain. Whereas in the United States, in France and in Germany voluntary societies and official organisations vie with one another in cultivating social and intellectual as well as commercial relations with Argentina, any movement of the kind in England is recent and occasional. While from those countries men of science, professors, lecturers and public men make frequent visits to Argentina, it is rare, if not unknown, to hear of such visitors from Great Britain. Yet any effort of this kind is welcomed, as is shown by the numbers who visited the exhibition of modern English art which was held in Buenos Aires in 1928.

The present book is meant as a small contribution towards filling the want. Its inception and production are due to Sir Malcolm Robertson, who was the first British Ambassador to the Argentine Republic; to Dr José Evaristo Uriburu, the first Argentine Ambassador at the Court of St James'; to Mr H. Reincke and to a group of Englishmen and Argentines who desire that the two countries shall be better known to each other. The character of their intentions is best indicated by the fact that they turned to the University of Cambridge for the accomplishment of those intentions.

A compendium which attempts to comprise in one volume the history of four centuries obviously can lay little claim to extensive research, and must be chiefly based upon the work of Argentine historians. But considerable use has been made of published documents; the third chapter, dealing with a period which has received less attention from historians, is based largely on documents published by the Archivo General de la Nación Argentina and by the Instituto de Investigaciones Históricas. A special debt of gratitude is due to the Director of the latter institution, Professor Emilio Ravignani, and to his colleagues, Señor Cánter and Señor Caillet-Bois. These three historians not only placed at the writer's disposal their collection of printed and manuscript materials, but were always ready to impart, with free generosity, the results of their own researches. The late Señor Mallié, Director of the National Archives, was no less generous in his anxiety to help—particularly in the gift, on behalf of the nation, of all the printed publications of the Archives, which are now to become the property of the Cambridge University Library. The Director of the National Historical Museum, Dr Antonio Dellepiane, spared no pains in showing the collection committed to his charge, and added a gift of his own publications.

Warm thanks are due, for gifts of books and for valuable help and advice, to Dr Ramón C. Cárcano, formerly Governor of Córdoba; to Professor Ricardo Rojas, at that time Rector of the University of Buenos Aires; to Professor Luis Terán, Rector of the University of Tucumán; to Señor Ricardo Freyre, Counsellor of the same University; to Monseñor Pablo Cabrera, Director of the Historical Museum of Córdoba; to Dr Mariano Vedia y Mitre and to Dr Correa Luna. Cordial acknowledgment must be made to Dr Ricardo Levene, President of the Junta de Historia y Numismática, and to his colleagues for their sympathy and encouragement, and also to the Jockey Club of Buenos Aires for permitting the use of their fine Library.

Sir Herbert Gibson was unstinted in placing at the writer's disposal his exceptional knowledge of Argentine and Anglo-

Argentine conditions, in searching out information and facilitating enquiries; he was kind enough to read the proofs of the earlier chapters and made many valuable suggestions. In the passages relating to British and European diplomacy Professor Temperley has freely given help and advice.

Finally the writer is much indebted to the hospitality of the State Railways and of the various British Railway Companies. The managers and officials of those railways, in various parts of the Republic, spared no pains in smoothing travel and in aiding enquiry. The Mihanovich Navigation Company, whose steam-boats ply upon the great rivers, were equally generous; as also were the Forestal and the Liebig Companies.

It is impossible to acknowledge individually and by name all the help and encouragement which were accorded to the writer in the Argentine Republic, particularly in the University towns of Buenos Aires, Córdoba and Tucumán. The conclusion can only be a comprehensive word of gratitude and of pleasant memories.

F. A. K.

20th November 1930

GEORGE CANNING

From a miniature by E. Scotney, by kind permission of
The Earl of Harewood

INTRODUCTION

OVER twenty years ago I was talking at Cambridge over Argentine affairs with one who, even then, was a leader of thought and literature of Latin America, and has since attained great eminence in both. Dr Ricardo Rojas talked with me as to the best method of getting Englishmen and Argentines to understand one another. We could think of no better one than of setting the historians and writers of both countries to study one another and thus sustain and promote cultural intercourse. In this connexion I called the attention of Dr Rojas to two chapters in volume x of *The Cambridge Modern History* which dealt with the wars of independence in Spanish America. We spent the best hours of one Sunday reading them together. At the end both agreed that the author ought to write the *History of the Argentine Republic*. After more than twenty years, the writer, Mr F. A. Kirkpatrick, has at last realised this dream. To write such a book it was necessary to have an intimate acquaintance with the Spanish language and literature, an eye for nature trained by travel in South America, and a comprehensive knowledge of the many specialised works of Argentine historical scholarship. The book bears traces of all these, and is one which should appeal to Argentines and Englishmen alike.

If there is one part of the story on which the author touches a little lightly, it is that of the circumstances attending upon England's recognition of the Argentine Republic. This is quite right, for the aim of the author is to display the Argentine Republic from within rather than from without. But it will perhaps justify me in devoting some attention to that decision, which is inseparably associated with the name of George Canning. The reputation of that statesman is nowhere higher than in Latin America, and the reason is that he was the political godfather of that continent and introduced it into the 'Comity of Nations'.

The recognition of young States was then comparatively a novelty, so that Canning was laying down principles not only for the moment, but for posterity. It is no small tribute to his genius that the doctrine of recognition has changed so little since his day. The view then current on the Continent of Europe, at a time when despots still governed Russia, Austria, Spain and Prussia, was that no recognition should ever be accorded to a revolting State if it called itself a republic. The view adopted by Canning was that it was political stability, not one or other political form, which mattered. All his views had the same massive simplicity. If a district like the Argentine Republic had in fact maintained its independence of Spain for some years, it was absurd for nations to go on saying that it had not. Portugal had indeed recognised the independence of the Argentine Republic in 1821, and the United States in 1822, but—strange as it may seem to-day—the United States was not then very important in the eyes of Europe. Also the United States was a republic, and had an interest in recognising other republics, which England had not. The decision as to the admission of a State into the 'Comity of Nations' has in fact always been determined by the decision of a Power of first importance. Consequently the United States' recognition had produced little effect in Europe. Far more excitement had been shown at some tentative steps taken by Lord Castlereagh in 1822. He had relaxed the Navigation Acts, and had allowed ships bearing the Argentine flag to enter British ports. That was a recognition of a commercial flag, but the establishment of consuls (the final stage in commercial recognition) was still not granted. But Castlereagh, just before he took his own life in August 1822, had stated that recognition of South American States in the future was a matter to be decided by 'time and circumstance' and that it was no longer dependent upon principle. This was the position when Canning became Foreign Secretary.

On November 8, 1822, Canning wrote to Wellington at Verona: 'Every day convinces me more and more that in the present state of the (Spanish) Peninsula and in the present state of the country, the American questions are out of all proportion more important to us than the European, and that, if we do not seize them and turn them to our advantage, we shall rue the loss of an opportunity, never, never to be recovered.'

In April 1823 a French army invaded Spain. After occupying Madrid, the French reached the last Spanish stronghold at Cadiz, and this news brought Canning on the scene. On October 10, 1823 (the day that he heard that the French had entered Cadiz), he accredited consuls to the chief towns of Spanish America, thus affording them full commercial recognition. It is an interesting fact that he immediately despatched Commissions of Inquiry to Colombia and Mexico, to report on the question of how far they were politically stable enough to justify diplomatic recognition. He took no such step towards the Government of Buenos Aires, for he had long known that she had in fact already won her independence of Spain and was politically stable enough for his purposes.

If the Pyrenees had been passed by the French, they would not be suffered to cross the Atlantic. If Old Spain was to be occupied by Frenchmen, Canning would not allow them in the New World. In October 1823 his interview with Polignac (as mentioned on p. 135) caused France to renounce any project of intervention by force in Spanish America. But attempts were made early in 1824 to call a European Congress to discuss Spain's relation to her Colonies. Canning declined to join this Conference, intimating that the question of the independence of the Spanish Colonies was decided and, if Europe could settle such things independently of England on the land, she would not do so across the sea. To make quite clear his resolve to resist by force European aggression in Spanish America, he published in March 1824 the Memorandum of his conference with Polignac.

This, of course, fitted in with 'the Monroe Doctrine'—wherein on December 2, 1823, President Monroe declared the United States could not view with indifference the attempt of a European Power (other than Spain) to intervene in South America by force. The publication of Polignac's Memorandum in March 1824 made clear that England would resist any such attempts by force, but discussions during 1824–5 in Washington revealed that the United States would not commit itself to so strong a declaration but would judge of each such attempt as occasion arose. Whether there was, in fact, any real danger from France or Russia is questionable to-day, though a certain ultra-loyalist party in France was undoubtedly anxious to intervene. But the reality of the danger was believed in at the time, and Latin America was grateful to Canning for his bold stand.

Canning's Consul-General, Woodbine Parish, started for Buenos Aires in January 1824. He carried with him not only commercial instructions but a copy of the Polignac Memorandum for publication in Buenos Aires, and three gold snuff-boxes bearing the portrait of King George IV. He subsequently sent for more snuff-boxes, and for a number of framed portraits of His

Majesty, which were duly distributed. These matters are not trivial, for they show that Canning was determined to make clear to the South American States his power to defend them at need, and at the same time to familiarise them with the idea of relations with a monarchical State. In March 1824, as already mentioned, the Polignac Memorandum was broadcast to the world. In April Canning tried a last negotiation with Spain to get her to recognise the independence of her colonies. On its failure he determined to recognise them himself. One of them—the States of the Río de la Plata—stood first both in importance and stability. Even his colleagues who were most opposed to recognition of republics admitted that. Accordingly on July 23, 1824, the British Cabinet decided to negotiate a commercial treaty with Buenos Aires and forwarded instructions and a full-power for the purpose to Parish, the Consul-General. The negotiation of a successful treaty was a foregone conclusion. Woodbine Parish signed the treaty at Buenos Aires on February 2, 1825, and received the ratification of the Government of the States of the Río de la Plata on the 19th. In doing so, he referred publicly to 'this event, which places you (the United States of the Río de la Plata) in the rank of the nations recognised in the World'. Canning, in a rather conservative vein, preferred to make diplomatic recognition depend upon ratification of the Treaty by England.[1] Even that did not take long. Early in May all sorts of rumours about South America began to fill the air in England. The text of the Argentine Treaty got out to the British public, through 'an extraordinary channel', on May 5. The formalities of exchange

---

[1] This was rather a pedantic view. In fact, recognition was accorded by the mere fact of the signature of a Treaty between a representative of England and one of the States of the Río de la Plata.

of ratifications were completed in London on May 12. On May 16 Canning laid the Argentine Treaty, in the form of a Parliamentary Paper, on the table of the House of Commons, when, we are told, it was received 'with loud applause'. The only comment was, however, that of Sir Robert Wilson, a veteran champion of liberty, who said that a free air was at last breathed in Latin America.[1]

It has been worth while to recount these stages in some detail, because the question of the recognition of other South American States took a stormier course. In the middle of December 1824 the Prime Minister (Lord Liverpool) and Canning both sent in their resignations to the King in order to enforce recognition of the independence of Mexico and Colombia. This step caused their colleagues (including the Chancellor Eldon and the Duke of Wellington) to give way, and the victory was won. King George IV still resisted. He argued that the decision over Buenos Aires had been commercial, not diplomatic, and that in any case it did not carry the other States. But events had gone too far, and on the last day of December 1824 Canning issued a circular to the different European Governments, and a formal despatch to Spain, intimating that commercial treaties would be negotiated with Colombia and Mexico which, when severally ratified, would confer diplomatic recognition on those two countries. Buenos Aires was also mentioned in this despatch as about to receive recognition. It was of course to take months before any treaties could be negotiated with Colombia and Mexico.

On February 2, far away in Buenos Aires, the Treaty securing the recognition of the Argentine Republic, and indeed that of

---

[1] These details are from the *Star*, the only newspaper which bears traces of inspiration from Canning's entourage.

the other States, too, had already been signed. On that very day in England, the intention of recognising the New World was proclaimed in the King's Speech at the opening of Parliament. The King had reluctantly accepted the decision and pleaded the gout as a reason for not delivering his own speech in person. Ironically enough it was delivered by Eldon—the Chancellor— the greatest opponent of Spanish-American republics. Canning, who had 'called the New World into existence', stood humbly among the crowd of other listening commoners. The storm of indignation this recognition provoked from the Spanish King, from the French Government, from the Emperors of Russia and Austria, was a measure of the services rendered by England to the New World. It will be seen, however, that Buenos Aires enjoyed the peculiar advantage of being recognised without hesitation or dispute. It was the first State to whom overtures involving recognition were made, and its actual recognition preceded that of Colombia by six months and that of Mexico by two years.

The only question that arose was not over the emancipation of Buenos Aires from Spain, nor was it over the question of her political stability as such. Canning had taken that for granted, but in his instructions to Parish of August 23, 1824, he still asked for information 'as to the power of the Government of Buenos Ayres to bind by its Stipulations with a Foreign State, all the Members of the Confederacy constituting the United States of Río de la Plata'. He drew the 'full power' and instructions on the assumption that such a federative union existed and informed Parish that he was not to negotiate the treaty save on that assumption. It was at least partly due to these instructions that the several States of the Río de la Plata moved towards union and that the law of the Congress (January 24, 1825) placed power in the hands of the Government of Buenos Aires. So here again Canning proved a benefactor.[1] A trace of this uncertainty is however preserved in the letter of King George of January 28, 1826 (the first Royal Letter addressed to any Spanish-American State). He addresses the United Provinces of the Río de la Plata directly as 'Our Good Friends'.[2] The King saluted 'the States' as individuals.

It was perhaps difficult to discover the formal sovereign. Such anomalies existed both in the United Provinces of the Netherlands and the Swiss Confederation, who were formerly addressed in the same way.

Canning selected a Minister of the rank of peer (Lord Ponsonby) as a special compliment to Buenos Aires and sent him out by instruction of February 28, 1826. He was to visit Brazil (which had an Emperor) on the way, but was specially instructed that England had no 'partiality for existing (i.e. monarchical) institutions'.

'We stand not upon a preference for this or that form of government with which (whatever may be our speculative opinions) we have practically no concern, but . . . upon the broad general principle of non-interference with the internal institutions of other States.'[2]

It is worth while examining what the doctrine of 'non-intervention' meant. For, at the time that England recognised the

---

[1] References to the records are unnecessary, as most of these details are in F. L. Paxson, *The Independence of the South American Republics*, Philadelphia (1916), pp. 232–41.

[2] Public Record Office, F.O. 118/6: instructions to Lord Ponsonby, encl. to Sir C. Stuart, No. 41 of Dec. 28, 1825.

States of Buenos Aires, of Colombia and of Mexico, they were weak enough. They might, very probably, have been influenced or induced to depend on a strong and wealthy State, like the British Empire. They could have, perhaps, been put into tutelage by a system of loans, which would have permitted interference with their internal institutions, or promoted a perpetual economic penetration. To all these methods Canning was in principle and in practice opposed. He wished the States of the Río de la Plata to be free, happy and rich, and he thought that the best way to enable them to become all three was to leave them alone.

These principles triumphed and it is significant that, since Canning's recognition, the most serious trouble that ever arose between England and the Argentine was over the Falkland Isles, that being a dispute inherited from old Spanish days. The principles of Canning were so exactly suited to an intercourse between a strong, mature state and a rising, infant one, just because they rested on a solid basis of common interest. Canning had renounced political influence to promote commercial intercourse, and the bargain held. Relations could be safe and amity could be lasting since no attempt at interference was made by the stronger Power, and because there was no threat of external force. These principles have remained and the best proof of it lies in the fact that even Lord John Russell, one of the most aggressive of our Foreign Secretaries, maintained them. When the question of the revolt of Buenos Aires came up in 1861, Russell refused to receive one of the representatives of the rebels, and put his views in a minute thus:

'H[is] M[ajesty's] G[overnment] do not at all wish to interfere in B[uenos] A[ires]. We may in concert with France offer our good offices or, if necessary, mediation but we do not mean to use force to support our friendly counsels.'[1]

This is exactly what Canning wrote to Ponsonby in offering to mediate in the war between Brazil and the Argentine Republic.

It will be seen, therefore, that Buenos Aires, or the Argentine Republic, was of all South American States not only recognised first in point of time, but that she was placed first in point of importance, by Canning. He believed in her future development, in her ultimate political stability, in her immense potential resources. The admiration felt by Latin-Americans for Canning was heartily returned by him. Woodbine Parish, the famous Consul-General at Buenos Aires, was thrown into great agitation in August 1827; for he feared that Canning's ministry would not last. 'And no one but him (*sic*) will take the same interest in South American affairs'.[2] It is this fact which accounts for Canning's renown in a continent which he claimed to have 'called into existence'. He was not only the most American, he was the most Latin-American, among British statesmen.

It is not fitting to suggest that only an Englishman should be celebrated in this Introduction. The careers of two contemporary Argentine figures, of San Martín and Rivadavia, are in themselves full of interest and importance and are interestingly displayed in this volume. Of Rivadavia there will always be critics in the Argentine itself, even though all admit his ability. Because he is unfamiliar in type he is for that reason the more worthy to be studied by an Englishman. With San Martín the case is different. His character—slow, persistent, resolute, austere,

---

[1] Brit. Museum Add. MSS. 38,987, f. 179: Lord J. Russell, Sept. 7, 1861
[2] Public Record Office, F.O. 95/591: Parish to Stowell, Aug. 25, 1827.

disinterested—is one which Englishmen readily understand and with which they can sympathise. It is by comparison or contrast of such types that nations understand one another. In fact it might be said that no more valuable service could be rendered by this book than to make Argentines understand Canning and Englishmen understand San Martín. It is by such supreme types that nations are properly represented, and it is from the study of such men that nations will learn to understand one another.

HAROLD TEMPERLEY

25th November 1930

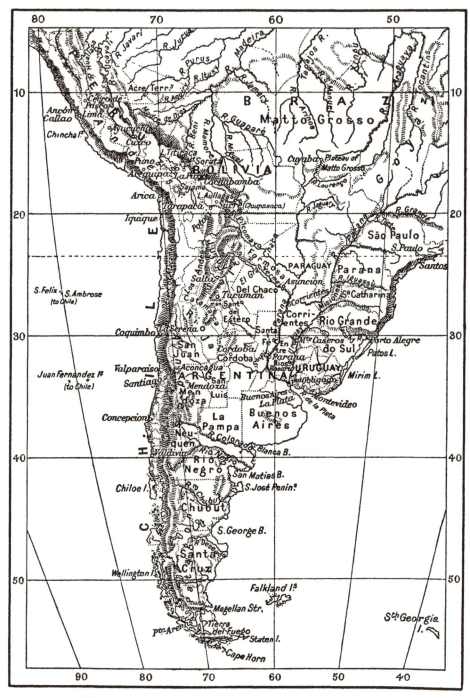

ARGENTINA AND ADJOINING COUNTRIES

CHAPTER I

THE LAND OF ARGENTINA

OF the three continental land-masses of the Southern Hemisphere, one only, South America, thrusts itself far southwards into the temperate zone. Much the greater part of this southern temperate region is occupied by the Argentine Republic or Argentine Confederation. It is a region marked out by nature to be the seat of a great civilisation mainly European in character, where the immigrant from southern Europe finds a climate resembling his own, and can follow his accustomed ways of life. Argentina, together with the small republics of Uruguay and Paraguay, forms the 'sub-continent' commonly known as the River Plate, from the great river system—one of the greatest in the world—which gives navigable access to the northern provinces and, beyond them, to Paraguay and western Brazil.

The Argentine Republic extends from latitude 22° S. to latitude 55°, from the tropical forests of the Chaco to the icy cliffs of Tierra del Fuego battered by Antarctic storms—a total length of above 2300 miles. The greatest width, in latitude 37°, is about 750 miles. The country tapers thence southwards to Tierra del Fuego and Cape Horn. The area exceeds 1,200,000 square miles, ten times that of the British Isles.

So vast a region, with so great a range of latitude and also of altitude—from the height of Mount Aconcagua, 23,000 feet above sea level, to the flat Atlantic shore—comprises a great variety of physical features, soil and products. There are lofty peaks, immense treeless plains, extensive forests, rich sub-tropical soil, salt deserts, swamps, rivers pouring voluminous waters into the ocean, and others which lose themselves in the soil. But the country, viewed as a whole, is divided with a certain vast simplicity into mountain, forest and plain. In order to define the subject and give clearness to the narrative contained in the following chapters, it seems well here to anticipate, to begin by pointing to the end, and to give, in broad outline, some account of present conditions.

The word 'Argentina' at once calls up the image of the vast flat expanse of the Pampa; and rightly so, for although the country possesses much else besides the Pampa, it is this immense plain which has made modern Argentina and has given to the country its wealth, its chief industries and its prevailing character; the plain contains most of the great cities and the bulk of the inhabitants: it has shaped the habits and the outlook of the people.

These boundless level spaces, once covered with coarse grass, but now waving with corn in summer or green with alfalfa, have the monotony but also something of the majesty of the sea. A man may ride day after day and always alight on a spot hardly to be distinguished from his starting-point. To the eye the land is dead level, but in fact it slopes imperceptibly downwards from the Andes to the Atlantic. The plains extend approximately from the River Salado in the north to the Colorado in the south, only broken by ranges of hills in the south of the province of Buenos Aires: westward they extend to the mountains of Córdoba, which run north and south half-way across the continent: farther south, the Pampa is yet wider, reaching to the spurs of the Andes. It is stoneless and, by nature, treeless,[1] although now dotted, as with islands, by the plantations surrounding the *estancia*

---

1 Near Córdoba the plain is no longer treeless, but covered in part by low scrubby woods.

houses or homesteads. The plough could be driven for hundreds of miles without meeting a pebble, a hillock or a bush.

Once the bed of an inland sea, the Pampa is covered for the most part with deep rich soil, through which the roots of wheat, maize, oats, linseed and alfalfa penetrate to the moisture beneath. In the west, where the soil is dry and rain is scanty, the need is in part supplied by artesian wells and by stored-up water, notably the great reservoir in the Córdoba hills which irrigates an ex-tensive district. Moreover, dry tracts, once sterile, have become rich cattle lands through the almost magical effects of sowing alfalfa (lucerne). This plant sends its taproot down to astonishing depths to find water: and once the root reaches water, the plant flourishes and turns a desert into a rich expanse of green. A great engineering work has turned the region of the Río Negro, once a desert, into a garden of fruit, vegetables and corn by confining the surplus water of the river in a great natural hollow so as to control its flow and make it available for irrigation.

The plain extends northwards beyond the River Salado, along the valley of the Paraná and its tributary the Paraguay: but here the plain changes its character: it is diversified by forests, inter-spersed with open spaces and by many swamps and watercourses, and so stretches northwards into the Chaco, a region of thick forests, intervening savannas, swamps and sluggish rivers, where there still lurk some scanty tribes of savage Indians. But two railways now traverse the Chaco, and there are 'tame In-dians' working on the cattle farms, and in factories which extract tannin from the hard quebracho timber. North-eastwards the plain stretches into the undulating and wooded country of Misiones.

To the north-west the Pampa merges into the hilly, wooded sub-tropical region of Tucumán, Salta and Jujuy. About

Tucumán, to the east of the lofty mountain range of Aconquija, is a sugar-growing region, favoured by mists from the mountains, summer rains and a rainless winter for harvest.

To the south of the Pampa, beyond the Río Negro, stretch the bleak wind-swept terraces of Patagonia, seamed by ravines and covered with snow in winter. This country used to be called 'The Great Shingle Desert'. Darwin thought it absolutely barren. It is now a vast sheep-farm which extends through the dry region to the more grassy lands of the far south and of Tierra del Fuego. It was found that sheep could subsist on the scanty tufts of herbage even through the snows of winter: and although it takes several acres to support one sheep, the flocks amount to many millions.

The great mountain chain of the Andes stretches between Argentina and Chile for a distance of 2000 miles. In so great a range of climate there is naturally much diversity in the mountain system. In the north is the lofty barren plateau of Atacama. Southwards thence through the north-western provinces the Andine region is treeless and almost rainless, but contains oases irrigated by streams descending from the snowy heights—notably the wine-growing district of Mendoza, intersected by water cuts bordered by poplar trees. Farther south, from about latitude 36°, there is a beautiful Alpine country where the Andine peaks, here less towering in height, rise above mountain lakes surrounded by verdure.

The outstanding fact of modern Argentina is the great economic expansion, the creation of new wealth, during the past fifty years. The extension of steam navigation, the building of railways, machinery applied to agriculture, the influx of immigrants from southern Europe and of capital from northern Europe, the growing demand in Europe for foodstuffs and raw materials —all these things favoured a rapid and very remarkable economic development which accompanied and aided a consolidation of the social and political fabric. This notable movement has been described in many modern books, and in consular reports which read like romances. The Pampa has become one of the great granaries of the world; and Buenos Aires, the greatest city of the Southern Hemisphere and, after Paris, the largest Latin city in the world, is the centre of a railway system 23,000 miles long, which gathers into other nuclei in the great ports of Rosario and Bahia Blanca. It is not the purpose of this book to dwell particularly on these matters, which can be studied elsewhere. But this brief preliminary survey may help the reader. Moreover this economic movement fills a large part in the political and social growth of the Argentine people.

The Argentine Republic is a confederation of fourteen autonomous provinces, every province having its own Governor and Legislature. There are besides, in the outlying and little developed parts of the Republic, ten territories (*gobernaciones*), six in the south and four in the north, which are administered directly by the federal authorities. These territories comprise three-sevenths of the area of the Republic, but contain only a fraction of the inhabitants. The capital, Buenos Aires, is a federal district belonging to the nation. Here resides the Federal or National Government, consisting of the President of the Republic, a Cabinet of eight ministers and a Congress of two Houses; also the supreme federal tribunal of the nation.

It is the purpose of the following pages to trace the origin and growth of that nation, which now numbers above ten million inhabitants.

CHAPTER II

THE CONQUEST

WITHIN twenty-five years of Columbus' westward adventure, Spanish explorers coasted all the Caribbean shores, crossed the Isthmus of Panamá to the 'South Sea' and made their way by the 'North Sea' along the Atlantic coast of South America beyond the Tropic of Capricorn. In 1516 Solís, Piloto Mayor of Spain, sailed up the great estuary which he named *El Mar Dulce,* 'The Freshwater Sea', landed on its north-eastern shore and was killed by cannibal 'Indians' who had beckoned him ashore. Three years later Magellan, seeking a passage to the South Sea and the Spice Islands, looked into the 'Río de Solís', found that this was not his way and turned southwards again. But in 1526 Sebastian Cabot or Gaboto, who had left England to take service in Spain, undertook to explore once again the westward route to the Far East, disobeyed his instructions in hopes of richer discoveries, and spent three years in exploring the immense waterways which led to the central recesses of an unknown continent and might perhaps lead, so he hoped, to the dominions of 'The White King', of whose opulent magnificence he heard tales from the Indians. Having obtained from the natives some silver ornaments, he gave to the Río de Solís its high-sounding name *El Río de la Plata,* 'The River of the Silver', a delusive title, for its shores are destitute of metals, although rich to-day in wealth of a less precarious kind. The silver had in fact come from the country of 'The White King', the Inca monarch of Peru. Gaboto carried home to Spain these first tokens of Peruvian treasure. The ruins of his fort, destroyed by Indians and its garrison slain, remained a landmark, known as 'Gaboto's Tower', for later explorers, thirty miles north of the site of the present great city of Rosario.

The reports of Gaboto, the sight of the Peruvian silver, the tale of Pizarro's recent discoveries, the hope of crossing the continent to those rich western regions, and, in addition, the rivalry of the Portuguese, who were pushing southwards from Brazil, led to the greatest Spanish expedition yet dispatched from Spain to the Indies. Pedro de Mendoza, a wealthy soldier-courtier, received in 1535 a commission to found three cities as Adelantado or Frontier Commander, to cross the continent and to occupy 600 miles of the Pacific coast. Mendoza sailed with eleven ships and probably about 1000 men,[1] also some horses and mares. He led his fleet to the low south-western shore of the estuary, the margin of the Pampa or vast South American prairie, and there he traced out a city of mud huts thatched with reeds, for the neigh-bourhood yields neither stone nor timber. The only inhabitants of the vast plain were groups or tribes of nomadic barbarians sheltering under rude booths of skins, and owning no domestic animals, for neither cattle, horses, nor sheep are indigenous to the country. The neighbouring Querandí Indians at first brought game and fish. When they wearied of feeding these numerous guests, forcible demands provoked a disastrous fight in which Mendoza's brother was killed by the *boleadora,* the

---

1 Schmidel's estimate of 2500 has been generally accepted. But M. Paul Groussac, whose recent death is a loss to Argentine letters, has proved that this is a wild guess and puts the number at about 800. Schmidel, one of the Germans who accompanied Mendoza, wrote long after the event. He is an excellent authority for the events which he witnessed. But his chronology is confused and inaccurate and his statistics must be rejected. Mendoza undertook to find 1000 men and certainly had no more.

typical weapon of the Pampa. The Querandís, summoning more distant tribes, attacked in multitudes. The huts and some of the ships were burnt by fiery missiles. Within the earthen city wall were famine, pestilence and cannibal horrors. Expeditions sailing in search of food brought momentary relief, but some of the searchers themselves died of hunger. Mendoza led part of his men to a site higher up the river, but finally sailed homewards, to die on the voyage, leaving the most devoted of his followers, Juan de Ayolas, as Lieutenant-Governor, with orders to pursue the quest for the rich regions of the west.

Ayolas sailed northwards against the current to latitude 25° S. Here on the left bank of the River Paraguay he found Guaraní Indians, submissive or friendly or easily subdued, people living in villages and raising crops of maize. On a bluff overlooking a bay sheltered from the strong current was set up a stockaded fort, 'Santa María de Asunción'. Leaving a small garrison, Ayolas sailed north far into the tropics, plunged westward into the forest and there perished with all his company.

Ayolas had named as his deputy Martínez Irala, a typical soldier-adventurer, ambitious, self-indulgent and unscrupulous, but a capable and inspiring leader. Irala is the patriarch of the River Plate: he was now elected Governor by virtue of a royal edict which empowered the settlers to fill any vacancy, pending the royal decision; and he contrived to retain this command, with a short and stormy interval and some sanguinary faction fights, for twenty years, until his death in 1557.

In 1541 the remnant of the settlers at Buenos Aires were brought to Asunción, which thus became a 'city' with its Town Council (Cabildo) and two annually elected magistrates (alcaldes), a city which for eighty years was the capital of the River Plate.

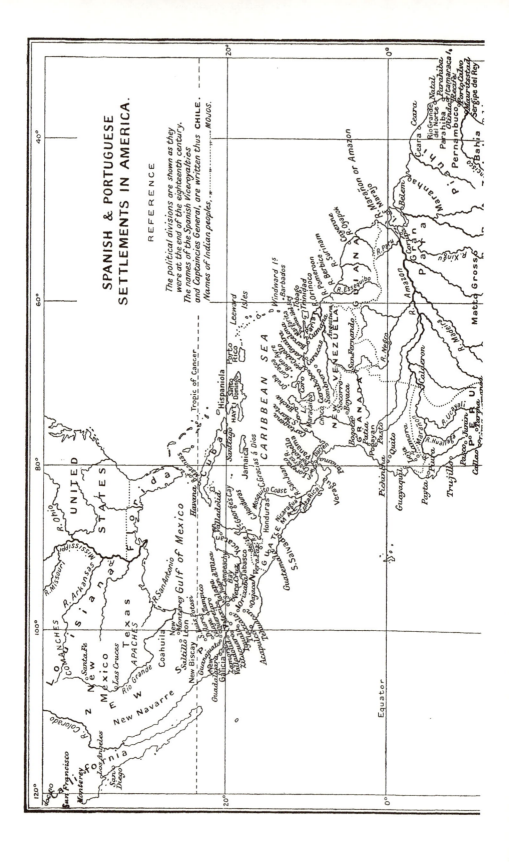

SPANISH & PORTUGUESE
SETTLEMENTS IN AMERICA.

REFERENCE

The political divisions are shown as they
were at the end of the eighteenth century.
The names of the Spanish Viceroyalties
and Captaincies General, are written thus CHILE.
Names of Indian peoples, - - - - - - - - MOJOS.

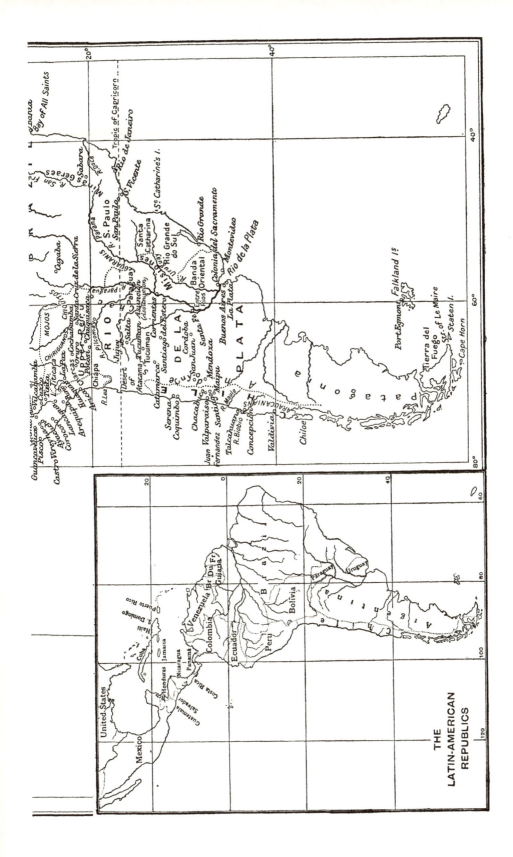

THE LATIN-AMERICAN REPUBLICS

Soon afterwards 400 immigrants arrived from Spain, led by the famous explorer Alvar Núñez, who had been sent out as royal Governor. The four months' march of Alvar Núñez overland through unknown country from the coast of Brazil to Asunción stands out as an extraordinary achievement even among the records of Spanish exploration. But this intrusive Governor was deposed after a year by Irala's followers and later shipped to Spain as a prisoner. Irala's ambition has been blamed for the concentration at Asunción; but an almost contemporary historian gives a commonsense explanation: 'Buenos Aires was abandoned because there was no service of Indians'. The Spanish settlers in America were not colonists, but *conquistadores*, a dominant aristocracy whose settlements were supported by *encomiendas*, that is to say by fiefs of Indian vassals or serfs granted to each conquistador. Where Indian labour was wanting, the newcomers starved. In Paraguay Irala rewarded his followers with rich encomiendas; he encouraged them to make captives in war and to take Indian concubines after his own example.

Before his death Irala nominated his son-in-law as successor. Upon the death of the latter another son-in-law was chosen by popular election and ruled for seven years. Later Governors were nominated by the Crown or by the Viceroy of Peru or by the Royal Council (*Audiencia*) of Charcas. These events in Paraguay cannot be ignored, for early Argentine history comprises the whole River Plate region: indeed Buenos Aires owes its second and final foundation to Paraguay.

But the oldest Argentine cities are those of the far north-west, remote from the river and connected with the southerly confines of the Inca Empire. In 1542 Diego de Rojas, 'a noble and honourable caballero', a veteran of various wars, led 200

Spaniards, a crowd of attendant Indians and a few horses down the steep passes from the plateau of Upper Peru (now Bolivia) into the wooded plains and valleys of Tucumán. For four years they marched, encamped and fought, shifting their ground in search of food, suffering the extremes of hunger, fatigue and danger, hoping to reach 'Trapalanda, the City of the Caesars', the fabled capital of some rich country still awaiting its con-querors. The Indians of Tucumán were tillers of the soil, not wholly barbarian. Among them the new-comers found some allies, but many enemies. Three Spanish cities, one of them named Londres in honour of the King's English marriage, perished by Indian onslaught. Rojas died by a poisoned arrow, and his captains fought for the command. They followed the Río Tercero to 'Gaboto's Tower' on the Paraná, where they found Indians speaking Spanish, but failed to get into touch with the Spaniards of Paraguay. Finally they returned to Peru, disappearing into a fresh vortex of civil war. But they had shown the road and prepared the way for the hispanisation of a vast and productive region.

For a fresh expedition came south from the Peruvian heights in 1547: these Spaniards clashed with another body of Spaniards who were marching to Chile. The latter element prevailed, and for sixteen years the settlers in Tucumán, mostly men of Peru, reluctantly submitted to Governors nominated by the Captain-General of Chile. Finally in 1563 Philip II decreed that the province of Tucumán should be separated from Chile, should have its own Governor, and should be placed under the juris-diction of the Audiencia or Royal Council and Tribunal of Charcas, which in 1559 was set up in the city of Chuquisaca, which the Spaniards named La Plata from the neighbouring silver mines.[1] The Viceroy of Peru, holding his Court at Lima, had superior dominion over all these regions.

These disputes hindered the work of settlement. Of several cities one alone survived a disastrous Indian rising in 1561, namely Santiago del Estero, the oldest city of the Republic, which was founded in 1553 by a veteran warrior, Francisco de Aguirre, a ruthless conqueror and despotic governor, precursor of the *caudillos* of the nineteenth century: he mocked at all authority except his own, mounted a cannon on his fortified house, exacted unquestioning obedience from his Spanish subjects, suppressed any rising of Indians and kept his word to them when they submitted. By his command was founded in 1564 the city of San Miguel de Tucumán, to the south of the present city of Tucumán. Nine years later this interior movement from Peru reached a notable goal, when Jerónimo de Cabrera, 'a person noble, affable, with other good qualities of a caballero', solemnly inaugurated the city of Córdoba, 330 miles south of Santiago. Córdoba stands at the edge of the forest country, at the foot of a range of wooded hills, and looks out upon the immense grassy plain which stretches thence to the Atlantic and to the Río Negro. Cabrera was beheaded—after torture, so it was said—by a brutal successor, Abreu, who in turn was beheaded by Lerma, his successor. This second slayer, a rapacious and sanguinary tyrant, founder of the city of Salta (1582) in its beautiful northern valley, died in the prison of Madrid. Under more settled conditions the province of Tucumán was consolidated and extended by the foundation of the

---

[1] Nomenclature is here confusing. Charcas was the province, Chuquisaca or La Plata the city in which the Audiencia sat. The name La Plata has no connexion with the Río de la Plata. The modern name of the city is Sucre.

city of La Rioja (1591) in the far west, and of Jujuy (1593) on the road to Peru.

Meantime the sub-Andine region farther south was being occupied by settlers from Chile who crossed the lofty Andine passes and set up the cities of Mendoza (1561), San Juan (1562) and San Luis (1596). All that country, comprehended under the name of Cuyo, formed part of the kingdom or captaincy-general of Chile down to 1776.

But in order to facilitate intercourse with Spain and secure the entry to all this region, a port on the estuary was a pressing need. Some attempts at re-settlement had been made. A more serious effort was urged in 1566 in a remarkable State paper by Juan de Matienzo, one of the *oidores* or magistrates of the Audiencia of Charcas. 'The port of Buenos Aires must be settled from Spain', he writes. 'The settlers will be rich through trade with Spain, Chile, Peru and the up-river regions.' He urges that navigation to Spain will be safer from corsairs by the open Atlantic than by the route from the Isthmus of Panamá, past the Caribbean bays, coasts and islands; that at least three new settlements should link Buenos Aires with the interior, that 500 citizens should be sent from Spain, traders and farmers, but not many *caballeros*.

A wealthy Biscayan citizen of Chuquisaca, Ortiz de Zárate, took up Matienzo's great plan, was appointed Governor of the River Plate by the Viceroy of Lima and departed for Spain to secure confirmation, leaving a deputy who enjoyed a short but tumultuous reign at Asunción, agitated by a furious quarrel with the Bishop. Zárate's return voyage from Spain to the River Plate with his company of immigrants was an Odyssey of ship-wreck, famine, mortality and disaster. But in 1573 his nephew Juan de Garay, a soldier-citizen of Asunción, carried out part of his design. Garay sailed from Asunción with sixty-six Spaniards, of whom fifty-nine were creoles (*criollos*), that is to say Spaniards born in America, to a spot about 600 miles down the river, and there founded the city of Santa Fe, the oldest Argentine city in the riverine region. He subdued, in part at least, the neighbouring Indians, and distributed encomiendas to his followers.

There is a touch of personal romance about Garay's later and more famous achievement. In 1575 Zárate died, bequeathing to his daughter, a descendant of the Incas, and to her future husband his Government and his designs. Garay, his nephew and executor, brought about the marriage of the heiress to the man of her choice. By his command and as his deputy, Garay in 1580 again sailed southwards from Asunción upon the mission which has immortalised his name, conducting sixty Spaniards, of whom fifty were creoles, together with 200 Guaraní families. Near the site of Mendoza's ruined settlement, he set up, in the King's name, with the usual solemn ceremonies, the *rollo*, the pillar which was the symbol of justice, and thus inaugurated El Puerto de Santa María de Buenos Aires, 'necessary and convenient for the good of all this Government and that of Tucumán'. The central *plaza* was marked out, with sites for the church and town hall. Streets were traced from it at right angles enclosing equal blocks, upon the chessboard pattern prescribed by authority throughout Spanish America. Garay, nominating two magistrates (*alcaldes*) and ten town councillors (*regidores*) instituted the *Cabildo* or Town Council—the most characteristic and valuable institution of the Spanish Empire. His sixty followers became *vecinos* or householders, every man receiving a building site within the city and land outside for tillage and pasture, and undertaking in return to defend the city with horse and arms. The founder rode at the head of his threescore armed horsemen against the Indians, drove them in rout and taught them to keep their distance. He then distributed encomiendas to all his men. Some of these grants, consisting of Guaraní Indians living on the banks and islands of the Paraná, were of some temporary value until fatal epidemics reduced these encomiendas to little or nothing. Other grants, consisting of Pampa Indians, indomitable nomadic savages, amounted to no more than hypothetical and valueless promises.

Returning northwards after three years spent in this work, Garay was caught asleep in the wilds and killed by Indians near the city of Santa Fe which he had founded.

The settlements on the Pampa, Buenos Aires and, in a less degree, Córdoba, differed in character from all the other Spanish settlements in America in that they were true colonies, not being supported by the labour of an Indian peasantry. Córdoba, it is true, possessed Indian subjects 'well-disposed and valiant: they serve when they choose; otherwise they run wild'. But Buenos Aires had not even this resource. The Cabildo constantly complains of scarcity of labour, petitions the Crown for leave to import negroes, and decrees that in autumn all artisans shall go to work at harvest. The conquistadores and their descendants despised manual labour, and a servile class gradually grew up, consisting partly of Indians brought from a distance, partly of imported negro slaves. But Buenos Aires possessed no dependent Indian peasantry. The vast prairie had few inhabitants and it would have been better for the settlers if there had been none. The people of Buenos Aires were colonists, just as the slave-owning British settlers in North America were colonists.

Garay's men were not *chapetones,* raw new-comers from Europe: they knew how to adapt themselves to their surround-ings: they contrived to maintain a not very clearly defined southern frontier against the Indians: they raised crops on the river bank: they caught and tamed wild horses descended from the barbs introduced by Mendoza. Horned cattle, now brought from Paraguay and Tucumán, multiplied rapidly and soon gave to the country its pastoral character. Within ten years cattle owners registered their marks and slaughter was regulated by the municipality. Buenos Aires was a community of farmers.

The new city soon outstripped the capital, Asunción. The most capable and active of the early Governors, the creole Her-nandarias de Saavedra, a son-in-law of Garay, who in his three periods of office, held at intervals between 1591 and 1609, did much to extend and consolidate the white settlements, to protect the Indians and to carry out the royal policy, commonly resided there, appointing a deputy in Asunción. Finally, in 1620, upon the petition of the Cabildo, Buenos Aires became the capital of a province separate from Paraguay, with a royal Governor who resided in the capital and appointed deputies in Santa Fe, in Corrientes, founded in 1588 as a fresh link upon the river, and in Concepción del Bermejo, which was an outpost in the savage Chaco. The last-named city had a tragic history. Within half a century it was destroyed by Indians. The Lieutenant-Governor and forty of the men were killed: women and children were made captives. The survivors fled to Corrientes.

From the separation in 1620 down to 1776 the Argentine region, apart from Paraguay, comprised four political divisions: (1) Cuyo, which depended upon Chile, (2) the province of Tucumán, with a royal Governor residing at first in Santiago and afterwards usually in Córdoba, (3) the province of Buenos Aires, (4) the Jesuit missions or 'reductions' in the region of the Upper Paraná, great part of which lay within the present Argentine territory. No white man was allowed in this region except the two Jesuit Fathers who ruled each 'reduction'.

The foundation of Buenos Aires marks approximately the conclusion of the period of conquest. The later foundations, Corrientes, Salta, Jujuy, Rioja, are rather the filling-up of gaps than fresh advances. Before the end of the sixteenth century, twelve Argentine cities were in existence, the nuclei of twelve out of the fourteen existing Argentine provinces.[1] The movement which has been here summarised, with the omission of many striking efforts and achievements, is a characteristic prologue to later history, characteristic in its violence, its sudden vicissitudes, its disregard for authority, its vigorous individuality, its strong local sentiment, and, finally, in the audacity, the failures and the triumphs of the conquistadores.

'Of those who went into Peru eighty out of a hundred died', wrote a contemporary. Among the conquistadores of the River Plate, the mortality must have been as much or more—by shipwreck, famine, pestilence, fatigue, exposure, warfare with savages and the various dangers of forest and wilderness: and to them no less than to their more famous predecessors of Peru may be applied the words of Raleigh:

'Here I cannot forbear to commend the patient virtue of the Spaniards: we seldom or never find that any nation hath endured

1 The two other capitals are of later foundation or re-foundation. Catamarca was established on its present site in 1683, through the transference thither, in two stages, of the population of Londres (London) 250 miles distant. Paraná, capital of the province of Entre Ríos, grew from a small village into a city some time after Entre Ríos was constituted as a separate province in 1814.

so many misadventures and miseries as the Spaniards have done in their Indian discoveries; yet persisting in their enterprises with an invincible constancy, they have annexed to their kingdom so many goodly provinces as bury the remembrance of all dangers past. Tempest and shipwrecks, famine, overthrows, mutinies, heat and cold, pestilence and all manner of diseases, both old and new, together with extreme poverty and want of all things needful, have been the enemies wherewith every one of their most noble discoverers at one time or other have encountered. Many years had passed over their heads, in the search of not so many leagues; yea more than one or two have spent their labour, their wealth and their lives in search of a golden kingdom, without getting further notice of it than what they had at their first setting forth. All which notwithstanding, the third, fourth and fifth undertakers have not been disheartened. Surely they are worthily rewarded with those treasuries and paradises which they enjoy; and well they deserve to hold them quietly, if they hinder not the like virtue in others, which perhaps will not be found.'[1]

1 *History of the World,* Book v, chapter 1.

CHAPTER III

THE MUNICIPAL PERIOD, 1580–1776

The study of Spanish history is the study of our history. ALBERDI

SPANISH and Spanish-American history is a series of contrasts. The half-century of conquest and advance introduces a period of two centuries which in comparison seems inactive. The wave of enterprise has spent itself. The port, founded in order to provide a safe and open road to Spain, is closed to direct Spanish trade by royal orders which hinder the natural growth of these colonies. But in the colonists themselves, now mainly creole or native-born, one seems to miss the forward spirit of an earlier age, partly perhaps owing to the royal prohibition of aggression against the natives, although that prohibition was often conveniently ignored. The colonists seem content to hold, and not even to hold securely, the regions already won. They treat the Indian problem in an intermittent and ineffective fashion, sometimes with a strange apathy and acquiescence, which remind one of the oriental tinge in the Spanish character. In 1619 the armament of Buenos Aires was found to consist of nine cannon without balls or powder and forty-eight rusty useless muskets. The cavalry militia had no lances, and the infantry no muskets or pikes. Even the many wars of Spain barely sent a ripple upon these shores, until the conflict with Portugal broke upon them after 1678.

Yet this period of incubation was not dull or uneventful. Its history cannot here be narrated in detail, but certain features must be indicated, namely the Indian question, the restrictions of trade, the territorial rivalry with the Portuguese, and particularly two main characteristics which are strongly contrasted and complementary to each other. These are, first, the robust virility of a rude and hazardous pastoral life, and secondly, the activities of the Cabildos which largely conducted internal affairs, so much so that this may be called the municipal period.

The main feature of the Conquest was the foundation of cities, each with its Cabildo consisting of two alcaldes and six or more regidores or town councillors; and the record of the two centuries from 1580 to 1776 is the history of cities which divided between them the whole of the intervening territory, the jurisdiction of every city extending to that of its nearest neighbour, however distant. Córdoba is 430 miles from Buenos Aires: accordingly the jurisdiction of Buenos Aires extended about 300 miles towards Córdoba, about 170 miles to the limits of Santa Fe, and southwards as far as the land could be won or held from the Indians. It extended northwards across thirty miles of water into the Banda Oriental, now the Republic of Uruguay, as far as the savage Charruas and Minuanes could be held in check.

Every city had a similar, if less extensive, jurisdiction, and was in fact the capital of a wide region, however doubtful might be its authority among hostile or independent Indians. 'Our Cabildo', says a Porteño[1] historian, 'often acted as a Provincial Parliament.' If not quite a Parliament, every Cabildo was an administrative and governing council, possessing even some legislative faculty by interpreting law and by decision upon emergencies, under the Governor's authority and under the remote and tardy supervision of the Audiencia of Charcas. Every city had the right to send a deputy or agent (*procurador*) to Spain to represent its interests and lay its petitions before the Council

[1] The people of Buenos Aires are called Porteños, i.e. 'men of the Port'.

of the Indies and the King—a right which was constantly exercised. Santa Fe and Buenos Aires, although subject to the same
Governor, send envoys to each other to treat matters of common
concern. The Cabildo of Buenos Aires repeatedly complains of
trespass by Santafecinos, Cordobeses and Mendocinos who hunt
wild cattle properly belonging to Buenos Aires; and in 1721
Buenos Aires concluded an agreement with Santa Fe concerning
annual cattle-hunting in the Banda Oriental. The export of
wheat to Santa Fe is permitted or prohibited, as the harvest in
Buenos Aires is plentiful or scarce. Aid against the Indian peril
is sought by one city from another, sometimes granted, sometimes
refused. These villages of four or five unpaved streets, with a few
hundreds of inhabitants dwelling in houses of mud walls thatched
with reeds, had all the conscious dignity of political communities: and the rectangular plan, though rigid and monotonous,
supplied the outward dignity of orderly design.

The founder of a city nominated the first alcaldes and regidores. Afterwards the outgoing Cabildo, on every New Year's
Day, elected its successor and also two alcaldes and two or more
minor officials: re-election was allowed only after two years' interval in order that all suitable persons should serve; but continuity was commonly secured by electing one or more of the
outgoing *cabildantes* to administrative posts. In 1618 it was
ordered that, as in Spain and other parts of America, seats in the
Cabildos should be sold by the King's Treasury and tenable for
life. Six regidores of Buenos Aires bought their posts at public
auction at the gate of the Royal Treasury at Potosí, the 'Imperial
Town', famous for its silver mines. Thenceforth as vacancies
occurred, they were sold by auction. But the Cabildo still con-
sisted of townsmen, and still elected annually, not from their

own number, two citizens as alcaldes, who were in general charge of the administration and sat as judges in a court of first instance, with an appeal to the Governor.

Towards the end of the seventeenth century the auction of *regimientos* in Buenos Aires found no buyers 'owing to the poverty of the city'; and from 1705 the outgoing cabildantes usually elected their successors, subject to confirmation by the Governor. This gradually became the rule in the other cities; but there was much variety in the activities and even in the constitution of different municipalities.

Upon emergency the Cabildo, inheriting medieval Spanish rights, might summon, with the Governor's consent, the principal vecinos to a civic assembly known as *Cabildo abierto* or *Cabildo pleno*. Sometimes these town meetings merely listened to a message from the King, asking for monetary aid in his costly wars against infidels and heretics. But when the Indian peril was menacing, they were real deliberative assemblies to concert measures against the marauding savages.

The royal Governor in the capital and his deputies in the other cities had superior authority. For in these remote and neglected colonies, which yielded no revenue to Spain, the Crown did not send, as in the more settled parts of the Empire, royal officials (*corregidores*[1]) to rule for three or five years, but left the Governor to appoint a deputy in each place. He usually named one of the vecinos: indeed, he often named as Deputy

[1] The title *corregidor* was often given, with convenient or complimentary laxity, to the Governor's deputy: but the real system of *corregimientos* was never applied to the River Plate. The death of the Governor of Buenos Aires in 1714 produced an armed conflict between competitors for authority. Thenceforward a Deputy Governor in Buenos Aires was nominated by the King, and in Córdoba from 1743. But the Governor still appointed his deputy in the other cities.

Governor the senior of the two alcaldes, and occasionally did so even after the practice was forbidden in 1707. Thus the royal authority was often represented by a fellow-townsman, virtually chosen by the municipality. In normal times, except upon the intervention of some unusually active Governor, these cities were, in respect of internal affairs, self-contained communities (*repúblicas*) of the native-born; for there was little immigration from Europe; the creole element prevailed during the seventeenth century in Buenos Aires and was predominant in the interior cities to a much later date. In 1671 the Governor of Buenos Aires addressed the municipal officials as *criollos e hijos de esta tierra*— 'creoles and native-born'.

In Buenos Aires royal authority was more definitely repre- sented by the presence of the Governor, usually a military officer sent from Spain, but sometimes a creole. The Governor was judge, military commander and ruler. The citadel, which con- tained his residence and the quarters of the garrison, stood upon the shore and faced the Cabildo across the plaza. The Governor, with the two 'royal officials', namely the Treasurer and Account- ant, formed a Committee to represent the King's interests. Yet municipal jurisdiction was a reality. The executioner main- tained by the Cabildo of Buenos Aires, who was also town-crier, sometimes a Portuguese, sometimes a negro, sometimes a par- doned criminal, frequently applies for arrears of pay. The Cabildo maintained the prison with its rack and its *garrote*, a wooden post with an iron neck-ring and screw, the instrument of execution by strangling. In 1772 one hundred pesos were voted to a French smith for making a new garrote, since the existing instrument was so ineffective and tedious that in the end it was usually necessary to shoot the criminal. The activities of the Cabildo depended partly on the character of the Governor. One of the early Governors, Francisco de Cérpedes, a resolute and capable man who did much for the security and improvement of the colony, arrested three of the regidores, procured the election of his son, aged twenty-two, as senior alcalde, and appointed his second son to be commander of the militia. For a time the Cabildo held its meetings in the prison, in order that the arrested members might take part in its deliberations.

A Governor's legal term of office was eight years: but, owing to vacancies and temporary appointments, there were frequent interruptions and intervals of weakness. Moreover the Governor on assuming office had to find bail that he would duly submit to the *residencia*, the judicial enquiry held, usually by his successor, at the end of his term of office, when anyone might bring complaints against him. The Governor's authority often clashed, sometimes in a violent and spectacular fashion, with that of the Bishop, who was usually a European Spaniard and was nominated by the King, by virtue of the ecclesiastical patronage granted to the Crown by successive Popes.

As in Spain, so also in Spanish America, the very success of local institutions hindered united action. A strong regional or local sentiment everywhere prevailed, finding expression in the municipal action of every separate *república*. The separatist and divergent movements of the nineteenth century, the difficulties of union which were only overcome through a long series of conflicts and experiments, had their roots in earlier generations. From the beginning, the cities of Buenos Aires, Santa Fe and Corrientes, as well as the six cities of Tucumán and the three of Cuyo, were virtually and consciously the capitals of separate regions. It was only through the recognition and clearer definition of this separation in the nineteenth century that union finally became possible by means of federation.

Both in their local diversities, and also in a general unity prevailing in spite of those diversities, the colonies were the precursors of modern Argentina. All the cities were conscious of a certain geographical and economic unity, embracing the whole plain which stretches from the Andes to the Atlantic. That plain is separated from Chile by a gigantic mountain barrier: Cuyo, politically Chilian down to 1776, was already Argentine geographically. Again, the mountain passes to the north of Salta and Jujuy led to a totally different region: the high plateau of Upper Peru with its silver mines and its submissive Indian villagers. The Argentine region on the whole was not tropical: it was not metalliferous: its life was pastoral and agricultural. It was the land of horned cattle and daring equestrian cowboys, of the boleadora and the lasso; for the spirit of the Pampa penetrated even into the wooded and mountainous regions of the north and north-west. Defence against the Indians was a common concern; so also the question of the wild cattle, which were hunted for the hides and tallow or often for the hides alone. There were disputes, agreements, frequent intercourse. The intellectual centre of the whole region was the University of Córdoba founded by the Jesuits in 1613. In spite of royal prohibition this country faced towards the Atlantic and resented, as a burdensome anomaly, its political and juridical dependence upon the Audiencia of Charcas, although the expenses of the royal Government in these poorer colonies were provided by the treasury of Peru. In response to petitions from the Cabildo of Buenos Aires, an Audiencia was there established in 1663, but it was abolished ten years later, having been found ineffective in checking contraband and costly to the impoverished Treasury of decadent Spain.

Every city had to defend itself against the Indian peril, either singly or by concert with neighbours. Relations with the Indians differed. In Buenos Aires the problem was to protect the out-lying cattle-farms from the sudden raids of the savages, expert horsemen and cattle thieves. Not until 1735, and then only owing to a strange mismanagement, were the port and its suburbs in imminent danger. But the cities of the north-west and also the up-river cities of Santa Fe and Corrientes had as neighbours numerous Indian tribes, some of them nominally allies, most of them inveterate enemies. In these places the white colonists were *encomenderos*, lords of Indian vassals, who suffered much hard-ship and rapid diminution, largely owing to smallpox, measles and alcohol. These *Indios encomendados* (vassals subject to an encomendero) were often ready to welcome incursions of savages from the forests and plains. Some towns were swept out of existence: others were always on the watch to maintain existence, every citizen being enrolled as a militiaman.

In 1627 a wanton affront to an Indian chief provoked a revolt and a ten years' war in Tucumán. In 1666 an attempt was there made to gather the Indians into 'reductions', and 200 families of Quilmes Indians were conveyed from Tucumán to Buenos Aires and settled in the village of 'Quilmes,' where they became *mitayos*, serving Buenos Aires in alternate shifts of labour. But thirty years later savage Indians swept through the streets of Tucumán, butchering the inhabitants. In 1711 Tucumán again sent 500 Indian captives to serve in Buenos Aires, where the Quilmes Indians had diminished much in number. In 1735, the Indians raged through the streets of Salta, scattering death. Santa Fe, eighty-seven years after its foundation, thirty-six of which had been spent in Indian warfare, was moved to a safer site: yet in 1717 the Santafecinos were confined within their wall and town-ditch: in the following years the active and able Governor Zabala tried, with some success, conciliatory measures, gathering the neighbouring Indians into villages under Christian instruction and municipal organisation; but the danger and intermittent fighting continued into the nineteenth century.

In Buenos Aires occasional expeditions were organised against marauding Indians after 1670—with little effect owing to the rapid mobility of the enemy. In the eighteenth century the In-dians became more daring, raiding domesticated cattle from the estancias near the city, killing men and carrying away women. After 1735 reprisals by the white men, who sometimes ignored treaties and slew friendly and hostile Indians alike, provoked furious Indian assaults. The Cabildo instituted a war-chest to provide a paid militia on the frontier: but their efforts were ill sustained. In 1741 Jesuit missionaries travelled south with messages of peace and dwelt for years in the desert. One of these was an Englishman, Falkner, whose story was published at Hereford in 1774. But the raids continued. 'The Indians', says Falkner, 'fell upon the village of Luján, killed many Spaniards, took some captives and drove away some thousands of cattle'. Next they attacked 'the district of the Magdalen, four leagues from Buenos Aires and...scoured and dispeopled in one day and a night above twelve leagues of the most populous and plentiful country in those parts: the inhabitants of Buenos Aires were in the most terrible consternation'. Invasions of Pampa Indians were frequent down to 1780, when Luján suffered another onslaught. About that time the Viceroy Vertiz established forts on the frontier and also tried conciliatory measures with some success both on the Pampa and in the northern forests. During the Viceroyalty there was comparative peace, and in 1806 many Indian chiefs offered help against the 'red' invaders, that is to say, the British red-coats.

In September of most years a caravan of carts, draught oxen, horsemen, cattle to provide food and an armed guard, travelled 150 miles south-westward to supply Buenos Aires with salt from the deposits which had been discovered in 1662 'within the jurisdiction of the city'. Sometimes this expedition attempted to clear the country of enemies: sometimes blackmail—gifts of alcohol, tobacco and *yerba mate* (Paraguayan tea)—secured safe passage.

Corrientes, in the Guaraní region on the confines of Paraguay, was in a peculiar position owing to the animosity between the Correntinos and the Jesuits of the neighbouring Indian missions, who opposed the encomienda system and were therefore regarded by the Correntinos as interlopers who deprived them of the fruits of conquest by enticing away their serfs. In 1732 Corrientes was attracted by the *comunero* movement in Asunción, which was partly a protest against Jesuit activity, partly a revival of the independent spirit of the conquistadores. The Correntinos refused to serve against the Paraguayans, raised the cry of *Viva el común* and deposed the Deputy Governor. But the discreet attitude of the Governor Zabala and more moderate counsels in Corrientes averted serious trouble. The autocratic action of the stubborn soldier-Governor Ceballos, conqueror of Colonia and protector of the Jesuits, provoked another revolt in 1764, when Corrientes in Cabildo abierto elected a Governor, who proclaimed, 'We defend our country and shall know how to defend it even though it were against the King'. The revolt was suppressed by armed force. There were arrests and thirteen death-sentences—whether meant in earnest cannot be known: for amnesty and peace followed when Ceballos was succeeded by Bucareli, who came commissioned to expel the Jesuits.

Jesuit activities throughout are best treated separately. The 'Company of Jesus', from its arrival in 1586, both in its colleges (i.e. houses of residence), in the cities and in its missions in the wilds, strove to protect, instruct and civilise the Indians. Their reports to the Crown had two results, 'The Ordinances of Alfaro' and the famous Jesuit missions of La Guaira. In 1609 Alfaro, a magistrate of Charcas, was sent into these colonies to examine the treatment of the Indians and to make reforms. His Ordinances aimed at checking the excesses of the encomenderos, limiting and regulating forced labour and forbidding the removal of Indians from their homes. His action was resented by the colonists, who complained of consequent unrest among the natives; and his rules were neither obeyed nor enforced.

In the same year, 1609, some Italian Jesuits undertook, under royal authority, the pacification of the savage country on both banks of the Upper Paraná. This became an isolated Indian reservation, closed to colonisation and to the entry of white men. Many of the Guaranís, who were menaced on the north by ferocious cannibals and on the east by Brazilian slave-raiders from São Pãolo, were gathered into villages, each ruled by a Jesuit priest, with one or two assistants. After a destructive raid of Paulistas in 1630 an Indian militia was formed, which was repeatedly sent by the Jesuit chiefs to protect the colonies and to fight for Spain against the Portuguese. Great part of this curious commonwealth of thirty Indian villages, administered by Indian officials under the rule of the priests, lay within the present limits of the Argentine Republic. In 1730 their Indian inhabitants numbered 141,000: but they were reduced by epidemics, by military service and by the results of an iniquitous treaty which in 1750 ceded seven villages to the hated Portuguese and drove those villages into revolt, followed by destruction through a Hispano-Portuguese military expedition. Part of the lands to which the Jesuits had established a Spanish title passed into the possession of the Portuguese and, afterwards, of Brazil.

There was much tension between the Jesuit missionaries and the colonists, who welcomed the expulsion of the Order in 1767-8. The motives of that expulsion from the whole Spanish Empire belong rather to European history: but among those motives were exaggerated and distorted accusations of independent aims in these missions. With needless violence and brutal suddenness the Jesuit fathers were taken both from their colleges and estancias in or near the cities and from their missions in the wilds. Some attempt was then made to administer these through civil magistrates and through the Regulars of other Orders. But the region soon sank into depopulation and barbarism. Ruins of solid and richly adorned churches, overgrown by forest, attest the tragic past of a region which to-day is being opened out to European settlement.

The failure of Mendoza's enterprise in 1535 was a great economic misfortune. When Garay traced out the existing city in 1580, the prescribed course of annual trade convoys, adopted first as a measure of safety and continued as a fiscal system, had prevailed for a generation: and neither Philip II nor his successors were willing to modify that rigid system in accordance with the changing needs of their growing Empire. Matienzo's prophecy of wealth and prosperity through trade with Spain, Chile and Peru was not fulfilled for two centuries, simply because the port was closed by royal authority. That the European trade of the Spanish dependencies should be limited to Spain and to Spanish ships was a matter of course according to the views of those days. But the River Plate was actually forbidden to trade directly with Spain. The only permitted course of trade was by the fleet of galleons which sailed annually from Seville to Nombre de Dios, later to Portobello. From the fair of Portobello European goods were conveyed by mule-trains across the isthmus to Panamá, and thence by sea to Callao, the port of Lima.

Any merchandise which could be conveyed from Lima to Buenos Aires over 3000 miles of indescribably difficult and dangerous country cost in Buenos Aires eight or ten times the original value. Trade by the easy sea route could not be entirely stopped, but it was a matter of infractions, exceptions and concessions: and every concession was vehemently opposed by two powerful bodies, the chambers of commerce (*consulados*) of Seville and of Lima, in defence of their long-established and lucrative monopoly. The Board of Trade at Seville, in reports to the Crown, supported the consulado of Seville, and successive Viceroys of Peru supported the consulado of Lima. During the decade following its foundation, Buenos Aires had some trade with Brazil, and in 1595 a Portuguese, Reynel, made a contract with Philip II for supplying annually to the Indies for nine years 4250 negro slaves, of whom 600 might be introduced through the River Plate. He probably never used this latter concession, which would have meant return cargoes and considerable incidental commerce; for in 1598-9 there are repeated petitions for the opening of the port 'through which all entrance and egress was forbidden', from the Cabildo, from the Bishops of Tucumán and of Buenos Aires, and from the royal Governor, who reported the lack of all the necessaries of civilised life except food. Philip III, in response, permitted in 1602 to the people of the Plate a limited export in their own vessels of grain, dried beef and tallow for six years to Brazil and Angola, and import of goods needed, forbidding however direct trade with Spain and import of negroes. The permission, which did not include goods from Tucumán, was renewed at intervals down to 1618.

In 1607 a ship's boat, manned by forty Dutch and English corsairs, entered the port and pillaged two ships laden with Peruvian silver—a proof that the prohibition of trade with the interior was not fully effective. In 1608 the Cabildo represented that poverty and bad harvests had prevented the export of the full quantities permitted and asked leave to make up the deficiency in future years: and in 1616 the Governor, Hernandarias, permitted export in Brazilian ships, since the Porteños owned none: evidently the limitations as to ownership had never been observed. In 1618 the Brazilian trade was forbidden; but two ships of 100 tons were to sail annually for three years from Seville to Buenos Aires; the Cabildo, apparently with success, claimed permission for three ships. Petitions continue, particularly for leave to import slaves from Angola; and the permissions of limited trade from Seville are renewed. Moreover, in addition, occasional licences (*registros*) were granted in Seville for the sailing of ships known as 'register ships'. But local interests in the River Plate were as narrow as in Seville or Lima. The arrival of a cargo from Seville in 1621 was not welcomed by Porteños interested in Brazilian trade, who at the time dominated the Cabildo, notably one Vergara who had bought the post of

senior regidor and in concert with a resident Portuguese merchant pursued a lucrative contraband trade with Brazil. Conflict
of interests or perhaps the conflict between interest and the jealousy
of more industrious and wealthy aliens appears in a petition to the
Crown that the Inquisition be established in Buenos Aires to
deal with Portuguese judaizers. It may be remarked that the
early arrival in Buenos Aires of a number of Portuguese, mostly
Jewish by descent, who made haste to marry into Porteño
families, indicates that there were more opportunities for business
than those recorded in documents.

After the revolt of Portugal (1640) and the recognition of
Dutch independence (1648) the Dutch were the most active
traders or smugglers, especially during the war with France
(1635-59) and with Cromwell (1656-9). In 1657 a French
trader, passing as a Spaniard, visited Buenos Aires in a Spanish
register ship and found twenty-two 'Dutch' ships, two of which
were in fact English, anchored in the roads.[1] He travelled to
Potosí and returned with a mule-train conveying silver and
vicuña wool to be embarked at Buenos Aires for Spain, together with 14,000 hides. This traveller found the cities of Buenos
Aires, Córdoba and Salta to be about equal in size—each containing, as he guessed, 400 houses—a convincing proof of the

---

1 Obviously the presence of this great neutral fleet, openly trading with Peru by
a usually forbidden route, was not normal, but due to the exigencies of war, the
dangers of the West Indian route and the destruction of Spanish shipping. In
1656 the English took Jamaica, an English fleet was cruising in the Caribbean
Sea, and part of Blake's fleet captured or destroyed most of the galleons outside
Cadiz. In April 1657 Blake's ships destroyed most of the Plate fleet in the harbour
of Santa Cruz in the Canary Islands. See *Trade and Navigation between Spain and the
Indies in the time of the Hapsburgs*, by C. H. Haring. The twenty-two ships were
probably a neutral war-convoy acting with the permission or the connivance of the
Spanish Government.

stunted growth of the port, which could not flourish by irregular and occasional trade.

In 1667 the Cabildo reports that no Spanish ships have arrived for four years, that the people cannot afford decent dress for attendance at Mass, and that the Governor, unlike some of his predecessors, had refused entrance to a slave-ship and to two English ships. In that same year the Board of Trade and the Consulado of Seville again reported to the Crown against the permission of trade with the Plate. In 1671, upon the destruction of Panamá by the Welsh buccaneer Morgan, the Cabildo wrote to the Queen Regent that Buenos Aires was now the only open port for South America and the natural destination for the galleons: the petition was ignored.

In 1678 the Portuguese, pushing southward from Brazil, established, opposite to Buenos Aires across the estuary, the forti-fied post of Colonia del Sacramento, which became an active emporium of contraband trade, both Portuguese and English. The Porteños welcomed the trade, but vehemently resented the encroachment on their cattle-grounds, and sent their militia to act with Spanish troops and Indian neophytes against Colonia, which, repeatedly taken by the Spaniards, was repeatedly re-stored and remained in Portuguese possession, with brief intervals, until it was finally taken by Spain in 1777.

The accession of the House of Bourbon and the War of the Spanish Succession (1702–13) open a new economic era. A French company acquired the Asiento de Negros or contract for supplying slaves to the Indies, with permission to send two annual shiploads of negroes to the River Plate, passage thence to Peru being forbidden. This meant a considerable trade in Euro-pean goods under cover of the Asiento, and an annual export of about 40,000 hides. The Cabildo organised cattle-hunts and arranged prices with the Frenchmen—a profitable business for the regidores. This slave traffic brought its nemesis—visitations of smallpox, one of which, so it was said, almost depopulated the city. From the Peace of Utrecht (1713) until the outbreak of the war of Jenkins' Ear (1739), the English South Sea Company held the Asiento with two brief intervals; they built at Buenos Aires a 'factory' with quarters for resident English agents, and for the imported negroes; and they cultivated the adjoining land. Four annual slave-ships returned to England laden with hides. The slave-trade covered much smuggling: one Captain King refused to allow the Spanish Governor and customs officers on board his ship *The Duke of Cambridge* and threatened to use his guns. Another ship, *The Carteret*, is said to have conveyed to London two million pesos in silver and hides worth 60,000 pesos. About 1725 the Governor Zabala advised the Crown to open the port of Buenos Aires, since smuggling could not be stopped unless Colonia were completely destroyed. Finding that the Portuguese were also about to occupy Montevideo, 120 miles nearer to the sea, Zabala anticipated them and founded the fortified city of Montevideo with all the civic privileges of Cabildo and alcaldes. The first inhabitants came, some from the Canary Isles, some from Buenos Aires.

In 1740 the galleons and the fair of Portobello were abolished; thenceforth Spanish trade with Peru passed round Cape Horn in 'register ships'. But trade overland to Peru through Buenos Aires was still forbidden in order to prevent contraband trade from Colonia to Peru. There is, however, evidence of increased trade with Spain, greater commercial activity in the city and a growing recognition of the political importance of those regions, largely owing to the territorial conflict with Portugal. One episode of that conflict demands mention. In 1762, Spain being at war with Great Britain, Havana and Manila having fallen to British arms, a privateering expedition, half-British, half-Portuguese, three frigates, a 'snow' and five store-ships, carrying 1050 soldiers, sailed against Buenos Aires, only to find that Colonia, which was to be their base, was in Spanish hands. They attacked Colonia, but the British flagship *Clive* caught fire and blew up with great loss of life. Eighty Englishmen swam ashore naked from the burning wreck: they were clothed by the Spaniards, treated 'more as sons than as captives' and merged in the population. Thus came the first English immigrants to the Plate, and thus ended the first British invasion, an attempt which illustrates the growing importance of the place.

Another clash with the British eight years later, in time of peace, further illustrates that importance. This matter demands some previous explanation. In 1764 the French navigator Bougainville established a French settlement in the bleak, wind-swept and uninhabited group of the Falkland Islands, which had been named *Les Isles Malouines*, in Spanish *Las Islas Malvinas*, by the sailors of St Malo. Spain protested against this encroachment on her American possessions, and two years later France, recognising the justice of this claim, ceded the settlement to Spain; and a Spanish Governor was appointed. But meantime, a year after the settlement by Bougainville, a small British naval post was established at Port Egmont, in another part of the group. For four years the two settlements, Spanish and English, subsisted out of sight of each other. But in 1769 they came into contact. The British commander, Captain Hunt, warned off a Spanish schooner which he met on a cruise. The Governor of the Spanish settlement sent him a letter of protest. In reply, Hunt warned the Spanish Governor to depart, since the 'Islands belong to his Britannic Majesty'. The Spaniard replied by warning Hunt to depart from the islands. Six months later Bucareli, the same able and energetic Governor of Buenos Aires who had expelled the Jesuits, sent, in obedience to orders from Madrid, a squadron and troops, which forcibly uprooted the British settlement[1] (June 10, 1770).

The reforms of Charles III brought practical recognition of the growth of his dominions in the River Plate. From 1767 a ship carrying mails and merchandise sailed from Corunna to

[1] This affront to the British Crown, together with Hunt's previous affront to Spain, almost led to war. But after long diplomatic fencing, the Spanish Crown, having failed to obtain support from France, gave satisfaction for the affront in January 1771, by expressing displeasure at Bucareli's action and by undertaking that 'things shall be restored. . .at Port Egmont precisely to the state in which they were before the 10th of June, 1770'. This was done, and Port Egmont was formally restored to a British naval party by a Spanish officer in September 1771.

The Spanish Declaration stipulated—'that the engagement. . .to restore. . .the possession of the port and fort called Egmont cannot nor ought in any wise to affect the question of the prior right of sovereignty of the Malouine Islands, otherwise called Falkland Islands.'

Lord North, the Premier, speaking 'unofficially', as he was careful to explain, had told the French Chargé d'Affaires in London in November 1770 that if satisfaction for the affront were given, the British would evacuate the islands, which they did not value. It seems certain that Lord North did not pledge his Government; for Lord Rochford, the Foreign Minister, denied having ever given any such pledge; and this denial was borne out by Guines, the French Ambassador in London. Moreover, in March 1771 the Spanish Government made overtures for reciprocal abandonment of both settlements, Spanish and British:—overtures which are inconsistent with any previous official promise of abandonment by Great Britain alone. After three years, in May 1774, the British withdrew their settlement, leaving, however, a leaden plate bearing an inscription which claimed the islands for Great Britain. Meantime the Spanish settlement of La Soledad on another part of the group was maintained, and Spanish Governors of Las Islas Malvinas, subordinate to the Government of Buenos Aires, were regularly appointed down to 1811, when the Spanish authorities were withdrawn.

Buenos Aires every three months, and later every two months. In 1776 trade with the other American dependencies of Spain was permitted, but not overland trade with Peru, since Colonia was once more in Portuguese hands. But in that same year Ceballos, who had taken Colonia thirteen years earlier, was sent out with 9000 troops and a large squadron to pursue the Portu-guese war, with a commission as Viceroy as long as the expedi-tion should last. He took Colonia a second time, and having thus removed the obstacle to inland trade, he decreed, upon his own authority, permission to trade overland with Peru, and urged upon the Crown that the Viceroyalty should be permanent. His advice was taken; and in 1778 Buenos Aires, now the Viceregal capital of a vast territory, was opened to trade with all parts of Spain and of the Spanish Empire.

Notwithstanding oppressive restrictions of trade and lack of most of the refinements of life, the people enjoyed from the be-ginning a rude pastoral abundance, alternating with scarcity in time of drought when the crops failed and the unfenced cattle wandered far into the Indian country, seeking water and pasture. The garrison of the port and the crews of ships lost many de-serters, attracted by the easy hospitality of the open country and by a life of half-savage plenty, with little labour. Hunting wild cattle was at once a business and a sport. Groups of horsemen, armed with the 'half-moon', a sharp-edged steel crescent set upon a wooden shaft, galloped among the wild herds, hamstringing the bulls and sometimes, in spite of prohibition, the cows also. When enough animals lay helpless, the riders feasted on freshly-killed beef roasted in the hide and then proceeded to dispatch and skin the prostrate animals. A few tongues were cut out as a delicacy and the carcasses were left to the vultures and wild dogs. In 1719 the Cabildo of Buenos Aires called for the loan of 1600 horses for a great cattle-hunt in the Banda Oriental. One townsman at once offered 1000 horses, another 500, another 200, all ready in the Banda Oriental. The following year brings complaints that the Santafecinos have driven off 400,000 cattle, besides killing many. Then it is reported that vagabonds aided by Indians are selling cattle to the Portuguese in Colonia; that they live without justice, obedience or fear; that when threatened they flee to Colonia and serve the Portuguese settlers or French interlopers; that Spaniards, with Indian wives, are living among the Indians; and that there are gangs of criminals and runaway husbands. Frequent robberies of cattle and horses by white malefactors in the lands of Buenos Aires tempt Indian incursions. The Gaucho of the nineteenth century as well as the outlaw and the *Gaucho malo* have their precursors long ago. Martín Fierro and Juan Moreira, the Robin Hood and Dick Turpin of Argentina, have far ancestry. The two determining human elements in early Argentine history are the adventurous hazardous open-air life of the saddle and the camp-fire, remote from laws of cities, a native life springing from the soil, and the organised life of the civic communities which carried on the traditions and inheritance of Europe.

CHAPTER IV

THE VICEROYALTY, 1786-1810

THE modern history of Argentina opens in visible and picturesque fashion, particularly in the capital, with the setting-up of a Viceregal Court, centre of a cultured atmosphere, with the free ingress of all ships flying the Spanish flag, strings of negro slaves disembarking to march to the far interior, caravans of bullock-carts carrying European merchandise to Upper Peru, bringing back silver and vicuña wool for shipment to Spain; the rapid growth of population through the movement of trade and the arrival of Europeans. Thus was accomplished the first act of Argentine emancipation, namely release from economic dependence upon Peru.

In 1785 a group of long-gowned magistrates from Spain brought the fresh dignity of an Audiencia, at once a supreme Tribunal and an administrative Council. Nine years later full equality with Lima was granted with the institution of the *consulado*, a gild of merchants who annually chose from their own number three magistrates who sat as a tribunal in commercial suits and also as an economic council, disposing of a revenue from the customs. The merchants were Europeans, careless of rural interests. Accordingly in 1797 the gild of graziers and farmers (*hacendados*) was admitted to the *consulado*, equal in number to the merchants and holding the magistracies in alternate years with them.

The second Viceroy, Vertiz, a Spaniard born in Mexico, who had served long in the River Plate first as a soldier, then as Colonial Governor, then as subordinate to Ceballos, and now

(1778–84) as Viceroy, strove to make his capital more worthy of its new dignity, by cleansing, lighting and partly paving the principal streets. He founded the College of San Carlos for higher education, the germ of the later University. He introduced a printing-press which had lain idle in Córdoba since the expulsion of its Jesuit owners; he opened a theatre in spite of episcopal and clerical protests. He set up a medical school, a hospital, an orphanage, a foundling asylum. He did much towards the defence and pacification of the frontier and the exploration of Patagonia. Some settlements made in the bleak regions of the far south in order to anticipate possible British encroachment, were abandoned: but Patagones, a small settlement at the mouth of the Río Negro, endured.

Vertiz turned from these pacific tasks to undertake urgent military preparation in order to meet the great Indian revolt of 1780–3. That tragic event belongs to the history of Peru and Bolivia, countries having a settled Indian peasantry, rather than to that of Argentina. The conflict was fought out on the tropical Andine heights, remote from the present frontier of Argentina. But since Vertiz and Buenos Aires had to appease a turmoil within the confines of the Viceroyalty, it demands brief mention here.

The revolt broke out in the south of Peru, where an Indian noble, taking the Inca name of Tupac Amaru, gathered a horde of Indians and besieged Cuzco, but was finally defeated, captured and executed, with medieval tortures, in the plaza of Lima (May 1781). But the northern part of Upper Peru (now Bolivia) was also ablaze. The insurgents turned a flood of water upon the town of Sorata and killed the 20,000 people gathered within it. The city of La Paz, crowded with fugitives, was besieged for nearly four months and suffered extreme famine. Meantime

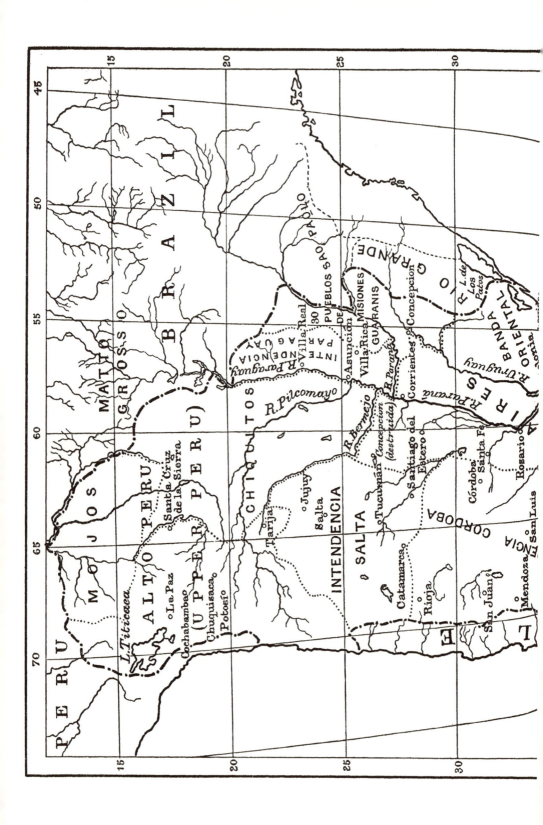

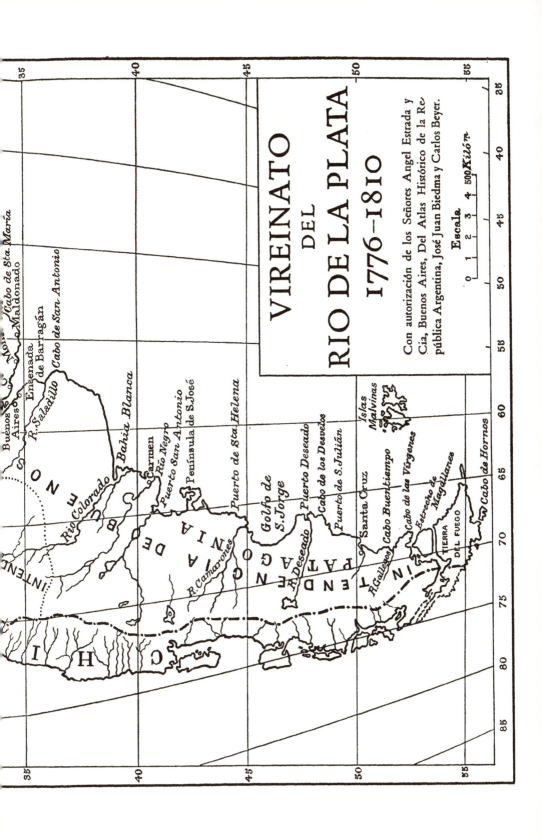

VIREINATO DEL RIO DE LA PLATA 1776–1810

Con autorización de los Señores Angel Estrada y Cia, Buenos Aires, Del Atlas Histórico de la República Argentina, José Juan Biedma y Carlos Beyer.

Escala.

0 1 2 3 4 500 *Kilóm*

troops dispatched by Vertiz from Buenos Aires were slowly approaching over their difficult march of 2300 miles: on their way through Tucumán they were joined by horsemen armed with lassos and knives—an interesting prologue to Gaucho activities in the War of Independence and in the later civil wars. La Paz was relieved, but suffered a second two months' siege when part of the relieving force was temporarily withdrawn, and there was much desultory fighting before the revolt was finally suppressed.

It would be a mistake to trace a connexion between this out-break in the distant tropical highlands and the struggle for emancipation in Argentina which began thirty years later. Although at first Tupac Amaru attracted many Peruvian mestizos and some creoles to his standard, the revolt soon became a struggle between insurgent Indians and white men, aided by loyal Indians. It was an attempt not to emancipate the Spanish colonies but to destroy them. The movement of emancipation in Argentina had nothing to do with Indian grievances. That movement was an effort on the part of the descendants of the conquistadores to detach themselves from the authority of the mother country.

In 1784, Vertiz, after long and laborious service, petitioned to be relieved and subjected to the residencia. The first petition was granted, but not the second: a man of such proved integrity and beneficent service was exempted from that ordeal.

A new system of local administration, French in origin, was introduced from Spain in 1782. The Viceroyalty was divided into eight *Intendencias*, extensive provinces ruled by *Intendentes*, magistrates of high rank and authority sent from Spain. Four of these provinces comprised Upper Peru: Paraguay formed a fifth.

The three properly Argentine Intendencies were Salta which included all the north, Córdoba comprising all the west, and Buenos Aires, where a Superintendente administered the riverine region.[1] Each Intendency was divided into districts (*partidos*) generally corresponding to the 'jurisdictions' of the cities, but now receiving a local administration which diminished the financial activities of the Cabildos. The system was intended not to divide, but to unify more effectively, the whole Spanish monarchy. The actual result was the strengthening of regional and local feeling. The system survived emancipation and influenced the early history of the Republic.

There were two divisions of a more distinct kind. The Audiencia of Charcas still held authority over Upper Peru, which thus formed a political entity, partly separated, as it was also ethnologically and geographically distinct, from the rest of the Viceroyalty; and Montevideo, a fortified and garrisoned city, was ruled by a military Governor only subordinate to the Viceroy. Montevideo became in great part the ocean port of all the River Plate and petitioned for a separate consulado, complaining of dependence upon that of Buenos Aires. Under the Viceroyalty official encouragement was given to leather-factories in Buenos Aires and in Salta and also to establishments for the salting and preserving of meat for export; but manufactures competing with those of the mother country were still forbidden.

1 The dual authority of Viceroy and Superintendente in the capital proved so unworkable that it was modified, and Viceregal pre-eminence was restored. The Superintendente, Paula Sanz, a man of engaging manners but corrupt, rapacious and extravagant, carried on a scandalous feud with the Viceroy Loreto (1784–9), a magistrate of austere integrity and difficult temper. Paula Sanz was withdrawn, only to be transferred—probably through some personal interest in Madrid—to a more lucrative post in Upper Peru, where he met a tragic end some twenty years later at the hands of the Porteños.

Throughout the period of the Viceroyalty trade with Europe was still confined, with occasional and temporary exceptions, to Spain and to Spanish ships. But from 1789 onwards—presumably in order to supply the growing demand for manual labour—the slave-trade was permitted to foreigners, who in return exported local produce. Moreover three wars with Great Britain (1779-83, 1796-1802, 1804-8) brought repeated concessions owing to the danger to Spanish shipping from the British navy. During the first of these wars permission to trade in Portuguese ships obviously involved trade with Portugal. In 1795 trade was permitted with the colonies of other nations; and in 1797, upon an outcry in Buenos Aires that the colonies were isolated, trade blocked and business conditions ruinous, trade was permitted in neutral ships, which meant trade with neutrals, especially North Americans. Two years later this general permission was withdrawn: but licences were still frequently granted for trade in neutral ships and with neutral ports, especially Hamburg. In 1801, owing to the naval predominance of the British enemy, the King's treasure from the Indies could only be brought to Spain through North American agency.

The impotence of Spain, repeated interruption of communication with the mother country, increasing intercourse with other nations, irritating efforts to check that intercourse, and a stupid censorship of books, tended to weaken respect for the monarchy. More stringent fiscal methods, due to the needs of war, were unpopular. In 1779-80 tobacco and playing-cards became royal monopolies and the price of tobacco was raised. King Charles III also called on his colonial 'vassals' for a poll-tax, styled a *donativo*, 'a free gift', to meet the cost of a war in which he was aiding the revolt of other colonies—the thirteen British colonies—against their sovereign. Moreover the wholesome neglect of earlier generations gave place to an officialdom, penetrating everywhere and encroaching on old municipal privileges. The gift of the higher posts to European Spaniards, contemptuously nicknamed *chapetones* by the creoles, whom in turn they regarded as inferiors, increased the 'decided aversion which the creoles feel for Europeans and for the Spanish Government'.[1] The Court, in the nervous uneasiness caused by the French Revolution, contrived that even the Cabildo should become a European preserve and a conservative stronghold. Yet some of the later republican leaders gained experience in subordinate posts of influence and dignity. One of them, Chiclana, in an official report on southern development, mentions the misfortune of administration by strangers to the country. Another, Mariano Moreno, an eloquent young lawyer with a fervent passion for justice, was councillor to the Cabildo and also *relator* to the Audiencia of Buenos Aires, charged with the responsible task of abridging and interpreting the multitudinous papers submitted to that body. Moreno had imbibed French and North American political ideas from a liberal-minded priest in the University of Chuquisaca and had pleaded the cause of the Indians before the Audiencia of Charcas. A third creole, Manuel Belgrano, son of a well-to-do Italian merchant domiciled in Buenos Aires, had studied in Spanish Universities, had qualified as a barrister, and was living in Madrid, keenly interested in economic theories, and, as he tells us in his autobiography, full of 'ideas of liberty, equality, security and just property', when he was appointed secretary to the consulado of Buenos Aires. He strove to push

1 The quotation is from the Spanish explorer Azara, who published his book on the River Plate in 1808. The origin of the nickname *chapetón* is unknown.

that rather inert body along the path of progress, and projected schools of mathematics and of design, but failed to get the sanction of the Spanish Court, which 'vacillated, making liberal and illiberal dispositions at the same time'. Yet under a sympathetic Viceroy, Pino (1801–4), schools were opened, chairs of medicine and anatomy established, and the first periodical was published, *El Telégrafo Mercantil,* followed by a second of a more serious kind, *El Semanario de Agricultura.* The feeling of the capital, and of the other cities, notably Córdoba, was speculative and uneasy, but not yet revolutionary. The impulse to revolution came from without, and the prologue was supplied by the British invasions of 1806–7.

CHAPTER V

THE BRITISH INVASIONS

IN 1804 the Marqués de Sobremonte, who had done good work as Governor-Intendant of Córdoba, was promoted Viceroy, and took up his residence in the citadel of Buenos Aires. In the same year, Spain was forced into open war with Great Britain by the capture of four Spanish frigates conveying treasure from Montevideo to Cadiz—treasure intended, there was reason to believe, for Napoleon. Sobremonte received warning from Spain of possible hostilities; and when a British squadron was reported to be anchored at Bahia in Brazil, he called out militia forces; for the regular garrison of Buenos Aires was depleted and neglected by a bewildered Home Government, in which the young guardsman Godoy, the Queen's favourite, was commander-in-chief of the army and navy.

News having come that the dreaded British squadron had sailed from Bahia for the Cape, Sobremonte dropped all precautions, and was completely surprised at the appearance of an enemy fleet in the river in June 1806. News that the invaders were disembarking was brought to him as he sat in the Viceregal box at a gala performance in the theatre. On the 25th the invading British squadron anchored off Quilmes, twelve miles from the city: armed men were quietly landed in boats: some skirmishing, chiefly with irregular creole cavalry, merely delayed their march. The Spaniards, in their retreat, burnt the wooden bridge across the intervening river, the Riachuelo, but omitted to remove or destroy a number of boats, with which the British constructed a floating bridge and so crossed the river. The Viceroy fled to

Córdoba, and 1640 red-coats marched on June 27 through the astonished city and hoisted the British flag on the citadel. Guards were posted, and the British soldiers were lodged in the barracks belonging to the Spanish Crown.

The author of this audacious adventure was not the British Government, but a naval officer of restless ambition and insinuating manners, Sir Home Popham, who had been privy to some proposals of the British Ministry for attempts to deprive Spain of her American possessions. All such proposals had now been dropped by the British Cabinet, and Popham, instead of leading, as he had hoped, an expedition against the American dependencies of Spain, was placed in command of the British squadron which was sent to occupy the Dutch settlement at the Cape in 1805 and which touched at Bahia on the voyage thither.

After the surrender of the Cape by the Dutch, Popham found his ships lying idle in Table Bay. Uneasy at this inaction in the midst of the world-wide Napoleonic struggle and still cherishing his former South American schemes, he listened readily to the talk of an American slave-trader whose brig happened to be in Table Bay; this man assured him that a sudden blow either at Montevideo or at Buenos Aires, places which he had often visited, could not fail of success. Popham thereupon persuaded Baird, military Governor of the Cape, to let him have a regiment under the command of General William Carr Beresford. Having taken this body of 700 men on board his ships, he sailed away to St Helena, where he induced the Governor of the island to give him a few more troops; and then set sail for the River Plate.

Eighteen months earlier, in October 1804, Popham, in concert with Miranda, the Venezuelan 'Precursor of Independence', had drawn up a written proposal for three simultaneous expeditions against South America, by way of Venezuela, by way of the Pacific and by way of Buenos Aires, not with a view to conquest, but in order to arouse and support revolt against the Spanish Crown. In that document he had declared that the expedition against Buenos Aires alone, as part of a much larger scheme, would require 3000 troops. Without orders and on his own initiative, he now made an isolated attempt, with about half that number, not at emancipation, but at conquest, a far greater undertaking.

Upon approaching the estuary, Beresford wished to carry out the only sound military plan, which had indeed been Popham's own original plan, namely an immediate attack upon the fortified and garrisoned city of Montevideo. But Beresford was overruled by Popham, who was now determined upon the easier and, in a sense, more profitable plan of an advance against the capital, where, so it was reported, there was a large amount of treasure, lately arrived from Peru and awaiting transport to the Peninsula. Accordingly the squadron sailed up the estuary to Quilmes and there disembarked the little army, which two days later marched into the city and hoisted the British flag over the citadel.

Had Beresford proclaimed republican independence, handed over the royal treasury to a governing Junta of Creoles and promised British protection against Spanish re-conquest—a promise impossible to make—success was conceivable, though improbable; for the European Spaniards were predominant in the Cabildo and among the official, professional and commercial classes: and the creoles, notwithstanding much discontent with their Government, still called themselves Spaniards, were under the influence of an age-long Spanish tradition, and held heretics in horror.

Beresford proclaimed British sovereignty, named himself Governor, required an oath of allegiance to King George III from all officials, and shipped more than a million pesos of royal treasure to England. Municipal, ecclesiastical and judicial institutions were left untouched. The port was opened to ships of all friendly nations, and customs duties were largely reduced, with a preferential tariff for British goods.

Realising his precarious position, Beresford wrote urgently to the Cape for reinforcements. But no reinforcements could arrive in time. All the inhabitants, above 40,000[1] in the city, besides the rural population, were hostile and indignant at this easy victory. A rising within the city was planned, under cover of the *tertulia*, the customary and apparently innocent conversational gathering in a bookseller's shop. A wealthy European merchant, Martín Alzaga, and other townsmen provided money: paid recruits were enrolled. Mines were dug and powder was stored to blow up the barracks where the British troops were quartered. Outside the city Juan Martín de Pueyrredón, son of a French immigrant, organised a volunteer force at his own expense, aided by another creole, Martín Rodríguez. Both these men afterwards played a notable part in Argentine history. But the effective leader was a naval officer, Santiago Liniers, a Frenchman of aristocratic birth and persuasive manners, who had started life as page to the Grand Master of the Order of St John at Malta, had then entered the French army, had passed

1 Beresford gives 70,000 as the population of Buenos Aires. The contemporary historian Funes, Dean of Córdoba, says 60,000: but there is evidence that the population can hardly have exceeded 45,000. A city of ground-floor houses, built round open courtyards, covered a much greater extent than an English town of the same population. Major Gillespie, Beresford's Commissary for Prisoners, estimates less than 41,000 inhabitants in his *Gleanings and remarks collected. . .at Buenos Ayres.*

thence to the Spanish service, and now at the age of fifty-three, after thirty-two years in that service and several campaigns, held a subordinate position in the river-flotilla. Liniers visited the conspirators in the city, crossed to Montevideo, obtained a few troops from the garrison, raised volunteers in the Banda Oriental and embarked at Colonia in the Spanish river-flotilla. The commodore of that flotilla, Juan Gutiérrez de la Concha, brought 330 seamen of the Spanish navy to reinforce the little army, and himself served as second-in-command under Liniers.

On August 1 Beresford led out 500 men and scattered Pueyrredón's volunteers at Perdriel, twelve miles from the city— a delusive success, for three days later Liniers landed north of the city with 1300 men. Heavy winter rains, making the road impassable, delayed his march for a week, and also prevented Beresford from sallying out to meet him. Meantime Liniers' force was gathering recruits and when finally he moved towards the city his numbers had doubled. On August 11 he approached the suburbs and summoned Beresford to surrender. The whole city joined in the attack. The British were driven first into the plaza and then into the citadel, where they were exposed to fire from all sides: on the 12th Beresford, having lost 300 men out of less than 1500, hoisted the white flag. Thereupon Liniers and his officers stopped, with some difficulty, the firing by the multitude in the plaza: the draw-bridge was lowered to admit a Spanish officer: the people, rushing across it to crowd into the citadel, were held back by the efforts of Liniers and his assistants. After some parley Beresford hoisted the Spanish flag and surrendered. The officers and men, as prisoners of war, received much kindness and hospitality from the creole inhabitants.

The popular excitement at this people's victory was immense.

The Cabildo met next day, and, following constitutional precedent, summoned the principal inhabitants, ninety-eight in
number, of whom fifty-three had some official position and only
a score were creoles, to a Cabildo abierto under the unaccustomed
name of 'General Congress'. This Congress decreed a solemn
thanksgiving, pensions to the widows of the fallen and measures
for future defence. During this session in the town hall the plaza
without was crowded by a multitude acclaiming Liniers as
commander. The Notables assembled within were averse from
such radical action. They held the view that the Viceroy was still
commander-in-chief, and might, by appointing Liniers as his
deputy, hand over to him the effective command. But the multitude at their doors was insistent, and finally the Congress gave
way to their clamorous demand. The appointment of Liniers as
commander-in-chief was announced from the balcony of the
town hall. Commissioners were sent to inform the Viceroy, who
was slowly approaching the city with troops raised at Córdoba
'for the reconquest'. Sobremonte protested against the action of
the Congress, but a fortnight later he resigned the military command in Buenos Aires to Liniers and the political government
to the Audiencia, and, still claiming to be Viceroy, crossed to
the Banda Oriental.

In effect Liniers became civil and military Governor of Buenos
Aires, the Cabildo acting as Parliament and War Council,
raising funds by subscription and by contributions from other
cities and even from Chile and Peru. Recruiting parties paraded
the streets. In November the Cabildo decreed the enrolment of
all men of military age. Ten infantry battalions were formed, five
of them consisting of European Spaniards: three were formed of
creole Porteños (Patricios), one of negroes and mulattoes, and

4-2

one of natives of the interior provinces (Arribeños): the cavalry were mostly creoles, among them a battalion of Correntinos. The recruits chose their officers and provided their own uniforms, with help from the Cabildo in cases of poverty. The efforts of Belgrano procured the election of Cornelio Saavedra, a creole of high character and integrity, as commander of the Patricios. Nearly 10,000 troops in all were raised, among them a few officers and men of the regular Spanish forces.

These measures were needed. Popham's squadron remained in the river and, reinforced from the Cape, occupied the port of Maldonado in the Banda Oriental. The British Ministry were carried away into schemes of conquest. In January 1807 General Auchmuty, an officer born in New York who had served as a loyalist in the North American War of Independence and had afterwards won distinction in India and Egypt, reached the River Plate with 4000 British troops. On February 6 he ordered a combined attack by land and sea upon Montevideo and took the place by storm with much loss on both sides, a loss which fell partly upon the townsmen who had been among the defenders. Montevideo remained in British hands for seven months.

When the news of the fall of Montevideo reached the capital, 'a great number of the People appeared at the door of the Cabildo of Buenos Aires, crying out that they all wished to go to re-conquer Montevideo and were ready to shed their blood, in order to preserve to the King his dominions and prevent the extinction, in any part of them, of the religion of Jesus Christ which their ancestors had professed'. They also clamoured for the deposition and arrest of Sobremonte. The Cabildo put aside the first wild petition, but granted the second: and next day a Junta of

Map
of the
ROUTE of the TROOPS
from their landing at
Barragan Fort.
to
BUENOS AYRES.

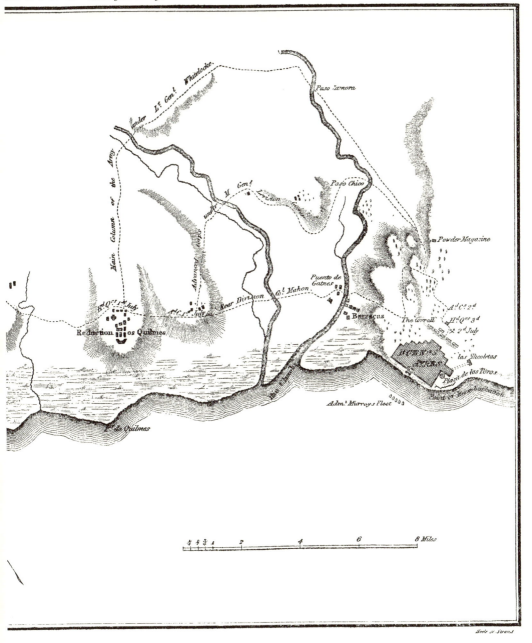

under L.ᵗ Gen.ˡ Whitelocke.

Paso Zamora

Main Column of the Army.

under M.ʳ Gen.ˡ Levison Gower.

Paso Chico

Advanced Corps.

Powder Magazine

H.ᵈ Q.ʳˢ 1.ˢᵗ July

Col.ˡ Mahon

Puento de Gaines

Rear Division

A.ᵈ C.ˢ 2.ᵈ

H.ᵈ Q.ʳˢ 3.ᵈ

The Corrall

& 2.ᵈ July

Redoubt on los Quilmes

H.ᵈ Q.ʳˢ 1.ˢᵗ July

Barracks

las Nicoletas

Plaza de los Toros

P.ᵗ de Quilmes

Adm.ˡ Murray's Fleet

Court of Recon.ᵗ

$$\begin{array}{c|c|c|c|c|c|c} 5\ 4\ 3\ 2\ 1 & 2 & & 4 & & 6 & \text{8 Miles} \end{array}$$

Neele sc Strand

Notables, mostly European Spaniards, sanctioned the verdict, which was duly executed, that Sobremonte should be deposed, arrested and shipped to Spain. The Cabildo now sat almost daily under the vigorous presidency of Alzaga, elected Senior Alcalde for the year 1807.

In May 4000 British troops under Craufurd—originally destined for an expedition to Chile—reached Montevideo: other reinforcements followed; and in June over 9000 troops were assembled in the Banda Oriental under General Whitelocke, who had been sent out as commander-in-chief to recover Buenos Aires. Whitelocke had served with credit in the West Indies, but had held no high command and probably owed his appointment to personal interest. Without waiting for further expected reinforcements of 2000 men, he embarked for the opposite shore. Leaving a garrison of 1330 men in Montevideo, he crossed the river to Ensenada de Barragán, thirty-six miles south of the capital, and there on June 28 he landed 7822 men, of whom only 150 were mounted, sixteen field-guns, and some heavier artillery to be kept in reserve. The four days' march to the city through much water and swamp was a series of blunders, confused orders, needless exhaustion and starvation of the troops, many of whom had been nine months on board ship and were unfit to march.

The improvised Spanish leadership was no better. Liniers, who had no experience of command in the field, led out 7000 volunteers southwards across the Riachuelo to meet the enemy. Half this force was never engaged: for the leading British division marched past it to the left. Thereupon Liniers, in a disordered march, hurried towards his right, to the western or landward outskirts of the city: and here, on the evening of July 2, he was defeated, losing ten guns, by the foremost British brigade. Defence in the field had broken down. The open city, almost devoid of troops, was in consternation, and Liniers spent that night in hiding, almost despairing. Had the British then advanced, the place would have fallen, says General Mitre, the Argentine historian. But there was a respite. The Cabildo sat night and day, and a group of subordinate officers, together with Alzaga, organised the street fighting in which the people were to defend their homes. The main defence centred in the plaza, across which the Cabildo and the citadel faced each other. Trenches were dug and cannon placed in the streets; and the infantry, as they returned to the city, were posted on the surrounding flat housetops. But in addition every householder barred his door and endeavoured to arm his family and slaves.

On the 3rd and 4th there was desultory musketry, and fugitives from the western suburbs drifted into the plaza, reporting that houses had been sacked and unarmed people killed by the invaders.

At daybreak on the 5th a cannon-ball passed through the window into the hall of the Cabildo: a cannonade from Whitelocke's headquarters in the western suburbs was giving the signal for the assault. Nothing could have suited the defenders better than Whitelocke's plan of attack: 5500 British troops, divided into thirteen columns, marched down thirteen straight parallel streets, their muskets unloaded, with orders 'to go, if possible, straight down the streets to the last square of houses near the river'; to take these houses and 'form on the roofs; if they find that they suffer from any interior defences, to lodge themselves as far in advance as they can'.

'Every street was a path of death and every house a fortress':

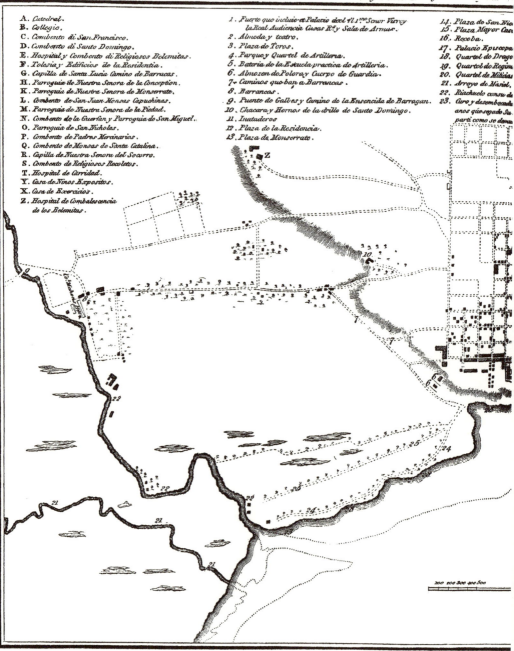

A. Catedral.
B. Collegio.
C. Combento di San Francisco.
D. Combento di Santo Domingo.
E. Hospital y Combento di Religiosos Belemitas.
F. Tolesia y Edificios de la Residencia.
G. Capilla de Santa Lucia Camino de Barracas.
H. Parroquia de Nuestra Senora de la Conception.
K. Parroquia de Nuestra Senora de Monserrate.
L. Combento de San Juan Monsas Capuchinas.
M. Parroquia de Nuestra Senora de la Piedad.
N. Combento de la Guerfan y Parroquia de San Miguel.
O. Parroquia de San Nicholas.
P. Combento de Padres Mercenarios.
Q. Combento de Monsas de Santa Catalina.
R. Capilla de Nuestra Senora del Socorro.
S. Combento de Religiosos Recoletos.
T. Hospital de Caridad.
Y. Casa de Ninos Expositos.
X. Casa de Exercicios.
Z. Hospital de Combalescencia
    de los Belemitas.

1. Fuerto que incluie el Palacio del 1ᵐᵒ Senor Virrey
    la Real Audiencia Casas Rˢ y Sala de Armas.
2. Almeda y teatro.
3. Plaza de Toros.
4. Parque y Quartel de Artilleria.
5. Bateria de la Escuela practica de Artilleria.
6. Almozen de Polora y Cuerpo de Guardia.
7. Caminos que ban a Barrancas.
8. Barrancas.
9. Puente de Galves y Camino de la Ensencida de Barragan.
10. Chacara y Hornos de la orille de Santo Domingo.
11. Inataderos.
12. Plaza de la Residencia.
13. Plaza de Monserrato.

14. Plaza de San Nic...
15. Plaza Mayor Cas...
16. Receba.
17. Palacio Episcopa...
18. Quartel de Drago...
19. Quartel de Regim...
20. Quartel de Milicia...
21. Arroyo de Marid...
22. Riachuelo consu d...
23. Curo y desembcad...
    anos que segado Su...
    parti como se dam...

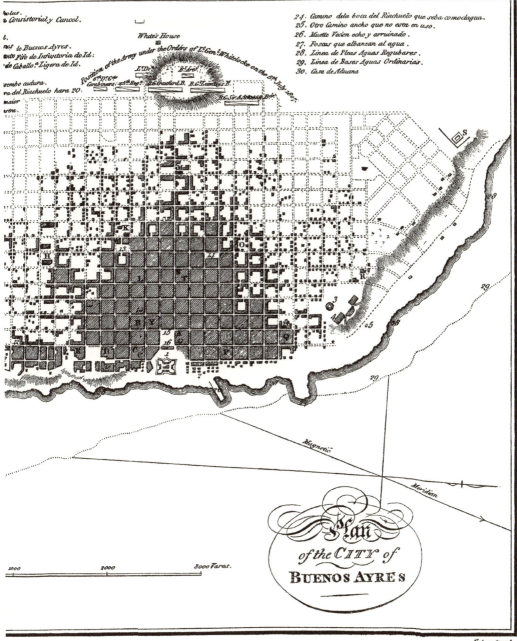

...itelocke taken in Short Hand by Mr. Gurney.

...holus .
...a Consistorial y Cancel .

...t.
...nos lo Buenos Ayres .
...onte Fiso de Infanteria do Id :
...'de Caballeria Ligera de Id .

...vembre audura .
...ra del Riachuelo hara 20 .
...maior
...ayre .

24. Camino dela boca del Riachuelo que seba comodagua .
25. Otro Camino ancho que no esta en uso .
26. Muette Vecien echo y arruinado .
27. Foscas que albanzan al agua .
28. Linea de Pleas Aguas Regubares .
29. Linea de Bases Aguas Ordinarias .
30. Casa de Aduana

Whate's House

Position of the Army under the Orders of Lt. Gen. Whitelocke on the 5th July 1807.

1st Div.   6th
Combiners   45th Reg: B.G. Crawford B.   B.G. Lumleys H.
B.G. Sir S. Achmuty Bde.

2000   2000   3000 Varas.

Plan
of the CITY of
BUENOS AYRES

Magnetic

Meridian

Neele sc Strand

every detached British column ran the gauntlet of fire and mis-
cellaneous missiles from the parapets of the flat roofs and from
the iron grills which barred the windows in Spanish fashion.
The two wings penetrated through the city to the shore and
occupied two strong and lofty buildings, the Residencia in the
south, and in the north the bullring with the adjacent artillery
barracks and arsenal, taken after heavy fighting by Auchmuty.
But most of the centre columns, isolated and entrapped, surrendered after heavy loss. Craufurd held the Church of Santo
Domingo, unsupported, for eight hours before surrendering.

In the afternoon Liniers stood upon the balcony of the
Cabildo, overlooking the plaza. Seeing the damage suffered by
the enemy, he remarked to the Second Alcalde and to the King's
Attorney who stood beside him that he thought of offering
terms to the enemy, the restoration of all prisoners and the re-
embarkation of the invaders. Alzaga presently joined them on
the balcony and, on hearing the proposal, objected, saying that
the prisoners taken with Beresford should also be restored on
condition that the enemy should evacuate Montevideo and the
whole River Plate 'with the understanding that if he does not
accept these terms all his troops will be annihilated'. Liniers
agreed about the restoration of Beresford's men and the evacuation
of Montevideo, but rejected Alzaga's truculent and vainglorious
threat. Passing into the Council Chamber, he wrote accordingly
a letter to Whitelocke, adding a clause, evidently in deference
to Alzaga: 'My troops are so heated that, if your Excellency
should reject these terms, I cannot answer for it that your
troops may not suffer all the rigour of war: my troops being all
the more exasperated because three of my aides-de-camp have
been wounded upon approaching where flags of truce were

displayed'.[1] This note, which was dispatched to Whitelocke on the following morning by the hand of a British captive officer, will not bear the interpretation which seems to have been put upon it that Liniers declared himself to be unable to answer for the safety of the prisoners if the terms were rejected. Liniers modified Alzaga's insolent threat that no quarter would be given into a warning that he might not be able to prevent his exasperated troops from refusing quarter. Liniers' position was difficult: his authority was not unquestioned; he had been defeated in the field; he had only a precarious hold upon the recently raised volunteer battalions who chose their own officers and had rudimentary notions, as Belgrano tells us, of military discipline. Moreover among Liniers' 'troops' might be reckoned all the inhabitants, including an agitated mob of the lower orders, infuriated at the attack upon their homes. 'Every male inhabitant', said Whitelocke in his defence, 'whether free or slave, fought with a resolution and perseverance which could not have been expected, even from the enthusiasm of religion and national prejudice or the most inveterate and implacable hostility.' There is evidence, it is right to add, that, when the famished, exhausted

[1] This account is taken from the published minutes of the Cabildo, of which Alzaga was chairman; that is to say it is Alzaga's own story, which magnifies the part taken by the Spanish civilian and minimises that taken by the French soldier. The story current at the time, and expanded later into a picturesque tradition, attributes even a greater share to Alzaga, implying that, but for his interposition, Montevideo would have remained in British hands. Alzaga's own account, signed by him and his colleagues, given above, does not justify that view; it cannot be asserted that Liniers, in drawing up the document, would have confined himself to his first conversational suggestion and would never have thought of demanding the entire evacuation of the River Plate. The terms were naturally a matter of discussion, and Liniers, as commander, was responsible for them. If Alzaga's insulting threat had been sent to Whitelocke, it might well have ruined the negotiation.

and ill-led British soldiers reached the outskirts of the city three days earlier, their discipline had suffered. Not only private houses, but a convent also had been sacked. Some of the outrages committed in the suburbs were the work of bandits from the surrounding country who, as often happens in such cases, took advantage of the occasion. But the invading soldiery were certainly not guiltless.

When night fell, the British had taken 1000 prisoners and held a strong position in and about the bullring: but they had lost over 3000 in killed, wounded and prisoners. Next morning, July 6, Whitelocke, who had shortly before moved from the western suburbs, where he had been quite out of touch with his troops, to the bullring, received the proposals for a capitulation, and after consulting the general officers, he accepted them in the main. All prisoners were to be restored, including those taken with Beresford, and the British were to re-embark at once and were to evacuate Montevideo within two months. Whitelocke incurred much obloquy by agreeing to these terms when, including a reserve outside the city, he still commanded nearly 5000 troops, held a strong position with much captured artillery and ammunition, besides a garrison at Montevideo and a naval squadron in the river. Sir John Fortescue, historian of the British army, holds that the capitulation, including the surrender of Montevideo, was Whitelocke's one wise action. Auchmuty, the captor and former Governor of Montevideo, held the same view, declaring that, since every inhabitant was an enemy, Montevideo could only be held if its 15,000 inhabitants were turned out and a reinforced British garrison were provisioned entirely by sea. It may be noted that a year later Great Britain entered upon a peculiarly

intimate alliance with Spain, which might have rendered difficult
the retention of a Spanish province in British hands.

In England two courts-martial sat: Popham was severely re-
primanded, and Whitelocke was dismissed from the service.[1]
From the Court of Spain the Cabildo of Buenos Aires received
the official style of 'Excelentísimo'. Concha, second-in-command in the *Reconquista*, had been already appointed Governor-
Intendant of Córdoba. Elío, second-in-command in the defence, was nominated by Liniers military Governor of Montevideo, an appointment which later had peculiar results. Liniers
himself was promoted admiral and soon afterwards was appointed Viceroy *ad interim*. He was the last Viceroy nominated
by the Spanish Crown.[2] When his commission as Viceroy
reached Buenos Aires in May 1808, the Spanish King was an
exile and a captive.

Among the memorials of the reconquest which are treasured
in Buenos Aires are the colours of a British regiment, the sword
of the British commander, a clock presented by Beresford to the
Cabildo of Buenos Aires and another clock presented by the
Seventy-first Regiment to the hospital where their wounded were
tended. This latter gift bears the inscription, *Fugit irrevocabile
tempus: beneficii haud fugit memoria.*

1 In this chapter the part concerning the movements of the British is largely
taken from the published Report of the Trial of Whitelocke by Gurney the
short-hand writer (London, 1808).

2 Cisneros was appointed by the Central Junta.

CHAPTER VI

PRELIMINARIES OF INDEPENDENCE

'I CONGRATULATE the Americans [*Americanos*]: they have proved the worth of those born in the Indies, showing that they are not inferior to the European Spaniards, that in valour and loyalty they yield to none.'

Saavedra, addressing thus the creole troops under his command five months after their victory, affirmed their loyalty, hinted at tension between Europeans and natives, and gave utterance to a strong local consciousness which might almost be called national. Although no single step in the defence and reorganisation of Buenos Aires was quite without precedent—local action had dethroned a Mexican Viceroy in 1624—yet the whole series of events amounted to a revolutionary development. Opinion had been educated not only by internal movements, but also by outside influence. For in Montevideo during the half-year of British occupation a newspaper, *The Star of the South*, was published in Spanish and English, and active trade went on, the bay crowded with shipping and people hurrying from the far interior to buy goods before the evacuation. Intercourse with the British had done much to widen views of commerce and of politics. A spirit of unrest and expectancy prevailed. Although the cities maintained allegiance, the lawless inhabitants of the plains had no regard for any Government; and in the capital itself, after the long interruption of normal life, after the months of military activity under lax discipline and the excitement of final victory, the young men were loath to resume a dull professional routine.

The Viceroy himself took an extraordinary and unprecedented course. Liniers, the representative of the Spanish Crown, actually sent an emissary to Napoleon, a foreign potentate, with a report of the recent victory. This anomalous and most uncon-stitutional action was approved by the Audiencia and the Cabildo owing to the exceptional emergency and the urgent need of aid from any quarter in case of further hostile attack. Spain was totally unable to protect her dependencies, which therefore turned elsewhere for protection and already pursued a foreign policy of their own, independently of Spain.

There was justifiable apprehension of danger from the north; for Rio de Janeiro was now the capital of the Portuguese monarchy and the residence of the Portuguese Court, which had fled from Lisbon before French invasion and had been conveyed in British ships to Rio in January 1808. And the Portuguese Court, in alliance with the British enemy, was at war with Spain and was threatening a movement against the Spanish dominions in the River Plate. Not only in his peculiar action of sending an emissary bearing dispatches to Napoleon, but also in his deal-ings with the Portuguese Court and in his preparations for meeting the Portuguese-Brazilian menace, Liniers acted as the head of an independent state: he even propounded a wild scheme for invading Brazil with the resources of the Viceroyalty alone.

Meantime the Cabildo, which was by no means fully at accord with the Viceroy, earnestly sought aid from the Peninsula against a possible Anglo-Portuguese invasion; but the Spanish monarchy, drained of men, money and ships by her imperious 'ally' Napoleon, was powerless to aid: she not only permitted but required her colonies to act independently. Some modifica-

tion of government was inevitable and had indeed been already
initiated on the spot. Few, as yet, envisaged the idea of 'independence', but the materials of revolutionary thought and
action had been prepared. The impulse to action came from
Europe, and it came in a startling form.

In July 1808, a Royal Order from Madrid came to Buenos
Aires. This official document declared that King Charles IV
had abdicated the throne, and that his son was to be proclaimed
King in his place as Ferdinand VII. Accordingly the proclamation of the new King was fixed for August 12, the anniversary of the Reconquista, but was postponed owing to con-
flicting reports. Meantime there landed in Buenos Aires an
emissary from Napoleon, carrying a bag full of papers, and
nothing more; for a consignment of arms and ammunition
which had accompanied him from Bayonne, destined for
Napoleon's allies in the River Plate, had suffered disaster at sea
from tempest and from British pursuit. Liniers refused to see the
envoy until he had summoned a committee representing the
Audiencia and the Cabildo. In their presence the bag was un-
locked and the envoy ordered to withdraw. The bag contained
packets addressed to the authorities of all the Spanish-American
provinces. The Audiencia and the Cabildo were then convoked
to a joint sitting, and listened to the reading of the dispatches
addressed to Liniers. These papers related that Charles IV and
his son Ferdinand VII, both being in France, had renounced
their rights in favour of Napoleon, who ceded these rights to his
brother Joseph, now to become King of Spain. Various other
'seditious prints' which emerged from the bag were burnt at
once. The assembly resolved that the Frenchman who had conveyed them should re-embark promptly for Montevideo *en route*

for Bayonne, that the Viceroy should issue an address to the people and that Ferdinand VII should be proclaimed King. The address which Liniers accordingly published reflects the prevailing uncertainties about this startling, obscure and fragmentary news which came from France concerning revolution in Spain. The address speaks respectfully of 'his Imperial and Royal Majesty Napoleon', indicates a hope of receiving military aid, expresses 'the fidelity of this people to their legitimate sovereign' and advises the people to imitate their ancestors, who during the war of the Spanish Succession 'awaited the destiny of the mother country in order to obey the legitimate authority which occupied the throne'. But notwithstanding these cautious and ambiguous warnings issued by official authority, the general determination found public expression in the solemn proclamation of the new King on August 21 amid popular cries of *Viva Fernando Séptimo.*

Two days later, another emissary arrived in Buenos Aires from Europe. This time it was a Spanish officer, creole by birth, Goyeneche, of later notoriety. He came bearing dispatches: 'All Spain had risen against the tyrant Napoleon, in order to restore their sovereign and preserve national independence: a Supreme Junta installed at Seville had declared war against Napoleon, was making peace with Great Britain and obtaining help from thence'. The Cabildo received the news with enthusiasm and appealed to the people, with prompt and remarkable success, for *donativos* to aid the mother country in her struggle against the oppressor.

Three weeks later came a presumptuous manifesto from Carlota, sister of Ferdinand VII and wife of the Prince Regent of Portugal, then reigning at Rio de Janeiro: she claimed to take charge of the sovereignty of the River Plate as depositary for her father Charles IV, whose abdication, she declared, was null, having been extorted by force. The Audiencia and the Cabildo replied with an emphatic repudiation of her claims, affirming their allegiance to Ferdinand VII.

Yet amid the various claims, of Charles, of Ferdinand, of Carlota, of the Junta of Seville and the Junta of Galicia—which also sent an envoy—and in the dubious light of inaccurate and incomplete reports coming from Spain some months after the events, it was difficult to define allegiance. When Napoleon's envoy reached Montevideo on his return journey, Elío, the stout ultra-royalist Governor of the place, imprisoned him, wrote to Spain denouncing the Viceroy as a Bonapartist and a traitor, sent to Liniers a defiant message, demanded the resignation of the 'Frenchman', and knocked down with his fists an officer sent by Liniers to supersede him. The mob of Montevideo carried Elío shoulder-high through the streets with cries of *Junta, as in Spain, viva Elío. Death to the traitor! Death to the Buenos-aireans!* A Cabildo abierto met in Montevideo and nominated a Governing Junta composed of European Spaniards, thus defying Liniers, the King's representative, by way of uncom-promising support of the King. 'South American revolution was initiated by its bitterest enemy', says Mitre.

The Audiencia, the supreme tribunal of the capital, pro-nounced this Montevidean movement to be illegal. Yet the stubborn and bitter chapetón Alzaga, with his colleagues and partisans, conspired to imitate Montevideo, and to decapitate the creole party by dethroning Liniers and replacing him by a Governing Junta. On January 1, 1809, the city bell rang for the election of the new Cabildo, and then changed its note to the

alarm. Some of the European troops, with arms and ammunition, crowded into the plaza. The cry was raised, *Junta, as in
Spain: down with the Frenchman!* A Cabildo abierto, carefully
packed beforehand for the purpose, hurriedly met and voted for
a Governing Junta. The Bishop, Lué by name, crossing the
plaza to the citadel, urged Liniers to resign. Saavedra, who had
marched his Patricios into the citadel by the river gate, protested.
Finally Saavedra led his Patricios into the plaza, added to their
number by calling out some European troops who were faithful,
entered the council chamber, where a Junta of Notables was
actually receiving Liniers' resignation, compelled the Viceroy
to withdraw that resignation and by this vigorous show of force
suppressed the 'revolution'. The word is appropriate, for the
whole movement closely resembles many of the 'revolutions'
which punctuate the history of Spanish-American republics
in the nineteenth century. Alzaga and four colleagues were
hurried on board a ship in their silken coats of ceremony to exile
at Patagones, whence they were rescued in a ship dispatched
from Montevideo by the stubborn reactionary Elío. It is typical
of the uncertainties of the time that Mariano Moreno, afterwards
the uncompromising champion of independent action, took the
part of Alzaga and of the European Spaniards in this attempted
revolution of January 1.

A week later all the authorities met in the citadel to swear
allegiance, amid popular rejoicings and illuminations, to the
Central Junta which had been set up in Spain, as 'supreme
Government of the kingdoms of Spain and the Indies...to hold
in deposit the authority of Ferdinand VII until his restoration'.
But this show of union was delusive. The Spanish monarchy,
the sole European authority over the American provinces and

the only legal link between the Peninsula and America, had disappeared: and in consequence Spain and Spanish America were inevitably drifting apart. Since the first news of disturb-ance in Spain, Belgrano, who knew Spain well, had been meet-ing in unobtrusive tertulias a group of men—Castelli, Paso, Pueyrredón and others—who aimed at independence, through monarchical continuity rather than through violent revolution: they held that Carlota might reign in the River Plate as con-stitutional sovereign, with a Parliament. The plan was unwork-able, both on account of the bizarre and intractable character of Carlota, a Bourbon princess of extreme absolutist proclivities, and also on account of the fantastic incongruity of a scheme for enthroning, in place of Ferdinand VII, a princess who was Spanish by birth and Portuguese by adoption. Such a scheme would have been blocked by the opposition of European Powers and would have been rejected by the common sense of the people of the River Plate.

Nevertheless, in June 1809, the moment for action seemed to have come. Admiral Cisneros, a veteran of Trafalgar, arrived in the River Plate, having been appointed Viceroy, not by the King, but by the Central Junta, that is to say by the provisional Spanish Government which had retired to Seville when Napoleonic armies installed Joseph Bonaparte as King in Madrid.

Belgrano now urged Liniers to treat Cisneros' commission as invalid, to retain the command in his own hands and to offer a constitutional throne to Carlota. The battalion commanders, arbiters of the situation, met at midnight: Saavedra was ready to act; but his European colleagues were irresolute and the meeting dispersed before dawn with nothing done. 'The figs are not yet ripe', remarked Saavedra. Liniers himself declined a perilous and illegal *pronunciamiento*: he crossed to Colonia, whither Cisneros, doubtful of his attitude, had summoned him, and there handed over to his successor his perplexing task.

Cisneros, welcomed with costly state by the triumphant European magistrates, occupied an uneasy seat for ten months in an atmosphere of pasquinades, of party tension, of growing disbelief in the possible revival of chaotic Spain. Although sent out with orders to favour the European party and to send Liniers to Spain, he adopted a conciliatory attitude, allowed Liniers for the time to retire to Córdoba, and showed by frequent proclamations a nervous anxiety to satisfy opinion and maintain authority.

Two matters demanded attention, political disturbance in Upper Peru and a growing debt due to military expenditure. Liniers had been about to admit British trade, in order to relieve the Treasury by the increase of dutiable imports which was certain to result from such a measure. Cisneros, perplexed by urgent financial need, was disposed to adopt the same expedient. There were abundant war-time precedents for such Viceregal enactments; but the Viceroy took no action without first consulting all possible advisers. The merchants, mostly Europeans, favoured the existing Spanish monopoly. Their attitude appears in the reluctant assent of the Cabildo: 'Although the admission of British trade is an evil, it is an evil necessary in present circumstances, and should be accepted in order to avoid greater evils'. A month later the farming community presented their famous 'Argument', signed by the representative of their gild, but written by Mariano Moreno. It is an eloquent and powerful plea for opening the port to British trade, not as a temporary financial expedient but as a necessity to economic well-being and particularly to pastoral and agricultural progress, which demanded free export: 'I sustain the cause of *La Patria*'. Cisneros finally summoned a Junta representing every class and interest, which sanctioned his proposal. The increased receipts from customs, as open trade replaced contraband, fully justified his action.

Señor Molinari in a recent monograph has shown that the effect of Moreno's pamphlet upon Cisneros' decision has been exaggerated; and he also argues that the whole proceeding was rather one in a long series of concessions than a considerable step towards emancipation. But at that moment of uneasy expectancy departure from law and tradition, although nothing very un‑usual, had unusual significance: it meant the opening of a window into the non‑Spanish world which could never again be closed. And the value of Moreno's pamphlet lies not in any immediate effect as an argument in debate, but in its implied condemnation of the colonial mercantile system and its oppor‑tune exposition of liberal economic principles—enounced, it is true, with considerable limitations, possibly due to motives of practical prudence on the part of the writer.

'I found', wrote Cisneros, 'two formidable parties in the capital...a popular tumult in the city of La Plata (Chuquisaca) which attacked and deposed the Governor...and a sedition yet more serious in the city of La Paz.' Long disputes, largely personal and trifling in origin, between the Spanish Governor and the Spanish Audiencia of Chuquisaca led to a popular outbreak on May 25, 1809, when the Audiencia deposed the unpopular and meddlesome Governor, assuming his functions. This act of a royal Court, consisting of European magistrates, the strongest pillar of Spanish authority, followed many pre‑cedents and was hardly unconstitutional: under normal con‑ditions it would have merely produced an interminable written 'process', passing into oblivion with the royal appointment of a new Governor. But under existing conditions it meant revolution: and the neighbouring city of La Paz, catching the infection, proclaimed autonomy under a creole Junta, which, in the name of Ferdinand VII, announced 'a new system of government, founded on the interests of *La Patria*, after three centuries of despotism and tyranny'.

The insurrection of La Paz was suppressed with sanguinary violence by an expedition sent by the Viceroy of Peru under the creole Goyeneche, who affixed the mangled limbs of executed townspeople to the milestones; Goyeneche wrote to Buenos Aires asking that a magistrate should be sent to try his remaining prisoners. Cisneros replied that summary justice should be done.

Meantime Cisneros sent a body of Patricios against Chuquisaca under Nieto, Governor of Montevideo, who imposed penalties of arrest and imprisonment. Opinion was shocked by the mode of suppressing these disturbances and by the different treatment of Europeans and of creoles. Cisneros by his callous severity forfeited the esteem gained by his moderate attitude in Buenos Aires.

Meantime news of further disasters in Spain aided Belgrano's efforts: his tertulia was becoming a Patriotic Club, separatist in aim. Saavedra, pressed to act, replied, 'When Seville falls'.

On May 13 an English ship brought news that Seville had fallen four months earlier, that the Central Junta, the source of Cisneros' authority, had fled to the remote island city of Cadiz and then dissolved, resigning its authority into the hands of an improvised Council of Regency. On May 18 Cisneros himself published the news, with an appeal for caution and patience. A week later he had ceased to rule; the moment had come to claim Saavedra's promise.

CHAPTER VII

EMANCIPATION

In the constitution of the Spanish Monarchy, the King was the sole link which bound together his various estates. MANUEL MORENO

THE stirring events of the week which followed the Viceroy's dubious pronouncement upon the fall of Seville are recalled with just pride, almost in hourly detail, by Argentines, whose ancestors carried through with prudent tranquillity the inevitable transition from external to native authority in so short a time.

The mother country had suffered, to all appearance, a fatal blow. Madrid had been occupied for a year by a usurping foreign monarch. A provisional Government which had established itself in Seville, claiming to represent Spain and the captive Spanish King, had now fled and dissolved. In Buenos Aires it was a moment of uneasy anxiety of hopes and apprehensions and of much excited movement among the creole troops. But Belgrano and his associates saw their opportunity to guide quietly these cross-currents to a definite issue. On May 19 they assembled in the house of Rodríguez Peña, who four years earlier had discussed plans of independence with Beresford during the captivity of the latter. Officers of all the creole battalions were present at this meeting, headed by the dignified figure of Martín Rodríguez, who had aided Pueyrredón to raise volunteers in 1806. Saavedra hurried to the city from a country residence and joined the gathering. They resolved to proceed by the constitutional method of Cabildo abierto. But a Cabildo abierto could only be legally summoned by the Cabildo, with the previous sanction of the Viceroy. With some difficulty Saavedra and Belgrano persuaded Lezica, the Senior Alcalde, an Americano, to assemble his colleagues. The Cabildo met and sent two of their number to ask the Viceroy's permission for the summoning of a Cabildo abierto. Cisneros expressed surprise at the request and deferred reply until he should have talked with the military commanders. These were at once summoned to the palace and were asked whether they were prepared to support the Viceregal authority. There was a pause, and then Saavedra spoke; he told Cisneros that the Viceregal authority no longer existed, since the power from which it was derived had disappeared. 'Your Excellency', he concluded, 'must not count upon the support of the troops under my command.' The officers then withdrew, but nothing was done until two emis-saries from the 'Patriotic Club', Castelli and Martín Rodríguez, entered, late at night, the Viceroy's private room, found him seated at the card-table, and, after a moment of astonished in-dignation on his part, extorted, by a peremptory demand, his consent that a Cabildo abierto should be summoned.

On May 21 the Cabildo met to consider preliminaries, while 'a considerable number of people gathering in the Plaza' clamoured first for a Cabildo abierto and then for the removal of the Viceroy. Four hundred and fifty tickets of invitation were issued: two hundred and fifty persons assembled in the early morning on May 22 for the Cabildo abierto which was to settle the future of the River Plate; the two hundred absentees, mostly European Spaniards, either discreetly stayed at home or else failed to get past the piquets of creole troops posted at every approach.

The Bishop, Lué, opened the debate, urging the continuance

of Cisneros in office. Castelli answered him with vehemence. Admiral Huidobro, formerly Governor of Montevideo, who had actually been nominated Viceroy while a prisoner in England but had never occupied that post, voted for the deposition of Cisneros. Tradition relates that a movement of dubious apprehension stirred the gathering when the attorney of the Audiencia argued for legal delay pending the assembly of deputies from the cities; but that the creole lawyer Paso, a man of small stature, having been pushed to his feet by a neighbour, urged immediate action in an impassioned oration and carried the assembly with him. The voting lasted till past midnight, every member rising in turn to pronounce his opinion. The decision of the majority was that Cisneros should be deposed and that the Cabildo should hold authority until they should appoint a Junta to rule, pending the assembly of deputies from the provinces to establish the form of government.

Next day the Cabildo, now half-European and half-Americano in composition, assembled, ostensibly in order to carry out the decision of the Cabildo abierto. But the Cabildo, a cautious and conservative body, shrank from so extreme a measure, and attempted to avert or mitigate revolution by means of a compromise: they nominated a Junta of five persons, two Americanos, namely Saavedra and Castelli, two European Spaniards and Cisneros himself as President of the Junta. The battalion commanders, among them Saavedra, were summoned to the Cabildo and agreed to this arrangement; and on the afternoon of the 24th this Junta of five members was solemnly installed, with Cisneros in the chair. But power lay elsewhere. This attempt to modify or nullify the decision of the Cabildo abierto and to bolster up the Viceregal authority aroused general indignation among the leaders of the movement and among the troops. All that night in the Patriotic Club and in the various barracks there were anxious discussions, preparing the programme, an entirely different programme, for the following day.

May 25, a date since annually observed as the birthday of the Argentine Republic, dawned with cold autumnal rain. The Cabildo met thrice. Early in the morning they received perforce the resignation of the short-lived Junta of five, while people crowded the corridors of the town hall, among them two ardent and youthful satellites of the Patriotic Club, Beruti and French, who forced their way into the council chamber, claiming to represent the people. The commanders, having been summoned once more to the Cabildo, reported unrest among the people and among the troops: blows fell upon the door of the chamber; and finally Beruti and French reappeared, presenting a list of nine names, eight creoles and one European. A written petition with many hastily gathered signatures, headed by those of the commanders, supported the demonstration. At a second meeting the Cabildo accepted the names proposed: Saavedra as President, Paso and Moreno as secretaries, Belgrano, Castelli and four others. At a third meeting these nine men were sworn in, pledging themselves, in presence of the Cabildo, 'to observe the laws of the kingdom and to preserve this part of America for our august sovereign Ferdinand VII'. Next day Cisneros, with apparent readiness, but with an intense chagrin which found expression later, signed a circular announcing his abdication and inviting the provinces to elect deputies to a Congress. Two days later all the officials and the troops swore obedience to the 'Provisional Governing Junta of the Provinces of the Río de la Plata in the name of Ferdinand VII'. British war-ships decked with flags fired a salute, and their officers landed to take prominent part in the celebration. On the same day the Junta dispatched an account of these events to Lord Strangford, British Minister at Rio, who sent a sympathetic reply. In an address to the battalions (May 27) the Junta publicly acknowledged 'the energy with which you have given a firm authority to your country...the wisdom which prevailed in your discussions'.

'A bloodless Revolution', remarks the contemporary historian Funes, 'produced by the very course of events.'

In January 1810 the Central Junta of Spain, just before its flight to Cadiz and dissolution, sent dispatches to Buenos Aires and to all the capitals of the Spanish-American provinces, inviting them to send deputies to Cortes, that is to say to a representative Parliament, which was to be summoned in Spain. These American provinces, they declared, were no longer dependencies of the Crown, but integral parts of the Spanish realm. One clause in this invitation ran thus: 'You are no longer what you were, bowed beneath a yoke harder to bear in proportion to your distance from the centre of power, regarded with indifference, vexed by greed and oppressed by ignorance. After nominating your deputies, your destinies will no longer depend on Ministers or Viceroys or Governors. They are in your own hands'. When this manifesto reached its destination the trans-Atlantic provinces were already taking their destinies into their own hands after another fashion than by sending deputies on a voyage of 5000 miles. It would not be easy to find a more striking justification of their action than this curious exhortation to revolution sent out by those who claimed to be the Government of Spain.

The Junta at the earliest opportunity sent an emissary to

England. He reached London on August 6, 1810; and on the following day news of the revolution in Buenos Aires appeared in *The Times*. Two Commissioners from Venezuela had recently arrived in London with news of revolution in that country. With regard to these two revolutions at opposite ends of the South American Continent, the policy of Lord Wellesley, the British Foreign Minister, appears to have been the same:—that Great Britain should protect the new Governments from any French aggression and should attempt mediation with Spain. In 1812, Lord Castlereagh being then Foreign Minister, a British mission was sent to Cadiz in hopes of arranging some accommodation between the Regency of Cadiz, which claimed to be the Government of Spain, and the revolted colonies. But the Regency was uncompromising, and nothing was done. During the following decade, the crucial period of the struggle for emancipation, Great Britain showed herself ready, whenever occasion offered, to act the part of common friend in any movement towards an agreement between her ally, Spain, and the new Spanish-American Governments, with which she maintained informal but friendly relations. But from the very beginning, from the critical date of May 25, 1810—however long the open declaration of independence might be delayed—the only possible issue of the movement was independence.

CHAPTER VIII

THE NEW STATE

CRITICS have complained that historians of Argentina write in fact the history of Buenos Aires. With regard to the years 1806–10 this is inevitable. Buenos Aires, with some aid from the provinces, had foiled invasion, had made and unmade Governments: her Town Council had acted as a Parliament for the whole Viceroyalty. And now a provisional Government, set up by the people and troops of the capital, claimed, in the King's name, with the public sanction of the Viceroy, all the authority previously exercised by Kings and Viceroys over the whole Viceroyalty; they treated disobedience as treason and denounced as 'rebels' and 'insurgents' those who resisted their arms even in the remote regions of Paraguay and Upper Peru. They issued a proclamation to the capital and 'to the Provinces under their superior command...the Provinces depending upon us', appointed and deposed provincial Governors, regulated the election of deputies, and sent out two of their number, Castelli to the north-west and Belgrano to the north, as commissioners with plenary authority, co-opting two members in their place.

This attitude was perhaps justified by the emergency and by the fact that the capital had to meet the menace of Brazilian aggression, to pursue the war in Upper Peru against the Viceroy of Lima and to bear the main brunt of war with Montevideo, whose people recognised the Cadiz Regency and opposed the Revolution, holding the reasonable view that allegiance to the dethroned King involved loyalty to the Spanish Government which ruled in his name and resisted the French intruder.

Prominent in the Junta was their young secretary, Mariano Moreno, who owes a semi-legendary reputation partly to the fraternal piety of his biographer, Manuel Moreno, partly to his own self-consuming zeal, his human impulses and utterances, his nervous and sometimes indiscreet vehemence and finally his tragic fate. An assiduous student of French political theory, he poured out in the weekly *Gazette of Buenos Aires* his arguments for the sovereignty of the people, speaks boldly of 'emancipation . . . state . . . nation' and insists on the lapse of the 'social pact' through the captivity of the King to whom he still professed nominal allegiance:—for he and his colleagues publicly observed all the outward forms of the hereditary Bourbon monarchy and sought to avert Spanish hostility and to conciliate both traditional sentiment and also foreign diplomatic susceptibilities by reiterating allegiance to Ferdinand VII.

Nevertheless, by shelving the question of recognising the Regency established in Cadiz, they assumed in fact a republican independence which the Argentine Provinces—alone among the countries of South America—have preserved unbroken from the first. The Spanish judges or councillors of the Audiencia were replaced by the appointment of native magistrates and later were deported, together with Cisneros, to the Canary Islands. The members of the Cabildo, who proved reactionary, were deposed, banished from the city, denounced as 'bad patriots' and replaced by nominees of the Junta. Steps were taken towards the liberty of the press. A public library and schools were founded 'in order that education might counter the barbaric influence of war'. For, notwithstanding the professed allegiance to Ferdinand VII, it was already clearly recognised that the Revolution meant war—war against the genuine supporters of the Bourbon monarchy, including the Viceroy of Peru, Abascal, an able and energetic ruler, who had been appointed to his post in 1806 by King Charles IV and therefore represented beyond all doubt the exiled King of Spain.

Two months after the revolution a mounted corps of 1150 men, commanded by Ocampo, colonel of the Arribeños and a native of Rioja, set out for the interior 'in order to carry the commands of the people on the points of their bayonets', says Mitre. They were to permit the formation of local juntas 'provided that these recognise absolute dependence on the Junta of Buenos Aires'.

Córdoba offered their first task. Here two officers of the royal navy, namely Concha the Governor and Liniers the ex-Viceroy, supported by the Bishop and other adherents, opposed the Junta and raised troops to co-operate with those of Upper Peru. Their followers fell away as the Porteño expedition approached. Liniers and Concha, who had been comrades in arms in 1806, retreated northwards, losing deserters at every step. They were pursued, found themselves almost alone, separated for greater safety, fled to obscure hiding-places, were tracked down and taken. The Junta commanded immediate execution: Ocampo pleaded for mercy; Castelli was sent to carry out orders; the two heroes of the reconquista were shot with three companions. The Junta appointed Pueyrredón Governor of Córdoba in the place of Concha, who had been appointed by the King.

Meantime all the cities of the purely Argentine region, successively, in Cabildo abierto, declared adhesion to the Junta and elected deputies to attend a Congress. But Paraguay and Montevideo declined; and most of Upper Peru was still held by royal Governors, obedient to the Cadiz Regency and to the Peruvian Viceroy. The Porteño expedition, gathering recruits on the march, passed through Tucumán and Salta, where Chiclana was appointed Governor. They climbed the steep passes to the plateau of Upper Peru. They defeated, after a slight reverse, the royalist forces at Suipacha and captured three Spanish officers, Córdoba, commander of the troops; Paula Sanz, Governor of Charcas, of undesirable memory as Superintendente of Buenos Aires; and the aged Nieto, Governor of Potosí, odious through his suppression of the 'Revolution' of Chuquisaca. All three were shot by order of Castelli. Success gained adherents, and for the moment all Upper Peru appeared to be subject to the Junta, which appointed Pueyrredón, who had been Governor of Córdoba, to be Governor of Charcas.

A month after the dispatch of the 'auxiliary expedition' to Córdoba, Belgrano was sent to offer the revolution to Paraguay. In December 1810 he crossed the Paraná with about 1000 men, half of them raw recruits. The royal Governor of Paraguay led against him a hastily raised and ill-armed militia force seven times greater. Belgrano showed high courage and remarkable skill in two skirmishes and an unavoidable retreat, as well as diplomatic readiness in concluding an armistice: this led, soon afterwards, to a commercial convention between the Juntas of Buenos Aires and of Asunción (October 18, 1811) which was in effect a treaty between South American Powers; for Paraguay soon deposed the Governor and assumed independence, though declining submission to Buenos Aires. Thenceforth, secure in her remote geographical position, Paraguay maintained an isolated independence without having to fight for it. Or rather she allowed the Argentine Provinces to fight her War of Independence for her without offering them any aid: for the defeat of the Argentines in their War of Independence would have exposed Paraguay to attack by the royalists; whereas Argentine victory meant security for Paraguay.

In December 1810 a triumphant article by Moreno greeted the arrival at Buenos Aires of a Spanish banner captured at Suipacha. A few days later Moreno resigned his post. His eager, uncompromising and somewhat doctrinaire temperament was in exasperating conflict with the conservatism of his chief, Saavedra, who occupied the Viceregal palace, supported by the battalions and generally esteemed. The conflict was exacerbated by personal incidents which embittered feeling and made co-operation between the chairman and the secretary impossible, and it came to a head in Moreno's opposition to the admission of the provincial deputies to the Junta. The original intention had been that those deputies should form a Constituent Assembly and that the Junta should act as the Executive until a Constitution should be promulgated: but the Junta, through some awkward confusion, had invited the provinces to elect deputies 'to be incorporated in the Junta as they arrive at the capital'. The deputies, headed by Funes, Dean of Córdoba, Rector of the University and protagonist of the Revolution in Córdoba, naturally claimed fulfilment of this promise, and as they successively arrived in the capital, they took their seats in the Junta. The result was an amorphous body, neither a strong executive nor a representative assembly, yet claiming complete authority. The nervous, uneasy, vehement Moreno, resolutely determined on strong government, hating half-measures and resenting the easy-going optimism of his chief, found his position an impossible one and resigned his post. The Junta at first declined to accept his resignation. Moreno replied that the resignation of a man of character was irrevocable. He accepted from the Junta a mission[1] to Great Britain, sailed in a British frigate in January 1811, and died at sea at the age of thirty-two. His body was buried at sea, wrapped in the British flag.

Emancipation had happened, almost of itself, through the collapse of Spanish government. The Argentines were now faced with the task of constructing a new State, with little foun- dation upon which to build except municipal institutions, which were clearly inadequate and were even a hindrance to permanent and effective union. Moreover the cities, nuclei of civilisation, were separated from one another by wide barbaric wastes. The result was a succession of short-lived experiments during twenty years, ended by a despotism which lasted another twenty years; and it was only after the fall of that despotism in 1852 that the constitutional organisation of the nation was gradually worked out.

[1] In the written Commission which he received as emissary to Great Britain, Moreno is styled 'Secretary of Government'. His mission, with the character thus assigned to it, was an honourable form of withdrawal from the Government, to serve his country in another field.

CHAPTER IX

DEFENCE AND SECURITY

THE experiments through which these scattered provinces, lacking cohesion, lacking political experience, lacking any comprehensive institutions, endeavoured to solve a strange and unprecedented problem, were carried out during years of warfare, wars against royalist attack and Brazilian aggression, wars which were waged at first by improvised armies and self-taught commanders, wars which were complicated by confusion concerning frontiers. This last complication was partly due to the natural but impracticable attempt to win for the young Republic all the territory comprised in the former unwieldy Viceroyalty.

The State had to defend her existence while struggling into form. Every triumph and every reverse were reflected in the political movements of the capital and in the activities of provincial *caudillos* (chieftains), the vicissitudes of government and of civil strife following the vicissitudes of war. The conduct of war and the simultaneous building-up of a new political order demanded a strong executive. Moreno knew this, but he lacked both physical strength and military backing: moreover he seems to have held, with Castelli, that revolution must be supported by Gallic terrorism, notwithstanding the wide dissimilarity between French conditions in 1790 and Argentine conditions in 1810. When Moreno was gone, there was no direct motive power which might guide the State to union and tranquillity. Men of high character and ability, it is true, served their country in the political field to the best of their power. But—perhaps fortunately for the ultimate development of the Republic—no commanding figure arose in that field, to cut the complex knot of politics, to crush ruinous rivalries, to compel and direct united action. On the other hand, after four years, a military genius adequate to the strategical situation came to the front, and the young Republic, at the very time when it was most shaken by internal disorder and disunion, achieved security against the danger of re-conquest from without.

Argentines naturally recall with intimate pride the activities of those who in rapid succession laboured at the machine of State or led armies among the Andine heights; and they trace particularly with affectionate admiration the career of Belgrano, a student and a man of peace, who with singular abnegation and zeal served his country in strange scenes of war: 'a dominie on horseback' Groussac unkindly calls him—a satirical epigram which is, in justice, high eulogy of the citizen who at need became a soldier and strove in every way to fit himself for the task. But it would be impossible, in this single volume, to make these rapid intricacies clear to an English reader. A summary and interpretation are needed rather than a detailed narrative: and although the movement of war and that of politics interacted continually, it seems best to trace separately the general course of each movement, and first that of war— war in two regions, on the plains of the Banda Oriental, just across the estuary, and at the same time among the remote mountain-heights of Upper Peru.

The war may be definitely divided into two periods of unequal length, first from the Revolution of 1810 down to the restoration of Ferdinand VII in 1814, and then from 1814 down to the crowning victory of Ayacucho in 1824. During the first four years of the conflict, Spain was herself struggling for national existence in her own 'War of Independence'. Her improvised governments, clinging to an unconquered fragment of the national soil, although treating as rebellion trans-Atlantic activities closely resembling their own, were unable to send men, money or munitions to America. Thus royalists and patriots alike fought with such resources as they could gather on the spot. But the war assumed a new phase, a definite struggle between the King and his insurgent 'vassals', when Ferdinand VII returned from exile in 1814 to reign in Madrid. From that time, veteran battalions of the Peninsular War were sent across the Atlantic to contend with 'patriot' troops—troops now also inured to war and commanded, in part at least, by experienced officers, some of whom had served in the Spanish army, while others, of no Iberian origin, had fought in the Napoleonic conflicts and now offered their swords to the cause of American emancipation.

The year 1814 marks a crucial epoch in the conflict; for in 1814 the royal Governor of Montevideo capitulated to an Argentine commander, and the royalists thus lost their base of operations in the River Plate. By that time also two unsuccessful invasions of Upper Peru from the south had proved that the Argentines could not conquer or retain that country, although a third attempt, foredoomed to failure, was made in the following year. Again, in 1814, San Martín, the military hero of the Revolution, assumed an almost independent command and began to prepare the movement which was to decide the contest through the liberation of Chile and the invasion of Peru by way of the Pacific Ocean. Moreover, in January 1814, it was realised that a Government, and particularly a belligerent Government, must have a personal head; and a 'Supreme Director' was appointed to replace the succession of 'Supreme' Committees and Triumvirates.

It should here be added that six years later, in January 1820, a

Spanish army which had been assembled at Cadiz, to be dispatched by order of Ferdinand VII for the re-conquest of Spanish America, mutinied and refused to embark. From that time no Spanish reinforcements came from Europe to America; and although the royalists in America continued the struggle, isolated and unaided, the issue from that time was hardly in doubt. Moreover, the military mutiny at Cadiz in 1820 developed into a political revolt against the absolutism of Ferdinand VII; and for three years a radical Spanish Government held the King in subjection, until he was reinstated in his absolute despotism by a French army in 1823.

The Revolution of 1820 in Spain caused uncertainty and division among the royalists in South America and thus weakened their resistance; for some of the royalist leaders, mainly European Spaniards, welcomed the Spanish Revolution and fought heartily for the radical Government in Madrid; other leaders, mainly Americanos, clung to the old tradition of personal allegiance to the King and resented the liberalism of their European comrades. Yet, notwithstanding these divisions and uncertainties, the royalists fought on, with characteristic Spanish stubbornness, for four years longer.

I. WAR IN THE BANDA ORIENTAL: 1810-14

The nearer war in which the Argentines were engaged, after the Revolution of May 1810, may be briefly narrated. Montevideo from the first recognised the Cadiz Regency and became the headquarters of the Spanish River Squadron, which blockaded the port of Buenos Aires. This blockade was at first recognised by a British naval officer; but Lord Strangford, British Minister at Rio, repudiated his action, and wrote privately to Moreno promising

support to the new Government as long as the Junta should recognise Ferdinand VII. Captain Ramsay of the *Mistletoe*, 'almost
an adopted son of Buenos Aires', broke the blockade, insisting
on the opening of the port to British trade, and received the thanks
of the Cabildo. Furthermore, an assembly of all the authorities of
Buenos Aires publicly conferred upon Lord Strangford honor-
ary citizenship of the United Provinces of the River Plate and
granted him a gift of a square league of land (6400 acres), 'for his
liberal attentions', attentions which included a decided opposition to Portuguese-Brazilian designs on the River Plate.

When Elío was succeeded as military Governor of Montevideo
by the Spaniard, General Vigodet, in 1809, the conflict between
the two cities of Buenos Aires and Montevideo became less intense. But in January 1811, the same Elío, the stubborn enemy of
all innovation and the upholder of Spanish authority, whatever
the Government of Spain might be, returned to Montevideo from
Spain, having been nominated by the Cadiz Regency to be not
merely Governor of Montevideo, but Viceroy of the whole River
Plate. He therefore claimed that Buenos Aires was by rights his
capital; and the hostility which had prevailed between the two
cities became open war. The Portuguese Court at Rio seized the
opportunity of fishing in troubled waters, hoping that this conflict
between the provinces of the Spanish Viceroyalty might open the
way for Brazilian expansion to the south. Accordingly Brazilian-
Portuguese forces came to the aid of Elío, as a means towards
territorial gains for Brazil. Had it not been for this external aid
from the north, Montevideo would have been almost isolated: for
the surrounding population was generally hostile to the royalist
Government which had been set up in Montevideo; and a guerrilla
warfare of the country against the city was carried on by gaucho

leaders. Prominent and finally supreme among these was the dominant figure of José Artigas, the first of the great gaucho caudillos or chieftains, men who by their personal prowess attached to themselves a following of mounted fighting-men, attracted by the qualities of their leader and by the prizes of war which he offered rather than by any cause which he might profess; for loyalty to the person of a chieftain was one of the first articles in the unwritten code of gaucho honour. These caudillos, one after another, came to rule whole provinces, and played a great but disturbing part in the early history of the Republic.

Artigas was a man of great physical strength, of resolute vigour and commanding personality, expert in all the rude science of gaucho life and, in addition, notorious for the atrocious cruelty which he either practised himself or permitted to his subordinates. He had been a smuggler and a bandit, then became an officer in the Spanish militia or police force, known as Blandengues. Impatient of all restraint, he left that service and gathered about him a horde of irregular semi-barbarian gaucho cavalry with many savage Indian auxiliaries. In his warfare against the royalists of Montevideo, he was ostensibly serving the Revolution as an officer in the armies of the United Provinces; but in fact he acted as an independent potentate, obeying no orders and affording no more than a loose and often insubordinate co-operation with the authorities of Buenos Aires. Although powerless to carry on effective warfare unaided, he ignored, on two occasions, armistices which had been concluded with Montevideo, continuing his raids and skirmishes; he also ignored an armistice which was concluded, through British mediation, with the Portuguese-Brazilian forces which had entered the Banda Oriental. The result was confused and dilatory warfare, the frequently changing

authorities of Buenos Aires being unable, owing to the simultaneous exigencies of the northern war, to dispense with the
capricious and arrogant aid of Artigas or to run the risk of turn-
ing him into an enemy. They were also powerless to reduce the
city of Montevideo as long as the Spanish naval squadron commanded the estuary.

Sarratea, one of the leaders of the Revolution, commanded the
Argentine forces in the Banda Oriental. Under his orders, Rondeau, an officer who had served in the Spanish army and had left
it to join the Argentine revolutionary army, laid siege to Montevideo in October 1812, for the second time, and won a notable
success in routing a sally of the besieged. But Artigas, furious at
the withdrawal, for the purposes of the siege, of some Argentine
troops which had been attached to his gaucho forces, insisted that
Sarratea should give up the command to Rondeau. In order to
avoid the collapse of the whole enterprise, Rondeau agreed to
satisfy the demands of the gaucho chieftain, and by an act of
mutiny displaced his superior officer and assumed the chief command. This proceeding was sanctioned perforce by the Government in Buenos Aires.

At the beginning of 1814 disaster seemed imminent. Artigas,
who held great part of the lines besieging Montevideo, withdrew
his troops by night and became an enemy rather than an ally. The
royalists, victorious in Upper Peru, were threatening the centre of
the Argentine Provinces; and the restored Spanish monarchy,
Ferdinand VII having returned from exile, was sending reinforcements to Montevideo and designing a great invasion of the
River Plate with that port as base. A decisive effort was urgently
needed, and was made. With the help of British merchant-captains,
a war-fleet was fitted out under the command of William Brown,

an Irish sailor who had already had an adventurous career as a British merchant-captain in European waters during Napoleon's Continental Blockade. Brown, after one reverse, defeated the Spanish squadron and drove it under the shelter of the Monte-videan batteries. He then blockaded the port, acting closely with the Argentine besieging army, now reinforced from Buenos Aires. The Spanish ships, sailing out to attack, were scattered or taken in a two days' fight. The royalists thus lost the command of the estuary, which lay open for the passage of Argentine ships. Ron-deau, who by an act of mutiny had superseded his superior officer, was himself superseded, apparently on the eve of victory, by the active and ambitious Alvear, who had now been appointed commander-in-chief of all the forces of the Republic. Alvear brought troops from Buenos Aires to reinforce the besieging army, assumed the command of that army, and in June 1814 received the capitulation of the Spanish Governor of Montevideo, General Vigodet, who had a second time succeeded Elío in that post and now gave up to the forces of the United Provinces the last foothold of Spain in the River Plate.

The fall of Montevideo was a signal triumph. It deprived the enemy of his base in the River Plate. It brought a store of arms and munitions, besides recruits gathered from the enemy's forces: it removed the danger, though not the apprehension, of a big Spanish invasion: it checked the southward advance of royalist armies from Upper Peru, since there was now no royalist strong-hold to welcome them if they succeeded in fighting their way through. Finally, by averting the immediate danger and by re-leasing forces hitherto engaged in the nearer war, the fall of Montevideo rendered possible the great design, already conceived, of an Argentine expedition into Chile and thence against Peru.

So ended the nearer and shorter war, that of the Banda Oriental. It remains to summarise the northern war, that of Upper Peru.

II. THE NORTHERN WAR

It has been seen (p. 78) that the Argentine army, victorious at Suipacha in November 1810 and advancing to Chuquisaca and Potosí, appeared to have won all Upper Peru. It was a delusive success: Goyeneche, ordered by the Peruvian Viceroy to mobilise the militia of the cities of Upper Peru, met the Argentine commanders, Balcarce and Castelli, at Huaquí, on the southern borders of Lake Titicaca, and drove back his opponents in complete rout.[1] The mob of Potosí, where the Porteños had been triumphantly welcomed six months earlier, fell upon the fugitives with sticks and stones and killed a hundred of them. Pueyrredón hastened to preserve the sinews of war by conveying the royal treasury from Potosí to Salta. There he gathered the remnants of the defeated army and retreated to Tucumán, where he remained inactive for many months and finally handed over the command to Belgrano.

The first invasion of Upper Peru foreshadowed the issue of the whole conflict. The 'auxiliary expedition' from Buenos Aires, was hardly, as its leaders claimed, aiding oppressed fellow-countrymen. They were entering an alien land, remote and distinct from their own cattle-bearing plains. North of Jujuy the mountain pass of Humahuaca forms a natural frontier leading northwards and upwards to a tableland, varying in height from

---

[1] This victory of Goyeneche is usually attributed to a deliberate breach of an armistice on his part, whereby he took the Argentines by surprise and gained the advantage of the ground. Mitre, in his *History of San Martín*, says that neither side observed the armistice. But Goyeneche's non-observance of it certainly seems to have given him the advantage and brought about his victory.

8000 to 13,000 feet above sea level, and bordered by towering mountain ramparts: the new-comer from the plains suffers from mountain sickness and from exhaustion upon any exertion in the rarefied air. The higher regions, including the city of Potosí and its neighbourhood, are bleak and barren, poor in crops and in cattle and rich only in subterranean mines. The attitude of the population was dubious and divided. In the north, La Paz, the first South-American city to proclaim independence, had been forced into reluctant submission by Goyeneche. Cochabamba, capital of a beautiful and temperate Alpine region in the north-east, flamed out into fresh revolt after every reverse. But these points of support were separated from the Argentine bases by a vast moun-tain region. Of the Indian peasantry many were ready to join successful revolt: others knew and cared little about the meaning of the struggle, or felt no desire for a change of masters. Upper Peru was a recruiting-ground for both sides, and both armies con-sisted mainly of Americanos. The Porteños, having no commis-sariat and living on the country, were regarded, when their rudi-mentary discipline broke down after defeat, as marauders rather than deliverers. Any success brought adherents to the Revolution, though not necessarily with any enthusiasm for submission to Buenos Aires. Defeat brought defection, desertion and stoppage of supplies.

The war was a struggle between royalist Peru and the re-publican River Plate for the possession of Upper Peru, the great mountain province (now Bolivia), which lay between the terri-tories of the two combatants. But the royalists were the defenders, with armies partly raised in the country, partly brought from Lower Peru. Each side had an ulterior object. The Argentines were aiming at Lima, distant 3000 miles from Buenos Aires, through co-operation with their many sympathisers in Cocha-bamba, La Paz and elsewhere. The royalists were aiming at Buenos Aires through co-operation with Montevideo. The final issue was that each side failed in attack and succeeded in defence. The Argentines never effectively penetrated Upper Peru. The Peruvians never got farther south than Tucumán and failed to keep hold of anything south of Humahuaca.

Descriptions of campaigns and battles would be here out of place. Even a scientific soldier would need many large-scale maps in order to trace movements amid 'a chaos of precipitous heights, detached crests and masses, thrown together without any ap-parent order'.[1] Moreover the armies on both sides consisting of militia and volunteers half-trained and ill-disciplined, success or failure was largely matter of accident and personal impulse: much depended on the attitude of the inhabitants, which in Upper Peru was dubious and variable, and on the Pampa was friendly. But between Upper Peru and the Pampa plains there extends, from Jujuy to the plain of Tucumán, a region of hill and forest, a country which is connected with the Pampa rather than with the Andine plateau, yet in some sort forms a link between the two regions. Here the population, which had a large indigenous element, were not so uniformly friendly: they hated invaders from the Peruvian north, but they did not love Argentine armies en-camped in their midst. This wooded hill region is traversed from north to south by a broad valley, which ever since Inca times has served for the passage of trading caravans and of armies. The marches and movements now to be narrated took place for the most part in this long and wide valley, along which the contend-ing armies advanced and retreated between Salta and Tucumán.

[1] From *Stanford's Compendium of Geography*.

In March 1812, Belgrano took over from Pueyrredón the command of the army which had been defeated at Huaquí and had retreated to Tucumán, much diminished by desertions and by casualties other than those of battle. The new commander, aided by Holmberg, a German soldier who had taken service in the Argentine army, strove to improve the morale and discipline of the dispirited soldiery. He recited the rosary daily on his knees in the midst of his troops, and appealed to their traditional feelings as well as to their new patriotism by displaying for ecclesiastical blessing on the second anniversary of the Revolution, May 25, 1812, the banner which was to become the national flag, but which the cautious Government of Buenos Aires declined as yet to sanction.

But the royalist army under the creole Tristán, second in command to Goyeneche, its rear secured by the temporary suppression of the revolution in Cochabamba, advanced southwards, confident of success. Belgrano retreated to Tucumán, where he resolved to give battle, disobeying the repeated orders of the Government to retire to Córdoba. Supported by the gaucho horsemen of the neighbourhood, and by the rudely armed citizens of Tucumán, he defeated Tristán on September 24, 1812, 'the day of La Virgen de Merced', whom Belgrano now nominated commander-in-chief, handing his baton of command to the image, carried in procession through the streets of Tucumán. The victory was a decisive one, for it averted the imminent danger of contact between the royalists of Peru and those of Montevideo; and proved in fact that even though the Argentines could not win or hold Upper Peru, neither could the royalists penetrate from the north into the Pampa.

Four months later Belgrano, advancing northwards in his turn,

upon crossing the River Pasaje, known ever since as the Jura-
mento, swore allegiance, followed by all his troops, to the banner
of *La Patria*. In February 1813, at the head of about 3000 men, he
defeated at Salta, although almost prostrated by illness, a larger
force. The defeated royalist leader was driven into the city of Salta
and only averted an assault by capitulation. Under this agreement, Tristán surrendered all arms and ammunition and evacuated Jujuy, but was permitted to depart with all his troops, under
oath not to serve any more against the Argentines. The two commanders, Belgrano and Tristán, both of them creoles, or rather
Americanos—to use the more dignified term which was coming
into use—sealed the capitulation by an embrace in presence of
both armies. The victors lost one-fifth of their number, killed and
wounded.

Belgrano has been censured for granting such unprofitable
terms after so decisive a victory. He was induced to do so by the
hope that the defeated soldiers—almost all of them Americanos,
like their commanders Goyeneche and Tristán, would thus be
led to fraternise with the Argentines. He was so far right that
the retreating soldiers scattered the seeds of revolution in Upper
Peru: but union with Buenos Aires was a more doubtful
matter.

The success of Belgrano's campaign, from Tucumán to Salta,
was largely due to the military skill and energy of Colonel Arenales, a veteran professional soldier and a keen student of the art of
war, a man of solid qualities, who served with unostentatious
and ungrudging loyalty under Belgrano, and was later to win
distinction in two theatres of war. Arenales, as a *vecino* of the city,
who had served as senior alcalde in Salta, knew the people and
had their confidence—a matter which was of great value in that

kind of warfare where the goodwill of the inhabitants counted for much.

After the capitulation of Tristán, Belgrano advanced north-wards to the heights of Upper Peru and entered Potosí, where he was welcomed with jubilant enthusiasm by the inhabitants. He appeared to dominate all the south of Upper Peru. Parties of In-dians armed with slings, pikes and clubs rose in his support. He sent secret emissaries throughout Peru proper to stir up revolution, and appointed Arenales, the most capable and the most trusty of his officers, to command in Cochabamba. He aimed at march-ing through a friendly country upon Lima—a delusive hope: 500 men deserted in Potosí; Dorrego, one of his finest fighting officers, he dismissed for scandalous indiscipline. The royalists still com-manded most of the country and recruited at their ease. Goyen-eche, at his own request, was replaced by Pezuela, a European Spaniard, in spite of the protest of the royalist troops, who de-manded an Americano as their commander. Belgrano, moving towards Cochabamba with 3500 men, was defeated at Vilca-pugio by Pezuela, losing all his artillery, much munitions and his best officers. During a difficult retreat he contrived to gather re-cruits, was joined by several guerrilleros, gave battle again, at the head of 3000 men, at Ayohuma, and again suffered defeat. The second invasion of Upper Peru had failed. Pezuela occupied Salta, while Belgrano retreated to Tucumán, where in January 1814 he yielded command to San Martín, with whom he main-tained relations of warm friendship and mutual esteem.

And here a brief retrospect is necessary. In March 1812 the ship *George Canning* reached Buenos Aires from London, con-veying several officers of the Spanish army who had been born in

America and now offered their swords to the Revolution. Among them were José de San Martín, whose devoted service and military skill were to bring decisive victory, and Carlos María de Alvear, the Alcibiades of the Revolution, who was to have an adventurous and varied career in the River Plate. Both men had belonged to secret revolutionary societies, first in Cadiz and then in London, and they now founded in Buenos Aires the 'Láutaro Lodge', a revolutionary secret society whose members were pledged by oath to aim at independence. This society exercised a profound unofficial influence on the Revolution by prompting the appointment of rulers and commanders and by guiding their policy. The handsome and aristocratic Alvear was the son of a distinguished Spanish officer who had served in the delimitation of the Brazilian frontier. The grave, cautious and reserved San Martín, now aged thirty-four, son of a Spanish district magistrate in Misiones, had served twenty years in the Spanish army, had seen many campaigns and reached the rank of lieutenant-colonel. On disembarking at Buenos Aires, he was at once recognised in that rank in the army of the United Provinces and was commissioned to organise a body of cavalry, which, under his training and strict discipline, grew into the famous regiment of Mounted Grenadiers, the backbone of later armies. His first notable action (February 1813) was the combat of San Lorenzo,[1] where with a handful of his grenadiers he ambushed and routed a landing party of thrice his numbers from the Spanish river-squadron—a success which opened the upper river to communication with Buenos Aires and aided the operations against Montevideo.

Being appointed to supersede Belgrano at Tucumán in 1814,

[1] This combat at San Lorenzo was witnessed by an Englishman, J. P. Robertson, who describes it in his *Letters on Paraguay* (London, 1838).

he spent four months in the reform and discipline of the demoralised army, in establishing a fortified camp or citadel at Tucumán, and in training officers. He then, on the plea of ill-health, handed over the troops to his second-in-command, and soon afterwards finally withdrew from the northern army, soliciting and obtaining a comparatively insignificant post, as it seemed, as Governor-Intendant of Cuyo, a western province remote from the scenes of war. This was the first step towards the great strategical movement which was to win victory and security for the Revolution. Before relating that westward enterprise, it is well to continue the story of the northern war.

In June 1814, Pezuela, the Spanish commander, was advancing southwards upon Tucumán, when, upon hearing of the fall of Montevideo, he turned back: for unless he could win through to Montevideo, advance meant isolation. Moreover the country had risen behind him; for the indefatigable Arenales now showed that he had all the qualities of an inspiring guerrillero leader, as well as those of a regimental officer and an experienced tactician. Some years earlier, as Governor of a district in Upper Peru under the Spanish Crown, he had befriended the Indian inhabitants and had striven to give reality to the little-observed ordinances and laws for their protection and well-being. And now he was trusted by the Indian peasantry as well as by the creoles of the city. Arenales held his ground in Cochabamba, harassing the royalists in an unceasing but elusive *guerra de recursos*. Undaunted by reverses and by surrounding disaffection and espionage, he gathered and drilled recruits, infected the Indians with his own enthusiasm, and on May 25, 1814, annihilated a royalist force at La Florida. The revolutionary infection spread, with various fortunes, even to the cities of Peru itself. Throughout Upper Peru sporadic foci of revolt flamed out, so detached and local in character that they were known as *republiquetas*—'little republics'. Out of one hundred and two local leaders of these insurgent groups only nine survived the war; the remaining ninety-three perished in fight or on the scaffold.

But, while the mountain region of Upper Peru was shaken by these tragic vicissitudes, the frontier of the truly Argentine region was more securely held by a leader whose dashing exploits and picturesque personality have particularly caught the imagination of the Argentine people. Martín Güemes, as a young officer in the Spanish service, had fought against Beresford and Whitelocke. Afterwards, in his home at Salta, he was noted as the gay ringleader of dissolute youths. On the outbreak of the Revolution, he carried these comrades with him to the patriot ranks and served in the war against Montevideo. He was obliged to leave that service owing to the mutiny of Rondeau, against whom in consequence he felt a peculiar resentment. Hearing of the dangers which threatened his native province owing to the defeats of Belgrano in Upper Peru, he hastened to Salta in order to raise fighting men for defence. By the attraction of his personality and his powers of leadership he soon achieved an extraordinary ascendancy among the people of the woods and the plains. By the audacious rapidity of his onslaughts he constantly harassed the royalists and gave encouragement and confidence to his own people. Finally he dominated the whole province and was acclaimed, or had himself acclaimed, Governor-Intendant of the Province of Salta by the Cabildo of the city of Salta, without much regard to the authority of the 'National Government' at Buenos Aires. The equestrian gauchos of Salta, expert in all the daring craft of forest and plain, held the frontier under their

idolised chieftain, who turned every one of his devoted subjects
into a soldier, forming a mobile militia, hardy, resourceful and indomitable. No detached party of the enemy was safe from them.
In the wooded parts many royalist officers were dragged from
their horses by the lasso of some stealthy gaucho.

Thus in 1814 the Argentines had won two signal successes,
the capitulation of the fortified city of Montevideo and the capitulation of Tristán's army at Salta. They had successfully defended
the region marked out by geography and ethnology as their own.
The remaining scenes of the northern war (1814–21) may be
briefly sketched.

The third invasion of Upper Peru, led by Rondeau, is a re-
petition of the two former invasions—initial success, occupation
of Potosí, attempt to reach Cochabamba, defeat at Sipe Sipe and
demoralised retreat. Güemes, the 'partisan patriot', withdrew his
forces in disgust and for a time treated Rondeau as an enemy; but
resumed friendly relations and a kind of remote and intermittent
loyalty to Buenos Aires when Belgrano, to whom he was heartily
attached, took over from Rondeau the command at Tucumán.
Thenceforth for six years Güemes and his gauchos defended the
frontier. An ambitious and carefully prepared royalist expedition
in the summer of 1816–17 was beaten back into the mountains.
Later invasions, or rather raids, got no farther than Salta, where
every man, woman and child in the country was an active enemy.
The eighth royalist 'invasion' in 1821 penetrated the streets of
Salta: Güemes, galloping through the suburbs, received a shot in
the breast and reached his camp to die, leaving to his lieutenant
the task of thrusting back the royalists for the last time. The equestrian statue of the bearded chieftain to-day looks out from the hill-
side over the beautiful little city which he loved, defended and

commanded. Thus the issue of the conflict followed the lines traced by physical features and racial divisions; and Upper Peru, when the inevitable emancipation came, broke off to form the Republic of Bolivia.

In the central plaza of the city of Salta there stands a monu-ment to another Salteño hero of a different type, General Arenales, who is there represented as a warrior protecting the women of the city. Arenales was a Castilian born in Spain, and bore himself with the reticent and almost stoical dignity of a Spanish *hidalgo*. He served many years in the River Plate as an officer of the Spanish army, married a lady of Salta and made that city his home. When, as is related on p. 67, the Audiencia of Charcas in May 1809 deposed the Governor and assumed his functions, Arenales, then aged thirty-eight, was Governor (*subdelegado*) of a neighbouring district. The Audiencia appointed him to the military command of the whole province. He accepted with reluctance: and then, seeing clearly the real significance of the movement, prepared for resistance as Nieto approached, sent by Cisneros to restore order. But the Audiencia resolved on submission. Arenales was sent a prisoner to Lima and suffered much hardship before he returned to his home in Salta. On the outbreak of the Revolution, he devoted himself to the cause of his adopted country. After his distinguished services throughout the War of Emancipation, he was for some years Governor of the Province of Salta.

CHAPTER X

SAN MARTÍN

THE war of Upper Peru was in fact a frontier war, although it took the Argentines nine years to realise the fact. But San Martín clearly grasped it from the time of his brief command of the northern army in 1814. In April of that year he wrote to a friend, 'Here is my *secret*: a small well-disciplined army in Mendoza to pass to Chile and finish off the "goths" there, supporting a government of firm friends in order to end the anarchy there. Uniting our forces, we shall pass by sea to take Lima. That is the road, and not this: until we have Lima, the war cannot end'. His plan was secret: for if divulged it would have stamped him as a madman and left him powerless from the beginning. During three years of patient effort he pursued this plan almost independently, educating and convincing his contemporaries, politicians and generals alike, by means of action and of facts.

This daring design of leading an army away from the Argentine plains, over the towering rampart of the Andes, at the very time when the royalists were constantly threatening and attempting invasion from Upper Peru, would have been impossible but for the persistent defence of the northern frontier by Güemes. San Martín fully realised this and cordially avowed his reliance upon 'Güemes and his valiant gauchos'.

San Martín's first step was the apparently modest request for a civil post as Governor-Intendant of the Province of Cuyo, comprising the jurisdictions of Mendoza, San Juan and San Luis; that is to say the region originally settled from Chile, then transferred from Chile to the River Plate Viceroyalty in 1776 but still remaining partly Chilian in character and sentiment.

In October 1814, a month after San Martín's arrival at Mendoza as Governor, the nascent Republic of Chile, which from 1810 had maintained close sympathy and intercourse with the Argentine movement, fell before royalist invasion from Peru, and fugitive Chilian soldiery streamed over the Andine passes into Cuyo under two rival leaders, the loyal, upright, impulsive O'Higgins, and the profligate, self-seeking, unscrupulous Carrera, who had proved himself a dashing soldier for Spain in the Peninsula and against Spain in Chile. Accordingly the first task which lay before San Martín was the re-conquest of Chile. He entered into close relations with O'Higgins and suppressed the turbulent arrogance of Carrera. The latter, in order to oust San Martín, passed to Buenos Aires, where Alvear, who was no friend to his former comrade, San Martín, became Supreme Director in January 1815. San Martín, in order to define the situation, anticipated dismissal by resignation. Alvear at once appointed a new Governor of Cuyo. This act provoked a clamorous popular gathering in Mendoza and cries of 'Cabildo abierto' —a movement singularly resembling the Revolution in Buenos Aires of May 25, 1810. The people and Cabildo of Mendoza, by an assumption of provincial autonomy, refused to admit the nominee of the National Government and insisted on retaining in his post the Governor who by force of character, good administration and devoted attention to duty had already acquired a singular moral ascendancy over his subjects: for such they were.

San Martín was strengthened by this 'Municipal Revolution', as Mitre calls it,[1] in the paternal despotism which he was

¹ Mitre, *Historia de San Martín*, chapter 9.

setting up. By means of persuasive coercion he formed in the course of two years an army of 4000 men, devising from the beginning or obtaining from the faithful Cuyanos uniforms, commissariat, munitions, transport—everything needful for the passage of an invading army through desert mountain-passes of more than Alpine height. A friar of mechanical turn set up an arsenal and cannon-foundry: a powder-factory followed. The country serge was dyed for uniforms which the women stitched. The selvages of cloth from the tailors' shops were made into straps for the men's accoutrements. Every man's household goods were at the disposal of the Governor. 'He turned to account even the children's toys', says a contemporary. A levy of a half per cent. on capital, extra taxes, gifts of women's jewels, supplied funds. He cajoled his people into manumitting two-thirds of their slaves and so formed a battalion of 710 negroes. Drilling, marching, military exercise were incessant. The Englishmen resident in Mendoza, fifty-five in number, formed themselves into a volunteer corps, although it does not appear that they accompanied the expedition over the Andes.

'Though none suspected it,' says Mitre, 'San Martín was the first potentate of the United Provinces: he had his province and his army in the hollow of his hand.'

'San Martín', so runs a confidential Spanish report, 'has a character apt for war. He is severe in discipline, honourable, austere and disinterested. He has experienced several commotions among his troops, and has suppressed these movements with success.' This striking testimony from an enemy justifies the feeling which his countrymen have concerning the character of their great leader.

But diplomacy was needful, too, to convince the Government of Buenos Aires and obtain thence such funds and supplies as were beyond the means of his thinly inhabited and not wealthy province. In December 1815, upon news of Rondeau's defeat at Sipe Sipe, a disaster which closed the cycle of attempts on Upper Peru, San Martín revealed his plan at a banquet to his officers. Six months later, in a two days' interview at Córdoba, Pueyrredón, now Supreme Director, was won over, and during his three years of office (1816–19) steadily supported San Martín. The Declaration of Independence by the Congress of Tucumán in July 1816—a declaration partly due to San Martín's own insistence—strengthened his hands.

An audacious Pacific cruise by William Brown (October 1815—September 1816), who took several Spanish prizes and threatened the ports of Callao and Guayaquil, was a prologue to San Martín's design. Meantime, by an ingenious system of propagating false news, the royalist commanders in Chile were induced to divide their forces and even to guard the Pacific ports on account of rumours of projected attacks by sea.

At the end of 1816 San Martín requisitioned from the Cuyanos 13,000 mules. In January 1817, the height of summer—for the Andine passes cannot be traversed in winter—all was ready: 4000 fighting men, 5200 men in all, crossed the Andes, the main force by the two passes of Uspallata and Los Patos, each 12,000 feet above sea level, while three detachments took more distant routes, the whole extending over a front of 500 miles. The movements were carried out according to plan exactly to the day fixed. The united force defeated the royalists at Chacabuco (February 12, 1817) and entered Santiago, the capital of Chile. Decisive victory was apparently achieved.

But San Martín, intent upon his great ulterior strategical design, instead of pursuing the fugitives and securing southern Chile, re-

crossed the Andes and rode to Buenos Aires, to seek naval aid in
the Pacific. Returning to Chile, he found the royalists victorious
in the south; and he himself suffered defeat in a night attack at
Cancha Rayada (March 19, 1818), but brought off his army
almost intact except for 500 desertions—the usual result of defeat
in these volunteer armies. The capital, menaced and filled with
consternation,[1] was saved by the victory of Maipú (April 5), the
most decisive battle of the war, in which the royalist army of
5500 men lost 1000 killed, 2200 prisoners, all the munitions and
the military chest. The Argentino-Chilian army of 5000 men
lost 1000 killed and wounded.

In the same year an improvised Chilian squadron, by an
astonishing and rapid success, captured a Spanish frigate and
four transports and thus deprived Spain of the command of the
Pacific. The sea road to Peru lay open. In November the greatest
living sailor, Cochrane, who had achieved sensational successes
as a British naval officer in the war against the French Republic
and Empire, took command of a much increased Chilian fleet,
which in three years was to sweep the Spanish flag from the
Pacific.

Yet the invasion of Peru was delayed for two years, by Argentine schemes for ending the war through diplomacy, by lukewarmness and party strife in Chile, and by the dismemberment
of the United Provinces of the River Plate, torn by civil war and
menaced by a Spanish expedition of 20,000 men assembled at
Cadiz. In 1819 the bewildered Buenos Aires Government sum-

---

[1] Mitre here humorously observes that whenever anything notable happens, there
is always an Englishman at hand to record it. Samuel Haigh, who was in Santiago
on business at the time, described the consternation of the capital in his *Sketches of
Buenos Aires, Chile and Peru*.

moned San Martín and his army to their aid. He disobeyed: he told his assembled officers to choose a chief, since the Government which had commissioned him no longer existed. He was at once acclaimed chief by the gathering of officers. The event justified his action: in January 1820 the mutinous army of Cadiz refused to embark for America: to throw his army into the civil war between Buenos Aires and the provinces would have wasted it in a welter of confusion. San Martín felt no particular attachment to Buenos Aires. *Toda la América es mi patria*, he was wont to say. Indeed his invasion of Chile in 1817 was an effort of the Province of Cuyo with some aid from Buenos Aires and from Chilian refugees, rather than a deliberate national effort on the part of the United Provinces of the River Plate.

At last all obstacles were overcome; preparations were completed and transports assembled. In August 1820, San Martín's little army set sail northwards from Valparaiso in seventeen transports, convoyed by Cochrane's armed ships. The troops disembarked at Pisco, 160 miles south of Lima, not indeed the 6000 troops which San Martín had declared to be necessary for complete victory, but the 4400 which sufficed to prepare for victory. Of the rank and file 2300 were Argentine and 1800 Chilian. The royalist forces in Upper and Lower Peru numbered 23,000, including a garrison of 8000 in Lima.

San Martín's main object was to rouse and support revolution in Peru. Some hopes were entertained that this might be effected without bloodshed, since news had reached America of the mutiny of the Spanish troops at Cadiz and the establishment of a radical Government in Madrid. Accordingly a brief armistice was concluded with the Viceroy Pezuela, the successor to Abascal,

and negotiations were opened. These had no result and hostilities
were resumed.

San Martín dispatched Arenales with two battalions into the
mountains and then sailed to Ancón, twenty-two miles north of
Lima, there to await Arenales, who in a surprising campaign
through the Andes gained adherents, won over cities and stirred
up revolt. Part of northern Peru, on San Martín's approach,
joined the Revolution, and there were daily desertions from the
royalists, now divided in sentiment, since a revolutionary and
radical Government in Spain had reduced the King to impotence. But San Martín, his army ravaged by a fatal epidemic,
confined himself to besieging Lima.

The arrival of Peace Commissioners from Spain in May 1821
led to another armistice and fresh negotiations, in which San
Martín proposed an independent constitutional monarchy under
a Bourbon prince. He had a cordial interview with the Viceroy
La Serna,[1] but the war continued. In July 1821 the royalists
evacuated Lima. San Martín peaceably entered the agitated
capital, proclaimed the independence of Peru and, under pressure
from the Láutaro Lodge, assumed the government, with the
title Protector of Peru.

But the occupation of the capital did not bring near, as he had
hoped, the end of the struggle. Cochrane had finished his naval
work; Arenales again marched victorious through the mountains;
Miller, a youthful veteran of the Peninsula, who had commanded
Cochrane's marines, carried victory and revolution to the southern
ports. Callao surrendered in September 1821. But San Martín

---

[1] The royalist officers had deposed the Viceroy Pezuela as not being sufficiently
zealous, and had put in his place the veteran La Serna, one of the defenders of
Saragossa.

and the bulk of the army remained almost inactive. The country, with its aristocratic traditions, did not respond to the Revolution as he had hoped. The epidemic sometimes left hardly enough sound men in his army to bury the dead; and he himself was hampered by illness, by the effect of drugs and by the difficulties of his position as a foreigner in the Viceregal city. The Viceroy and his officers held the southern heights, recruiting at their ease; and though divided among themselves and isolated from all the world, they fought on with Quixotic pertinacity for a mother country which left them unaided.

Meantime the Venezuelan Bolívar, Liberator of the North, and his lieutenant Sucre had beaten the royalists of Quito (now Ecuador) and won that country for the Revolution. The two movements of emancipation which had started from Buenos Aires and from Caracas, 6000 miles apart, were converging. In July 1822, the two chiefs, Bolívar and San Martín, met in a secret interview at Guayaquil. Two months later, San Martín, having assembled a Constituent Congress in Lima, resigned command, leaving to Bolívar the task of completing his work, a task which took two more years of effort. San Martín's troops fought on under Bolívar, and the remnant of the famous regiment of Mounted Grenadiers still bore the Argentine flag in the final battle of Ayacucho (December 9, 1824), where the last Spanish Viceroy yielded his sword to the creole Sucre. Thus Argentina played her part to the end in the continental war, which by freeing her neighbours gave security to her own independence. The fifty Spanish banners which adorn the walls of the National Historical Museum in Buenos Aires supply the best commentary on the course and the issue of that war.

The Argentine War of Emancipation differs in two respects from the contemporary movements in other parts of Spanish America. In the first place the Argentines, by a continuously successful defence, maintained their independence without in-terruption from the first movement of Revolution. No hostile army ever approached the capital; and only once, in 1812, did the royalists from the north advance far into the Argentine country —to meet with two decisive defeats. In the second place the Ar-gentines, alone among the peoples of Spanish America, while they were defending their territory against Spanish attempts at re-conquest, had to contend at the same time with the hostility of a foreign monarchy which was not Spanish.

The attempts made, first by the Portuguese Court established at Rio, and afterwards by the independent Brazilian monarchy, to encroach upon the Spanish lands in the River Plate, added much to the complication and the burden of the Argentine War of Emancipation. This additional contest with a neighbouring monarchy gave to that war a markedly national character. But under the leadership of San Martín, the Argentines, aiming at ends which were more than national, took a generous part in the wider movement beyond their own borders which was to deprive Spain of a vast Empire in the New World.

It may be said without much exaggeration that the Revolution of America was worked out on both sides of the Atlantic. The fifteen years of struggle, revolt and constitutional effort in America (1809–24) were years of revolutions and constitutional effort in Spain. The movement in America was begun, not by a deliber-ate revolt against Spain but by an attempt to repair or replace the fallen monarchy of Spain. First, the monarchy which was the only constitutional link between Spain and America disappeared.

Then Spain herself seemed to disappear, and the kingdoms and provinces of the Indies felt themselves to be standing alone, and attempted to provide for their own government. In so doing they found themselves in conflict with Spanish Governors and Peninsular authorities: the result of that conflict was separation.

CHAPTER XI

INTERNAL DEVELOPMENT

IT is time to turn from the foregoing rapid summary of the War of Independence in order to trace the efforts which were made, during those years of warfare, by those who were striving to achieve form and unity for the nation. The course of internal politics was an agitated one, partly owing to the inherent difficulty of tranquilly guiding a revolution to a firm conclusion, partly owing to the divergence which soon showed itself, as always occurs in such cases, between the advanced wing of the revolutionary leaders and the more cautious or more conservative elements. This divergence, increased by personal animosities, caused a split in the Junta itself which had been set up as a provisional Government by the Revolution of May 1810. It has been already related how, in December of the same year, the provincial deputies, claiming fulfilment of the invitation which had been sent to the provinces, insisted on taking their seats in the Junta—a proceeding which rendered that body ineffective as an executive Government and was the chief cause of Moreno's retirement from his post as secretary and of his embarkation for England.

After the incorporation of the provincial deputies and the departure of Moreno, the Junta sank into deeper discredit, while at the same time it provoked widespread resentment by the indiscreet assumption of more absolute authority. Four months later, in April 1811, it suffered an imitation or a caricature of the scene of the previous 25th of May. A tumultuous crowd, followed by troops, streamed into the plaza. Their leaders entered the council chamber, demanding the banishment or arrest of various 'Morenistas' and the dismissal of four members of the Junta, to be re-placed by four named by the 'petitioners'. The Junta consented, submitting to this blow inflicted upon their dwindling authority. This episode, the first of many interruptions to the peaceable con-duct of affairs, is known to Argentine historians as the 'Revolu-tion of the 5th and 6th of April'. It is generally agreed that there was little justification for it; at the time it was suspected that the supporters—even in the Junta itself—of the conservative and aristocratic Saavedra instigated or supported the movement in the strange expectation that by these violent methods they might strengthen the position of their chief and counteract the revolu-tionary activities of a popular club formed by the advanced liberals, men imbued with the doctrines of Mariano Moreno, who were known sometimes as the Sociedad, sometimes by the name of their place of meeting, the Café de Marcos.

Naturally, however, the Revolution of April, so far from strengthening authority, brought weakness and humiliation upon the governing Junta. The defeat of Huaquí in June 1811 and the retreat from Upper Peru of the army which had previously been victorious at Suipacha, brought fresh discredit. In August, Saa-vedra, the President of the Junta, departed for the north in order to re-organise the defeated and demoralised army—presently to hear that he had been deposed in his absence, later to be arrested and banished, a fate which afterwards overtook many politicians, as successive Governments denounced their predecessors.

Finally, amid 'general clamour and discontent', petitions, and manifestations, the Junta abdicated in September 1811, nominat-ing an Executive Triumvirate, consisting of Paso, who had been a member of the Junta; Chiclana, one of the most vehement revolutionary leaders, who accompanied the expedition to Upper

Peru; and Sarratea, who afterwards commanded the troops in the Banda Oriental and later was sent to reside in London as agent of the United Provinces. One of the secretaries was Bernardino Rivadavia, a man of notable capacity and integrity but comparatively new to political life. Rivadavia himself afterwards became a Triumvir, for it was arranged that one of the three members should retire at the end of every six months, to give place to a newly nominated Triumvir.

Meantime, although the Junta with which they had been incorporated had ceased to exist, the provincial deputies continued to meet, under the title *Junta Conservadora de los Derechos de Fernando VII*, claiming 'supreme authority' and legislative power. After six weeks this body was dissolved by the Triumvirate. Dean Funes, the most distinguished member, was imprisoned, and the others, suspected of complicity in a barrack mutiny, were ordered to return home—a *coup d'état* which was also a singular affront to the provinces. The attempt to form a Constituent Assembly had collapsed, as did also two other halfhearted attempts in the following year. The Triumvirate, assuming the title 'Provisional Superior Government', undertook in a 'Provisional Constitution' to summon a General Assembly in order to prepare for a Congress of the United Provinces. The 'General Assembly', predominantly Porteño in composition and by no means representative, met in April 1812, but upon assuming the title 'Supreme', was at once dissolved by the Triumvirate—in a second *coup d'état*.

Another Assembly was summoned for October 6; but the Triumvirate, clinging to power, annulled the election of any unwelcome deputy. On the 5th, news came that Belgrano, although unsupported and forbidden by the Triumvirs to fight, had triumphed at Tucumán. On the 7th, Triumvirate and Assembly were alike swept away by another demonstration on the lines of 'May 25th'—the Cabildo called from their beds at midnight, a crowd in the plaza, troops headed by their officers drawn up in front of the council chamber, a hastily signed petition, and finally dictation by soldiers, notably San Martín and Alvear, who commanded the Cabildo to assume authority and to nominate as Triumvirs three designated persons. Such, in brief, was the 'Revolution of October the 7th'.

Yet the First Triumvirate, thus ignominiously ended, had not been barren, thanks to the energy of Rivadavia. The Spanish system was reversed by his measures. Liberty of the press was decreed; the slave-trade was forbidden; various import dues were abolished or reduced; immigration was encouraged; schools were opened; the Royal Audiencia was dissolved and replaced by a Court of Appeal; jurisdiction was organised in tribunals of graduated authority; a military staff was created.

Three dangerous crises were handled with vigour and success. First the mutiny of a regiment, provoked by disciplinary measures and particularly by the order to cut off their queues, was forcibly crushed, and eleven ringleaders were executed. The Portuguese Brazilian menace was also averted. Aided by British diplomacy, which was powerful in Rio de Janeiro, Rivadavia concluded an armistice[1] stipulating for the withdrawal of the Portuguese forces from the Banda Oriental. This armistice facilitated the operations against Montevideo and also the handling of a third formidable

[1] The Portuguese Foreign Office at Rio, in correspondence concerning this armistice, spoke of 'the amity which should prevail between neighbouring nations', thus implicitly recognising an independence which had not yet been claimed!

danger, which threatened the State from within. The wealthy and active Spaniard Alzaga, who as alcalde had led the defence against Whitelocke in 1807, organised a conspiracy among his compatriots to restore Spanish authority by opening a way to the royalist armies. The plot was revealed: Alzaga and forty of his associates suffered death in the plaza where he had organised victory. Then an amnesty was proclaimed.

Rivadavia, a fervent patriot but a thorough Porteño, convinced, like Moreno, of the need of a strong Executive, provoked a fall by dictatorial methods, by ignoring the provisional character of the Government and by evading the promised creation of a representative system. It is impossible to call in question the unselfish patriotism and the good intentions of San Martín, who at the head of his troops helped to lead the 'Revolution of October the 7th'. Yet the overthrow of a Government by a military pronunciamiento, acting with an extreme radical party, was a matter of evil augury.

'The last rights of Ferdinand VII have disappeared.... The dignity of a nation legitimately constituted.' With such words the new Triumvirate summoned a Constituent Assembly of thirty-two deputies, chosen, in theory at least, by indirect election based on the suffrage of 'patriot' householders in the towns of the provinces—a limitation which favoured the electioneering activities of the Láutaro Lodge and the ambitions of Alvear.

Yet, even though the mode of election may not bear exact scrutiny, the creation of this Assembly was a notable achievement, and marks a real advance towards national organisation. After three abortive attempts, an authority had at last come into being which was more than local in origin and character, and was not merely improvised to meet some sudden emergency. Its members, whether strictly representative or not, came from all parts of the United Provinces; and thus the gathering had a distinctly national character. Argentine historians have called it 'The Illustrious Assembly'; and the title was earned by the remarkable series of measures enacted during the first half-year of its existence. Those measures showed that the Assembly clearly grasped the true significance of the Revolution, the ultimate end which was to complete that Revolution, and the general character of the political life which was to spring from it.

The Assembly, which met in January, 1813, declaring itself to be 'Sovereign' and its members to be 'Deputies of the Nation' —words which implied an assertion of independence—carried through in six months a series of measures which amplified that assertion. Judicial torture, the Inquisition, titles of nobility, external ecclesiastical control, royal symbols, Indian forced labour and tribute, entailment of estates; these were all swept away. All children born thenceforth were declared free—the first step towards the gradual abolition of slavery during the following decade. A National Anthem was sanctioned which announced the birth, 'in the face of the world, of a new and glorious nation'. In short, the Assembly of 1813, in every act, implicitly assumed independence. But they deliberately stopped short of the two ultimate issues, formal Declaration of Independence and promulgation of a Constitution.

There were motives for delay. Venezuelan independence, proclaimed in 1811, had apparently been crushed. And the constitutional problem was a thorny one: for the long conflict between federal and unitary tendencies, between provincial autonomy and centralisation in the capital, took definite form with the arrival of five deputies from the Banda Oriental. These deputies presented themselves armed with instructions to demand an immediate Declaration of Independence and a federal system, with complete autonomy for every province and a capital outside Buenos Aires. The Assembly, influenced by Alvear, evaded these unwelcome proposals by excluding the five deputies as not duly elected. This exclusion, whatever its wisdom might be, had some technical justification. But the next proceeding seems to show a somewhat arbitrary view of the meaning of free election. The Assembly ordered Rondeau, the Porteño soldier commanding the troops in the Banda Oriental, to hold parliamentary elections in that province. Artigas, self-styled 'Chief of the Orientales', protested. A rupture within the United Provinces themselves was imminent.

CHAPTER XII

THE DIRECTORY

I. INDEPENDENCE

THE Assembly, leaving these grave questions to the Executive Triumvirate, suspended its sittings in November, 1813, but was summoned two months later to inaugurate a new system, namely, Government under a personal Head of the State. It was justly felt that the divided and unstable authority of a succession of Triumvirs did not constitute either an efficient Executive Government for a State which was still in an inchoate condition or an adequate central command for the conduct of a war which was simultaneously waged upon two fronts. Thus there was the soundest reason for the appointment of a Head of the State, but perhaps not equally cogent reason for the personal appointment which was actually made. The Assembly was much under the influence of Alvear, who for a time had even been President of that body. In the absence of San Martín, who had recently left the capital for the theatre of war, Alvear was the most powerful personage in the State and had the valuable support of the Láutaro Lodge. The choice of the Assembly fell upon Alvear's uncle, Gervasio Posadas, an estimable citizen of unexceptionable character, who became 'Supreme Director of the United Provinces of the River Plate', with a Council of State nominated by himself. In the course of the following twelve months this new Executive attempted to solve, by means of monarchical schemes, which will be described later, the double problem of internal organisation and of external recognition. But immediate perils demanded prompt action. On January 15,

1814, news came of Belgrano's defeat at Ayohuma. On the 20th Artigas abandoned his post in the lines besieging Montevideo. Posadas, assuming office on the 30th, denounced Artigas as a traitor and put a price upon his head.

The militant efforts of the Directory, Brown's naval victories and the fall of Montevideo have been already told (pp. 87–88). Alvear, who had superseded Rondeau before Montevideo on the eve of victory, attempted to supersede him a second time five months later in the command of the northern army, now re-organised by San Martín at Tucumán. The officers of that army rejected Alvear's command and stuck to Rondeau: not only the provinces but the troops also were ignoring orders from the capital. However, in the following January (1815), Alvear, aged twenty-eight, stepped into his uncle's place as Supreme Director, to maintain a precarious military dictatorship for four months by strange expedients; he attempted to bribe Artigas by handing over to him the fortified city of Montevideo, taken by Argentine arms, and he even offered to Great Britain a Protectorate over the River Plate—an offer which never reached its destination and was in any case impossible of acceptance by Great Britain, bound as she was by alliance with Spain. Neither San Martín in Cuyo, nor Güemes in Salta, nor other prominent chieftains paid much regard to this strange 'National Government'.

After a time the capricious and self-assertive methods of the youthful Head of the State caused such discontent in Buenos Aires itself that the Cabildo of the capital in May 1815 sent a message to Artigas, the enemy of their city, requesting him to overthrow Alvear. The gaucho chieftain readily complied with a petition which was so flattering to his power and ambition. He moved towards the city at the head of his irregular cavalry. Alvear sent out troops against him; but the officers and men of the army of the Supreme Director mutinied and fraternised with the advancing gauchos. Alvear, finding himself deserted, escaped to Rio in a British ship. The National Government had collapsed.

The Cabildo of Buenos Aires now assumed 'National' authority, dissolved the Assembly, summoned a Cabildo abierto, and appointed Alvear's rival Rondeau to be Supreme Director. Rondeau being absent with the northern army, the leader of the recent mutiny became Director *ad interim*.[1] But he was not to rule uncontrolled, as Alvear had attempted to do. His proceedings were to be watched and checked by a rival authority, bearing the significant title of *Junta de Observación*. This body took a decisive step towards closing the cycle of oligarchical or personal Governments directed mainly by Porteños. They invited the provinces to elect a Constituent Assembly, which should meet at a distance from the capital. A year passed, a year of sporadic revolts and spreading disintegration, before this Congress opened its sessions at Tucumán in May, 1816, at a moment of extreme difficulty. The interim Director had just been replaced by another soldier,[1] more acceptable to the Cabildo and to Artigas. The Peruvian royalists, victorious at Sipe Sipe, were threatening invasion; a Brazilian-Portuguese army was preparing to advance through the Banda Oriental. The treasury was exhausted. Talk of monarchical designs brought suspicion upon all Governments and all politicians.

Furthermore, the nation had almost suffered disruption, or at least division into two parts; for three of the provinces, in addition to the Banda Oriental, had practically seceded, under the

[1] The first *ad interim* Director, leader of the mutiny, was Alvarez Thomas; the second was González Balcarce.

leadership of Artigas, from the rest of the provinces. Artigas, having assumed the title 'Chief of the Orientals and Protector of the Free Peoples', dominated not only the Banda Oriental, which was a distinct geographical region beyond the estuary, but also the three 'littoral provinces', Santa Fe, Corrientes and Entre Ríos. No deputies came to the Congress from those provinces, whose equestrian caudillos, at the head of their irregular gaucho cavalry, formed a loose federation of autocrats under Artigas, proclaiming a 'federalism' which meant disunion and local despotism. Córdoba, also influenced by Artigas, tardily sent deputies without hearty adhesion. Salta, under Güemes, held a yet tardier election amid cries of 'Death to the Porteños'.

Of the thirty-two deputies who finally assembled at Tucumán, some claimed to represent districts of Upper Peru which were occupied by the royalists. The others represented ten cities or provinces of the Argentine region. Most of the deputies, prominent in their provinces, were little known to Buenos Aires— a fact which indicates the imperfect and non-national character of the various Porteño essays at government. Four of the deputies, constituting an eighth part of the whole number, were priests; for the clergy in the United Provinces were not in general opposed to the Revolution, as they were in some parts of Spanish America. Owing to provincial sentiment and a tendency to aloofness from Buenos Aires, there was some hesitation about the nomination of a Porteño as Director. But the urgency of the case overcame those feelings, and Pueyrredón, who was marked out by his capacity and his previous services, was chosen to be Supreme Director of the United Provinces, a post which he held for three years.

The next question was the crucial one, concerning the Declaration of Independence. All, or almost all, were heartily in favour of publicly claiming an independence which had long been assumed in practice. But there were doubts whether the moment was propitious for an immediate declaration. Everywhere throughout South America, except in the United Provinces, the revolutionary Governments appeared to have fallen before royalist re-conquest. Ferdinand VII, to all outward appearance, was reigning once more over his South American kingdoms with the exception of the River Plate. But this hesitation or disposition for cautious delay was overcome, chiefly by outside pressure from two men who were not members of the Congress, Belgrano and San Martín. Both men had for years past been determined upon complete independence. San Martín, from his headquarters at Mendoza, wrote to the deputy for the Province of Cuyo in the Congress urging an immediate Declaration of Independence. Belgrano, now returned from his European mission—to be related presently—arrived at Tucumán at the beginning of July to take command of the army stationed there, and at once urged the same step. Their efforts were seconded within the Congress by the eloquence of Fray Justo de Santa María de Oro, whose name is remembered with honour as that of a priestly champion of Revolution. Finally on July 9, 1816, the Congress, by a unanimous vote, issued a solemn Declaration of Independence.[1] The nation which had come into being six years earlier, thus proclaimed itself in the face of the world.

[1] A translation of the Declaration of Independence is given in the Appendix.

II. MONARCHICAL SCHEMES

But that nation was not yet organised, and although two 'Provisional Constitutions' were promulgated by the Congress, the drafting of a definitive constitution was delayed for three years, partly owing to the prevailing anarchy and the conflict between centralising and local tendencies, partly owing to diplomatic efforts to win Spanish and European recognition of independence by establishing a constitutional monarchy under a European prince. The Congress was a Constituent Assembly, which had been summoned for the express purpose of promulgating a Constitution. Belgrano was invited to address the Congress in secret session, and warmly advocated a monarchical constitution, as being the form most prevalent in the world and most likely to conciliate the goodwill of European Powers. The members of Congress were generally disposed to agree with him. But in order to institute monarchy, it was necessary to find a king: and pending the conclusion of that matter, the promulgation of a Constitution had to wait. Meantime the Congress did not confine itself to its functions as a Constituent Assembly, but regarded itself as a branch of the Government and as the only link which maintained some semblance of unity between the Provinces.

During the previous eighteen months, schemes had been on foot for establishing a monarchy and finding a king. In December 1814 Posadas, as Supreme Director, had sent Belgrano and Rivadavia to England with a commission that they should attempt to bring about an understanding with Spain through British mediation. They landed at Plymouth amid the excitement produced by Napoleon's recent escape from Elba and his resumption of the Imperial Crown of France. When the two envoys arrived in London, they were welcomed by Sarratea, formerly one of the Triumvirs and commander in the war against Montevideo, who was now residing in London as agent of the United Provinces. Sarratea, who was a light-hearted and untrust-worthy optimist rather than a serious statesman, induced the two commissioners to pursue a chimerical design, or rather plot, hatched by a Spanish political adventurer, the Conde de Cabarrús. At the very time when Alvear was offering to Great Britain a Protectorate over the River Plate, Cabarrús travelled from London to Rome, as emissary from Sarratea, Rivadavia and Belgrano, charged with a mission to offer a South American crown to a Spanish Bourbon prince. The ex-King Charles IV, with his family, was living in exile at Rome, receiving a pension from his son, Ferdinand VII, the reigning King of Spain. Cabarrús was the bearer of a letter signed by the three Argentines, in which Charles was saluted as King and was requested to establish in the Provinces of the River Plate a kingdom which he should then cede to his younger son, Francisco de Paula. The disillusioned old King, after some hesitation, declined this attempt to disturb the peace of his retirement. The Prince, backed up by his mother, was eager to accept. But it was found that it was only by kidnapping him through Austria to London that he could be conveyed to the throne which awaited him in the Southern Hemi-sphere. The scheme, futile in itself, was rendered doubly impossible by Ferdinand's secure hold of the Spanish Crown after the final defeat of Napoleon at Waterloo.

After the failure of this design, Belgrano embarked for home; he landed in Buenos Aires in January 1816 and in July took command of the troops stationed at Tucumán, where, as has been related, he recommended to the Congress the adoption of a constitutional monarchy and urged them to proclaim independence. But when the Declaration of Independence was issued at Tucumán, Rivadavia, who had remained in Europe, was actually in Madrid, having been invited thither by Ferdinand VII. However, King and 'vassal' alike were uncompromising, the one demanding submission, the other independence: and Rivadavia's residence in Madrid ended abruptly when an Argentine corsair seized Spanish ships in sight of Cadiz.

Rivadavia then betook himself to Paris, whence he wrote to Buenos Aires setting forth proposals for an independent monarchy of the River Plate with a French prince as King; a settlement which would secure recognition by France. After a brief visit to London in the vain hope of obtaining British support for some such monarchical scheme, he returned to Paris to further the candidature of Louis Philippe, Duke of Orleans. This design was vetoed by King Louis XVIII. Rivadavia then pushed forward the candidature of Ferdinand's nephew, the Prince of Lucca, who, so the French Foreign Office now proposed, was to espouse a Braganza princess and reign over the United Provinces.[1]

[1] The later story of these fruitless negotiations may be briefly told. Gómez, a man of character and capacity, was sent to Paris as Argentine agent in order to continue Rivadavia's negotiations on the basis of complete independence and limited monarchy—conditions which were an insurmountable obstacle in view of the stubborn opposition of Ferdinand VII, who could not be left out of account by France. Meantime, one Le Moyne, a clever and adventurous Frenchman who was living in London, persuaded the French Ambassador in London to send him to the River Plate in order to push the interests of French monarchy. Le Moyne reached Buenos Aires in August 1818, and, although he had no credentials, contrived, after some difficulty, to be admitted to see the Supreme Director. Pueyrredón, who was the son of a Frenchman, listened to him, received him several times and warmly favoured the candidature of the Duke of Orleans. Pueyrredón's successor, Rondeau, afterwards supported the candidature of the Prince of Lucca. However, towards the end of 1819 the French Government withdrew all proposals and closed the negotiations.

While Rivadavia was pursuing these monarchical designs in Europe, his friend and former colleague Belgrano, on the other side of the Atlantic, was persuading San Martín and others to follow him into yet more fantastic schemes. Some Indian 'prince' of Inca ancestry might be sought out who should reign in Cuzco, the historic capital of the ancient Inca dynasty, over a united kingdom of Peru and the River Plate. Or, failing this, there was a king ready to hand in Rio de Janeiro, where the former Portuguese Prince-Regent now held his Court as King John VI of Portugal and Brazil. It was true that King John's armies had occupied Montevideo and the Banda Oriental, which was claimed as one of the United Provinces. But Belgrano argued that it might be possible to welcome him amicably and invite him to reign as Constitutional Sovereign. Or these two designs might be combined through the union of a Braganza prince with an Inca princess.

Those schemes were impossible for two reasons. Great Britain, whose favour was particularly sought, would have no French or Portuguese dominion in these Spanish lands. Moreover, an artificial and alien monarchy was in itself totally inappropriate, and was repugnant to the strong local individualism and the intuitive common sense of the Argentine people.

Moreover, the Government itself was in a precarious position; for a central authority which was necessary for the conduct of the

Pueyrredón's 'secret' communications with Le Moyne afterwards became known in Buenos Aires and did much to discredit the Directorial Government, and to win support for the attacks of Ramírez, since to the mass of the people the notion of an imported monarchy was hateful.

Castlereagh's extreme anger at these French negotiations suggests that he believed they had support in high quarters in France.

war was not acceptable to the regional sentiment of the Provinces. Immediately after the Declaration of Independence the Supreme Director, Pueyrredón, left Tucumán for the capital.[1] Six months later, early in 1917, the Congress followed him thither to avoid the inconvenience of the two branches of Government being separated by a distance which might take weeks to traverse. Now that the Congress was holding its sessions among the Porteños, it was viewed with yet greater dislike and distrust in the Provinces. That dislike and distrust now broke out into violence. A new and disconcerting force shook the State. The politicians, from Moreno onwards, had ignored, except as possible military recruits, the most virile part of the population, the inarticulate illiterate masses, alien to city life, to whom the term 'Government' meant some unintelligible unwelcome external power, and 'Justice' was something perilous and sinister. These were now making their unruly power felt in the *montoneras*,[2] that is to say, hordes of mounted gauchos led by local caudillos.

The gathering of these dangerous crowds of mounted men was due to the peculiar circumstances of the time, and to the interruption of normal economic life by years of warfare and disorder. The plains had been devastated and cattle destroyed by the exigencies of war, by civil strife, by Portuguese invasion, by raids of Indians who took advantage of conflicts among white men, and finally by extensive slaughter for the *saladeros*, factories in the open air where oxen were slaughtered and the carcasses were dried for export to Brazil and the West Indies, in order to redress the un-

---

[1] It was in the course of this journey that Pueyrredón had his momentous meeting at Córdoba with San Martín, who persuaded him to abandon the design of a fresh invasion of Upper Peru and to support the projected expedition to Chile. See p. 103.

[2] The word *montonera* is derived from *montón* = 'a heap' or 'mass': it has nothing to do with mountains. The individual riders in a montonera were called *montoneros*.

favourable balance of trade which had prevailed since the River Plate had been opened to British commerce. Such was the strange scarcity of meat on these immense pastures, that Pueyrredón ordered the closing of many saladeros. The hungry gauchos were ready to gallop after any leader who would arm them and give them beef and maté, their sole necessities.

Moreover, although many of the professional and well-to-do classes in the provincial towns favoured adherence to the capital with a view to preserving order and property, yet little regard was paid in general to a succession of 'provisional' central governments, largely local and municipal in origin, which could not protect the provinces from spoliation and yet claimed the rights which had been previously exercised by kings and viceroys, nominating the Governors of Provinces and even attempting to control the nomination of the Cabildos in provincial capitals.

These claims of the capital were now repudiated. Entre Ríos and Corrientes, which had been erected into Provinces by the Directorate in 1814, accepted or elected local caudillos as their Governors. The Province of Santa Fe shook off the authority of Buenos Aires by successful revolt in 1815, and the Cabildo of the city of Santa Fe elected as Governor the patriarchal and hospitable Candioti, an honourable man of some culture, lord of extensive lands and herds, enriched by the dispatch every year of thousands of mules to be sold in the markets of Peru. The death of Candioti a few months later led to destructive rivalries, in the course of which the vigorous, ambitious and unscrupulous Estanislao López made his way to the front, to rule the province for thirty years (1818–48). The Province of Entre Ríos, divided between rival caudillos, passed in 1817 under the authority of Ramírez, an ally or lieutenant, like López, of Artigas. Tucumán claimed independence under one Araoz, who was soon coercing Santiago and Catamarca and making war upon Güemes, lord of Salta. Rioja broke away from Córdoba, which in turn was at variance with Buenos Aires. It was a medley of disintegration and cross-currents of strife.

In 1816 Artigas, refusing proffered aid from Buenos Aires against the Portuguese invaders, assumed complete independence and made war on his own account against Portugal, issuing letters of marque to North American privateers, who with head-quarters at Colonia attacked Portuguese merchant-ships and openly sold their booty at Baltimore. Other North American privateers, with letters of marque from Buenos Aires, were attacking Spanish commerce. Thus the 'United Provinces' were at war with Spain, while three or four of those provinces were at war with Portugal, which was invading territory claimed by Spain. Artigas, not without reason, was accused of making common cause with the Spanish royalists; and Pueyrredón, the Head of the State, was accused of traitorous complicity with the Portuguese invasion and of equally traitorous surrender to schemes of Bourbon monarchy.

And indeed Pueyrredón's position was peculiar. The Portu-guese invasion of the Banda Oriental actually had the assent of Argentine envoys at Rio de Janeiro; yet Pueyrredón indignantly protested when the Congress refused to declare war on Portugal, although neither men nor money were available for the Banda Oriental. Pueyrredón was obliged to accept the assurances of Lecor, the Portuguese commander, that he came with no hostile designs, but merely in order to end anarchy in a province which touched Brazil and had declared itself independent of the United Provinces.

The invasion from the north was successful. Lecor entered Montevideo. Artigas and his irregular levies, repeatedly beaten by the Portuguese soldiery, retreated to Entre Ríos and still dominated the littoral provinces.

In 1819 the Congress, which had already issued two 'Provisional Constitutions', promulgated a unitary and centralised Constitution, providing for an elected Director and two legislative chambers. But this attempt at union merely hastened the growing disruption. Pueyrredón resigned. After the solemn swearing on May 25 of this republican constitution, in which, however, the word 'Republican' did not occur, his successor, Rondeau, like himself the son of a Frenchman, summoned the Congress to discuss in secret session the monarchical candidature of the Prince of Lucca, which they accepted under certain conditions. But López and Ramírez, caudillos of the Littoral, rejecting all that came from the Congress, led their montoneras against Buenos Aires. Rondeau summoned San Martín and Belgrano to his aid. San Martín disobeyed, as was related on page 105. Belgrano obeyed, but his army mutinied. Rondeau marched against the gauchos of López and Ramírez and was defeated at Cepeda (February 1820). Directorate, Congress, 'National Government' disappeared. The Cabildo, at the command of Ramírez, created a Government, not of the Nation, but merely of the Province of Buenos Aires. This Provincial Government, by the Treaty of Pilar (February 23, 1820), recognised the 'Littoral Federation', undertook to pay an indemnity and agreed that the United Provinces should have a Federal Government, to be arranged by a Congress. This Treaty of Pilar foreshadows the Federation which later came into being. And the bearded caudillo Ramírez, chieftain of cowboy cavalry, however independent and autocratic in his own action, deserves the credit of comprehending and declaring, in rudimentary fashion, the possibility which was realised forty years later.

But that union was remote. Nine months after Pilar the Buenos Aires Government agreed to pay López, as the price of peace, 25,000 head of cattle, to feed the hungry inhabitants of the Santa Fe plains. The cattle were provided by a young estanciero, Juan Manuel Rosas, who by his wealth in lands and herds, his aristocratic family traditions, his splendid horsemanship, his powerful personality, his handsome face and proud bearing, had become a kind of prince among the gauchos and Indians of the South. These wild horsemen submitted to stern discipline and even harsh punishments from the young *patrón*, who shared their labours and their dangerous sports, who beat them at their own feats, could ride an unbroken colt without saddle or bridle and sit a bucking horse with a gold ounce firmly held under each knee. Since, in the midst of the civil disturbances, Governments in Buenos Aires had been unable to check Indian incursions and cattle-stealing, Rosas had himself raised troops of gauchos and friendly Indians to protect his property and that of his neighbours from the savages. And in the recent wars he had led his scarlet-clad 'Rosista' cavalry in defence of his native province against the montoneras of the Littoral.

CHAPTER XIII

PROVINCIAL ISOLATION

IN 1820, the 'Terrible Year', as Argentine historians have called it, the term 'United Provinces' seemed to be no more than a name. The main thread of history is to be sought during this time in Buenos Aires. But even there the thread is repeatedly broken. Zinny, in his history of the Governors of the Argentine Provinces, gives a list of twenty-four successive Governments of the Province of Buenos Aires during the year 1820, and then, unable to complete the list, takes refuge in an 'etcetera'. In this rapid procession of rulers, Alvear held a fugitive place. He appeared from exile among the montoneras of López, thrust himself into the seat of power and passed again into banishment. One day, June 20, brought three successive Governments. On that day, Belgrano died: two months later San Martín sailed from Valparaiso to invade Peru, leading an Argentine army to victory abroad at the moment of national dissolution at home.

The issue of these troubles was the collapse of all central authority and the segregation of the provinces. From the confusion there emerged as 'Provisional Governor' of Buenos Aires, returning from exile in the United States, the genial figure of Dorrego, distinguished as a soldier by skill and gallantry in the field, and in the camp by a joyous and turbulent indiscipline. Although a townsman and a man of education, he represented the creole tradition, sympathising with the spirit of the plains and with regional patriotism. Under Dorrego elections were held and a Representative Chamber of the Province of Buenos Aires chose Martín Rodríguez, one of the *próceres* of the Revolution, who had helped to raise volunteers against Beresford, as Governor of the province. With Rivadavia as Minister and guiding spirit of his Government, Rodríguez initiated a four years' period, 1820–4, of peace, progress and beneficent legislation. A general amnesty, universal suffrage, abolition of the cabildos, now replaced by republican courts, improved police, posts, port facilities, the raising of a loan in London,[1] encouragement of agriculture and of immigration, organisation of archives and of statistics, regulation of the Treasury, a Provincial Bank, a University, new and more efficient schools, a Public Welfare Society which gave official sanction to organised feminine philanthropy, the reform of the religious houses, effected in the face of much opposition—a general effort at reconstruction which won the respect of foreigners and prepared the way for recognition by Europe: such were the fruits of peace in the Province of Buenos Aires.

But peace was not yet in the littoral provinces. Ramírez, caudillo and Governor of Entre Ríos, having been denounced as a traitor by Artigas for concluding the Peace of Pilar, turned against the 'Protector of Free Peoples' and drove him in flight to Paraguay, there to linger out an obscure old age. Ramírez himself had a more sudden fate. López, Governor of Santa Fe, disobeyed his call to attack Buenos Aires once more. The two chieftains fell out. Ramírez, beaten in the field, fled with a group of horsemen. His paramour, who rode with him on every adventure, cried out

---

[1] Already some British settlers had invested capital in Argentine land. This British loan is the beginning of a great movement of public British investment in Argentina. In this connexion Rivadavia, while Minister in the Province of Buenos Aires, assumed a national authority which he did not possess; in November 1823 he granted to an English company a concession to work mines in Rioja, Catamarca, Córdoba and San Luis. The Governments of those provinces naturally refused to recognise this concession.

that she was overtaken. Ramírez turned to save her and fell by a pistol shot (July 1821).

After his death, Entre Ríos succeeded in forming a more con-stitutional Government: and in every province some system was evolved, usually dictated by an autocratic caudillo, yet something which shaped every province into a self-conscious entity. The most notable of these provincial movements was that of Buenos Aires, which maintained a certain national predominance as being the wealthiest, most prosperous and most orderly region, and also the only convenient channel of diplomatic and com-mercial communication with the outside world.

It was during this period of national dissolution that, by a strange contradiction, the Nation, through Buenos Aires, achieved formal international recognition; received two missions dispatched by the radical Government of Spain (1820–3) in the vain hope of some accommodation short of complete independence; and also conducted negotiations, first with Portugal and then with Brazil concerning a national question, namely, the continued occupa-tion of the Banda Oriental. In January 1822, the four provinces immediately concerned in this territorial question, Buenos Aires, Entre Ríos, Santa Fe and Corrientes, concluded a 'Cuadrilateral Treaty' to defend the 'integrity of the National Territory', certain internal questions being remitted to a future Congress of all the provinces. This treaty, two years after that of Pilar, marks a further essay towards national union.

After an attempt at a Congress in Córdoba, frustrated, in part at least, by the reluctance of Buenos Aires and of Rivadavia to take part in an assembly held in the rival city of Córdoba, a Con-stituent Congress did meet in Buenos Aires in December 1824. This Congress obtained the consent of all the provinces to a

'Fundamental Law', providing that the constitution to be framed should be submitted to the judgment of the provinces, that mean-time the provinces should govern themselves, and that the Govern-ment of Buenos Aires should act as a provisional National Executive in charge of Foreign Affairs.

This last point was essential. War with Brazil was imminent. There was a frontier question with the newly founded Republic of Bolivia, which comprised the territory formerly known as Upper Peru. There were apprehensions concerning the possible ambition of the conqueror Bolívar, now supreme in that Re-public, who was proposing co-operation against Brazil and vast schemes of American union, schemes which found little favour in Buenos Aires. Moreover the nation was now 'called into ex-istence' through recognition by a great European Power. In April 1821, King John VI of Portugal had publicly recognised the independence of Buenos Aires; recognition by the United States and by the now independent monarchy of Brazil followed in 1822. Meantime Spain, in maintaining her claims over these independent countries, had the general support of continental Europe: but Great Britain, as the prospects of any agreement between Spain and her former dependencies faded away, gradually dissociated herself from the continental attitude, being disposed to acquiesce in any system of existing government which permitted the enforcement of contracts and therefore favoured commerce and peace.

In June 1822, a change in the British Navigation Acts ad-mitted the ships of the revolted Spanish dependencies to all the ports of the British Empire. This was the first step towards com-mercial recognition, though it was not, as Castlereagh suggested, 'substantially *de facto* recognition' and still less diplomatic re-cognition. But it granted a national character to the blue and

white flag of the United Provinces, which in Spanish eyes was a
piratical symbol. Furthermore, at the Congress of Verona, which
met in the autumn of 1822, Wellington, the British envoy,
instructed by Castlereagh, announced that Great Britain had
been obliged to recognise the existence *de facto* of several Governments so far as to treat with them; and he indicated that further
recognition was unavoidable.

In the following year a French army entered Spain, overthrew
the radical Government, under which the King was a prisoner,
and restored the absolute authority of Ferdinand VII. The possibility of further intervention in order to restore that absolute royal
authority in America was viewed with strong objection in the
United States and in England. For a time there seemed to be
some likelihood of a joint protest by those two Powers. But in
the end they acted separately. In October 1823, Canning, now
Foreign Minister, in a conference with Polignac, the French
Ambassador in London, signified uncompromising opposition
to any French interference in America: in December, President
Monroe in his famous message to Congress announced that 'with
the Governments . . . whose independence . . . we have acknowledged, we could not view any interposition for the purpose of
oppressing them, or controlling . . . their destiny, by any European
Power in any other light than as a manifestation of an unfriendly
disposition toward the United States'.[1]

[1] Monroe's message, of which a few lines are here quoted, referred not only
to Latin America, but also to Russian advance in Alaska; and it defined the
attitude of the United States towards European affairs and towards existing European colonies in America. This message was later interpreted by Adams as
meaning that the policy thus indicated would not necessarily commit the United
States to war against an aggressor. On the other hand Canning's published
memorandum of the Polignac conference, mentioned in the Introduction to this
book, was a pledge of defence against aggression.

In July 1824 the British Cabinet decided that the British Consul-General in Buenos Aires should be instructed to conclude a commercial treaty with the States of La Plata. This decision meant recognition; for the signature or ratification of a commercial treaty implies full reciprocal diplomatic recognition. The signing of this treaty in Buenos Aires on February 2, 1825, was celebrated by fireworks, banquets and public rejoicings. One clause stipulated for religious toleration to British subjects in the United Provinces—a stipulation which, as it were accidentally and by a side issue, introduced the principle of religious toleration, only to be fully accepted a generation later.

Thus in 1825 the international status of the young Republic was secured. Five years later France accorded recognition, and about the same time satisfactory relations were established with the Vatican, whereby the Roman Church remained, as it remains to-day, the officially recognised religion supported by the State, which in turn claims to have inherited both the ecclesiastical patronage, granted by successive Popes to the Spanish Crown, and also the right of refusing or granting the *exequatur* to Papal Bulls. To a country where the Church fills so great a place in public, social and domestic life, agreement with the Holy See was more important than the long-delayed recognition by Spain.[1]

But in 1825 this independent Republic had no Government: and the Constituent Congress determined to create a permanent National Executive by appointing a President of the Republic of the United Provinces. Accordingly, in February 1826, Rivadavia, now returned from his notable mission to England, was

[1] Spain granted recognition in 1859; but for some years before that date there had been intercourse between Spain and Argentina which implied a considerable step towards recognition.

chosen first President of the Republic. It was a victory for Buenos Aires and for the unitarios, a contravention of the Fundamental Law of 1824, and was therefore an affront to the provinces and to the caudillos. But this step, although unconstitutional, was perhaps justified by the urgent necessity of the case; for this form-less Republic was at war with Brazil.

The long-threatened conflict was precipitated by an audacious adventure. In April 1825, thirty-three 'Orientales' crossed the estuary from Buenos Aires and disembarked near Colonia in the Banda Oriental to rouse revolt against Brazil. The country rose at their call. They were victorious in several encounters. An Oriental Assembly proclaimed union with the United Provinces. The Buenos Aires Congress welcomed this incor-poration. The consequence was that in December 1825 the Congress was at war with Brazil for possession of the Banda Oriental.

This three years' war (1825–8) has left an Argentine tradition of victory by sea and by land followed by an unprofitable and un-stable peace. William Brown, Admiral of the United Provinces, once more led out an improvised fleet to break the blockade of the coast and beat the Brazilian fleet at Juncal. Alvear, returning from a diplomatic mission to Bolívar, commanded the army. Argentine troops, invading Brazil, proved their endurance and fighting qualities, particularly in the battle of Ituzaingo, a soldiers' victory, in which the Hollander Brandsen, a veteran of the Na-poleonic armies and now an Argentine colonel, fell in a cavalry charge. Yet an envoy, sent to Rio de Janeiro by Rivadavia to treat for peace, broke his instructions and agreed to the Brazilian possession of the Banda Oriental. Rivadavia repudiated this ar-rangement; and fighting was resumed. Buenos Aires, almost isolated and unaided, continued the conflict—an inconclusive conflict owing to the disruption of the United Provinces, the collapse of the Presidency and the civil wars of provisional caudillos, who preferred the perpetuation of their own 'federal' authority to the national interests. A forced paper currency and forcible recruiting ill supplied the wastage of war.

Finally under pressure from Lord Ponsonby, British Minister at Rio, and through British mediation, a Preliminary Convention of Peace was signed, which erected the Banda Oriental into the independent Republic of Uruguay,[1] to be a South American Belgium, a buffer State between two powerful neighbours. But the island of Martín García near the Uruguayan coast remained in the possession of Argentina, which thus commanded the only navigable channel leading to the up-river provinces. The independence of Uruguay was guaranteed by the two contracting Governments, but not by the mediating Power. The definitive Treaty of Peace was not concluded till 1859, when Uruguay was a party to it. But the validity of this convention was never disputed, although neither party strictly observed it.

Meantime the Congress at Buenos Aires had failed in its work. The Federal and Unitary parties, now clearly defined, debated their respective proposals with eloquence and ability. Dorrego, elected or rather nominated deputy for Santiago by his associate, the caudillo Ibarra, advocated the federal system which he had seen at work in the United States without clearly comprehending its origin and meaning. The provinces were consulted: six of them favoured federation; five were for a unitary system; the re-

---

[1] The country continued to be called the Banda Oriental and its inhabitants Orientales; but in this book the more convenient terms 'Uruguay' and 'Uruguayans' will henceforth be used.

maining six left the decision to the Congress.[1] Rivadavia, zealous for a strong Central Executive, declaring that Buenos Aires, as national capital, could be the seat of only one Government—that of the nation—abolished the Provincial Legislature and placed the territory of Buenos Aires directly under national authority, until a separate provincial Government should be set up outside the national capital. But he took no steps to create this projected provincial Government, and in effect he wiped out the autonomy and even the corporate existence of the province which he had done so much to create; and he himself, as Head of the Nation, assumed control over the territory of the Province of Buenos Aires with excessive and unpopular authority.

Finally in December 1826, the Congress issued a unitary and centralised Constitution. Emissaries were sent to the capitals of all the provinces bearing copies of the Constitution for the approval of the provincial Governments, in accordance with the Fundamental Law of 1824. The Constitution was rejected by all the provincial caudillos, in some cases with contemptuous insult; and in 1827 the country, in the midst of a foreign war, was distracted by civil strife, disruption and anarchy. Facundo Quiroga, Governor of Rioja, whose aquiline countenance and terrifying glance, framed in masses of black hair, symbolised the ogre-like legend of 'Facundo, the Tiger of the Plains', was extending his merciless despotism over all the west, leading his gaucho hordes under a banner displaying a skull and cross-bones, with the legend 'Religion or death'—an allusion to the supposed unorthodoxy of Rivadavia, reformer of the convents.

Powerless to pursue the Brazilian war effectively, to maintain

---

[1] Three of the votes were from regions which are not now Argentine provinces: hence the total number of seventeen.

internal peace or to construct a national Government, Rivadavia resigned the Presidency in July 1827. His resignation marked national dissolution. A month later the Congress dissolved, having named Dorrego Governor of the now resuscitated Province of Buenos Aires, charged with the conduct of Foreign Affairs and National Finance.

Rivadavia had been for seven years the prominent figure in Argentine history. His portrait, with features over-prominent and fleshy, but enlivened by a vivacious and energetic intelligence, is familiar to all his countrymen. His conduct is still hotly debated between followers of the federalist and of the unitary tradition. To the latter he is a constructive statesman, overthrown by barbarous lawlessness. The former, while conceding his executive merits, hold that his anti-federal attitude delayed national organisation and was responsible for much of the succeeding misery and oppression. His admirers regard his nationalisation of the capital as a statesman-like measure which anticipated the federal settlement of 1880. It was in fact an effort to reconcile the capital with the provinces and to settle a financial question which underlay the long conflict between them.

That financial question arose from the fact that Buenos Aires possessed the sole really productive custom-house in the United Provinces; and the customs duties, which in the opinion of the other provinces should have constituted a National Treasury, provided in fact the Provincial Treasury of Buenos Aires. On the other hand the burden of international affairs and of costly military operations was borne principally and sometimes exclusively—notably during the domination of Rosas—by the Province of Buenos Aires. The nationalisation of the capital might have been a remedy: but Rivadavia failed to accomplish the second and indispensable part of his design, namely the separate organisation of the Province of Buenos Aires with a capital outside the city of Buenos Aires. At that time the difficulties may have been insuperable: if so, Rivadavia's action was premature. In any case his nationalisation, in theory provisional, of the whole Province of Buenos Aires was a disastrous error. Some of his difficulties may be understood by reading Sir Francis Head's *Rough Notes of Journeys across the Pampas*, published in 1826. In England general incredulity greeted this vivid and accurate picture of primitive gaucho life on the vast plains in which the cities formed little oases of civilisation.

Dorrego, as Governor of Buenos Aires (1827–9), strove for peace and order. He accepted, on behalf of the nation, the Convention of Peace with Brazil: he concluded an agreement with Córdoba, the jealous rival of Buenos Aires and the leader of provincial activities. The assembly at this time of a Federal Congress at Santa Fe marks an interesting but ineffective effort towards union.

But the situation in Buenos Aires was unstable. The return from Brazil of the army, dissatisfied with the peace terms and sore about its sufferings in the field, enabled the fallen party to gratify their resentment against the 'anarchist' Dorrego. Lavalle, an officer of arrogant and impulsive courage, distinguished in the Peruvian and Brazilian wars, became their instrument or leader, was acclaimed Governor of Buenos Aires by an irregular gathering in the streets, and led his troops into the plaza. Dorrego, deserted by the garrison, escaped by the postern gate to join Rosas on the southern plains. Lavalle pursued him, found him already a captive in the hands of the soldiery, and shot him.

This homicide was the beginning of great evils. Civil war

flamed out everywhere. Several provinces had their own Foreign Office, War Office and Custom Houses. After a year of disorder Rosas, ablest and strongest of the caudillos, was at the age of thirty-six elected by the Provincial Legislature to be Governor of the Province of Buenos Aires for three years, 'with such extraordinary powers as he might deem necessary'. During the Brazilian war Rosas had been commandant of the southern plains, remote from the theatre of active war, had there held the Indians in check and had developed his scarlet-clad gaucho militia into a little army devoted to his person. After twenty years of brief experiments, of revolts, civil wars, confiscations, proscriptions, exiles, abortive essays at Government, the commonwealth of Buenos Aires accepted the strong hand of a dictator and gave perforce a power above all law, including summary power of life and death, to this capable and determined young chieftain, himself an educated man of aristocratic connexions and a successful business man, but at the same time the comrade and captain of cowboys and of Indian caciques, an expert in the craft of the lasso and the boleadora, of the rodeo, the camp-fire, and the savage frontier, a man who represented the creole tradition.

CHAPTER XIV

ROSAS, 1829-52

THE lurid melodrama of Rosas' tyranny is introduced by a prologue less intense in character, in his first term as Governor of Buenos Aires (1829–32). That Government, it is true, was an autocracy. For although Rosas ordered the term 'Argentine Confederation' to be thenceforth officially used, the word 'Confederation' signified to Rosas not any effort at union or organisation, but rather provincial despotism and suppression of unitarios. A submissive Legislature ordered the burning of all papers which had attacked Rosas or Dorrego and the legal prosecution of all concerned in the recent 'intrusive Government'. Already political prisoners were filling the gaols and prominent unitarios were escaping to Córdoba or to Montevideo. Yet this three years' Government in Buenos Aires, despotic and uncompromising though it was, compares favourably with some of the previous brief administrations: it was supported by the masses and by the general acquiescence of a bewildered and disillusioned society. Rosas threw himself into the work of economical administration, demanded honest and industrious service from all his subordinates and never spared himself. Like other Spanish and Spanish-American dictators, he held that the business of a ruler was to rule—to keep order in the city and province under his charge.[1]

But 'federalism' was not everywhere triumphant. Lavalle's

[1] During this first government of Rosas a dispute arose with the United States and with Great Britain concerning the sovereignty of the Falkland Islands. In orde not to interrupt the main narrative, this matter is treated in an Appendix.

associate, General Paz, a one-armed veteran of many wars and a scientific tactician, occupied Córdoba, thrice routed the on-slaught of Quiroga's gauchos and for two years (1829–31) main-tained a unitary league, first of five and then of nine provinces. A cultivated man, of sober, studious and humorous counten-ance, author of valuable historical memoirs, the very opposite of the headlong Facundo, he aimed at opposing urban civility to rustic *caudillaje*, but, like Rivadavia, failed to give due weight to regional sentiment and to gaucho individualism, forces which were to be recognised and regulated before national organisation should be possible.

Paz made overtures to the littoral provinces. The reply was the 'Federal Pact' of January 1831, between Buenos Aires, Entre Ríos and Santa Fe. Rosas and his ally or lieutenant López of Santa Fe made war on Córdoba. Paz, riding almost unattended, fell in with a party of López' men. As he galloped away, he was unhorsed by the boleadora, flung by one of the pursuers, and was led a prisoner to López' camp. Rosas treated his distinguished captive honourably, and after seven years released him. But eleven other captive officers, as well as a boy, aged fourteen, who had accompanied his father, were shot by Rosas' command: the murder of the boy was long remembered with horror in the village of San Nicolás, where it was perpetrated. Paz being gone, his unitary system was swept away with sanguinary thoroughness by López and Quiroga. Córdoba passed under the dominion of four unscrupulous adventurers, the 'Governor' Reinafé and his three brothers.

The victory of federalism was celebrated in Buenos Aires by civil and religious rejoicings, by a decree which muzzled the press and by a command that all men of any public position, including the clergy, should wear a scarlet badge, the Rosista colour, with the legend 'Federation'.

After his three years' term Rosas refused re-election as Governor and retired to his estancia. Aided by contingents from other provinces, he spent a year (1833–4) in a military expedition to push back Indian savagery and extend the southern frontier.[1] Having killed many Indians and explored the Pampa up to the River Colorado, he received a grant of sixty square leagues of land and later the title 'Hero of the desert'. The expedition did not achieve all that had been hoped; but it made known a region hitherto almost unexplored: savage incursions were checked—at least for some years; and white settlement near the Indian frontier was made more secure. But there was other work in hand. During his absence, Rosas had a watchful agent in Buenos Aires in the person of his wife; moreover his active supporters founded a Rosista association, 'La Sociedad Popular Restauradora', known as the Mazorca from its emblem, a head of maize, probably chosen as a symbol of unity.

The Governor, Balcarce, attempting to act independently, was compelled by organised revolt to resign. His successor, Viamonte, went the same way. No one would accept the post of Governor, which was therefore occupied provisionally by the President of the Legislature, Maza, an intimate friend and supporter of Rosas and now the faithful agent of his commands.

One such command had a tragic issue. Facundo Quiroga, who was now living in Buenos Aires, was commissioned to

---

[1] Darwin, in *The Voyage of the Beagle*, gives a vivid description of life on the Pampa at the time of this expedition.

compose disputes between the northern provinces. Travelling many days, he fulfilled his mission so far as possible. On his return journey by a route which he had been warned to avoid, his carriage was waylaid near Córdoba by a group of horsemen, who murdered him and his four companions, one of them a young boy. The immediate instigators of the crime were the four Reinafé brothers of Córdoba and Cullen, Secretary to López of Santa Fe. The complicity of Rosas, suspected by some and denied by others, cannot be proved: the supposed motives, namely Quiroga's possible rivalry and indiscreet zeal for some genuine scheme of federal organisation, seem hardly adequate. The brothers Reinafé and the assassin whom they had employed were brought to Buenos Aires, and there tried, condemned and executed under the Government of Rosas.

For, amid the general consternation aroused by the murder of Quiroga, Rosas, after repeated refusals and after demanding a *plébiscite*—with the inevitable affirmative result—accepted election as Governor of Buenos Aires for five years 'with the sum total of public authority'. All the provinces, that is to say all the provincial despots, in succession entrusted to him the National Executive and the conduct of Foreign Affairs.[1] Strange scenes of adulation welcomed him in Buenos Aires. 'Guards of honour' succeeded one another; the guard of citizens, of officers of the desert expedition, of militia officers, of merchants, of farmers. Respectable citizens, their wives and mothers, vied with one another in dragging through beflagged streets a triumphal car bearing the dictator's portrait, while men saluted and some women knelt. His likeness was exhibited in the churches, with

---

[1] Corrientes gave a tardy adhesion and repeatedly revolted, actually making an alliance twice with Paraguay against Rosas in 1841 and 1845.

eulogistic sermons and thanksgivings. In time the accepted effigy appeared everywhere, on cups and saucers, on fans, even on women's gloves.

Hundreds of military officers and public servants were dis-missed as unitarios, a term conveniently applied to all suspected of lukewarmness in servile submission. Three officers were shot, nominally on the charge of conspiring to assassinate the Governor, in fact probably as a warning. Lists, printed in red, of those who were to be elected as legislators were issued to the electors. All those suspected of being not heartily addicted to the 'sacred cause of federation', which meant Rosas' autocracy, retired into in-secure seclusion or abandoned their homes and occupations, migrating to Uruguay, where, in ever-increasing numbers, they lived the precarious life of political exiles, helping one another in crowded poverty, following humble avocations, but carrying on a vigorous propaganda against Rosas and seeking all possible aid to compass his fall.

Rosas, like other despots, sought popular support by a vigorous 'national' foreign policy. In May 1837 he declared war against Bolivia, where an ambitious dictator was encroaching on the Argentine frontier. The Argentine troops were successful in the field; but the war, which was ended after two years by the fall of the Bolivian dictator, taxed the resources of the State during a time when Rosas' power was assailed by a succession of shocks. The exiles in Uruguay found their opportunity in the internal conflicts of that country. The first Uruguayan President, Rivera (1835–9), had been obliged to defend his seat by arms. And now, taking to the open country and gathering gaucho followers, he attempted to supplant his successor Oribe. The exiles, headed by Lavalle, not only joined the shifty and untrustworthy adventurer Rivera in 1836, but they also found and welcomed two years later a strange ally in the maritime power of France.

For several years French envoys had protested against the compulsory military service of Frenchmen in Argentina. In November 1837, the French vice-consul, an arrogant and tactless person, renewed the protest, adding certain claims for injuries to Frenchmen—matters which might have been easily adjusted; but Rosas refused to treat with one lacking diplomatic credentials. His stubbornness brought upon him the blockade of the Argentine coast, declared in March 1838 by the French admiral Leblanc. A combined body of French and of Riveristas, beating down the stout resistance of a small Argentine garrison, took the island of Martín García, which became a base of operations for the exiles. Moreover, President Oribe, Rosas' ally, besieged in Montevideo by the victorious troops of Rivera and Lavalle, and rendered helpless by the intervention of the French admiral, was obliged to resign the Presidency in October 1838: he departed to Buenos Aires and took military service under Rosas, who, however, affected to treat him as legal President of Uruguay. The chiefs of the Argentine exiles in Montevideo now formed themselves into an 'Argentine Commission', a kind of anti-Rosista shadow Government on foreign soil.[1] Under pressure from them, the Uruguayan Congress declared war on Rosas in February 1839. A month later Rivera was legally elected President of Uruguay. But it was only by French marines and by a hastily raised militia of foreign residents, chiefly French

[1] In Chile an equally notable group of exiles formed, some years later, an 'Argentine Commission' in that country, and carried on a vigorous propaganda against the tyranny of Rosas.

Basques, that this fighting cowboy President was defended from Argentine attack.

The blockade caused much suffering in Buenos Aires, and cut off the main source of public revenue, the customs duties. Rosas issued paper money and practised rigid economy, abolish-ing posts, reducing salaries, closing many schools, and reducing the University to a nullity by withdrawing State support, a deprivation which meant in fact disendowment.

There were other blows. López of Santa Fe, resenting the injury done to his province by the blockade, was preparing a separate accommodation with the French when he opportunely died in June 1838. His secretary Cullen, attempting to succeed him and to oppose Rosas, fell after some months and was shot by Rosas' order. But Corrientes first and then Entre Ríos, hard hit by the blockade, withdrew the executive powers entrusted to Rosas, and for three years the Dictator's hold on the littoral provinces was insecure.

Even Rosas' supporters at home, sound federalists, were turn-ing against his tyranny. In 1839, Colonel Maza, son of Rosas' old friend the President of the Legislature, contrived a conspiracy in the capital to co-operate with a rising in the south and with a landing of Lavalle and the exiles. The plot was known through informers. Maza was arrested. His father, implicated in the conspiracy, was stabbed by two cloaked men in his room at the Parliament House: next morning the son was shot.

Though the conspiracy in the city had failed, the gauchos of the south, Rosas' own country, rose in revolt, but were defeated by the Dictator's brother, Prudencio Rosas, who fixed upon a pole in the village of Dolores the head of Castelli, son of the revolutionary prócer of 1810. Lavalle, who with 3500 troops was conveyed in French ships to Entre Ríos, won some success and caused alarm by approaching within twenty miles of the capital. But he effected little, failed to support the southern revolt, and was discredited by his alliance with the French. In October 1840, the blockade was raised, Rosas having concluded with the French admiral Mackau a Convention whereby the French claims were submitted to arbitration, but the allies of the French were abandoned: for Rosas agreed to respect the independence of Uruguay only 'so long as the rights, honour and security of the Argentine Confederation were not endangered'. The island of Martín García was restored to Argentina. Rosas by determined persistence had successfully emerged from a perilous and almost overwhelming crisis, as the national champion of Argentina against European aggression.

That same month saw an orgy of violence and murder in Buenos Aires; for the anxious strain of these conspiracies and attacks provoked Rosas to the savagery which has made his name a proverb.[1] The Mazorca, or 'Mas-horca' (= 'more gallows'), originally a comparatively respectable political association, had degenerated into a gang of authorised bullies and assassins. Assaults upon houses, floggings, nocturnal throat-cutting in the streets or in the barracks, military executions, were daily events. It was a dangerous offence to appear without the scarlet badge, to wear a beard in the form of U, the unitary initial, to possess a piece of blue earthenware, the unitary colour. The house of any suspected unitario was visited at night: any blue object was

---

[1] The vital menace to Rosas' authority is reflected in the variations of exchange. In 1835 the paper dollar was worth $7\frac{1}{2}d$. The French blockade reduced it to $4\frac{1}{2}d$.; the Southern insurrection to $2\frac{3}{4}d$.; Lavalle's invasion to $1\frac{1}{8}d$. After Lavalle's retreat it rose to $2\frac{1}{2}d$.

destroyed. The owner was either butchered at once or carried off to prison or barracks. Every newspaper and every public document bore the legend 'Death to the savage unitarios'. Spies and informers were everywhere. The houses, lands and cattle of unitarios were seized under the plausible pretext that, since unitarios had brought upon the country the cost of war, they should pay for it. Emigration, which might increase the ranks of the enemy exiles, was forbidden. The coast was patrolled by assassins who cut the throats of all whom they caught attempting to escape. Santos Lugares, a military camp, barracks and arsenal twelve miles from the city, was a place of brutal outrages and summary executions; the victim, before being shot, was sometimes tortured, stretched upon the ground for hours, face upwards to the sun, his limbs fastened to four stakes.

Meantime in the north, where five provinces had withdrawn the powers granted to Rosas, Lavalle was carrying on the war, but was defeated by Oribe, who massacred all his prisoners. Sporadic revolts were crushed with the usual butchery. Lavalle, attempting escape to Bolivia, was killed by a chance shot in October 1841. For another year Paz, the most capable of the 'liberating' leaders, carried on the struggle in the Littoral: but in 1842 he withdrew to Montevideo, being ill-supported by Rivera, whose aim was not liberty for Buenos Aires, but despotism for himself: he wished to imitate Artigas by detaching Entre Ríos and Corrientes from the Argentine Confederation and uniting them with Uruguay. When Paz withdrew, Rosas, notwithstanding much smouldering discontent, was once more the chief of fourteen despotic caudillos ruling fourteen provinces and suppressing by blood and terror any disturbances or revolts within

their respective dominions. There was peace within the Argentine Confederation. But it was 'a Federation without a Congress,
without a President, without Federal Tribunals. The only
factor of common life consisted in a delegation of powers by
the provincial chieftains to enable Buenos Aires to assume the
diplomatic representation of the country in dealing with foreign
nations'.[1]

In April 1842, another storm of murder and terror raged
through Buenos Aires. A word from Rosas checked the fury of
the assassins: but the terror, with frequent murders and summary
executions, continued ten years longer. The people were paralysed by an epidemic of dread as by a physical infirmity. Sometimes the intercession of Rosas' daughter[2] Manuela, a good and
attractive woman, saved a life or mitigated a punishment. But in
turn she had to witness the buffoonery and the rough practical
jokes, played upon men of formal rank or character, which were
the Dictator's recreations from his incessant labour:—for this
athletic horseman, this captain of Indians and gauchos, devoted
himself night and day, with no fixed hours for food or sleep, to
the sedentary labour of administration. His buffooneries may
have been partly a matter of policy, to maintain his reputation
among the uncultured masses and among half-barbarous caudillos. The strangest of those was the 'friar Aldao', a Dominican
who had doffed his habit to serve in the War of Independence.
He dominated Mendoza for some years to his death in 1845. A
drunkard and the father of a numerous illegitimate brood, he decreed that all unitarios were mad and sent a number of them to
hospital for treatment. Ibarra, despot of Santiago for thirty years,

[1] C. A. Villanueva, *Historia de la República Argentina*, Paris, 1914.
[2] Rosas' wife died in 1838.

bequeathed at his death his authority to Rosas, as though the province were his own private estate.

In 1842 there was peace, of a kind, in Argentina. But there remained the war with Uruguay. The Uruguayan Government had declared war and had attempted to dismember the Argentine provinces, allying itself with the French aggressors and with the exiles, who in Rosas' eyes were traitors; and those exiles, sheltered in Montevideo, carried on a press campaign of hot denunciation against Rosas. Early in 1841, the Uruguayan Government requested Mandeville, British Minister in Buenos Aires, who was on intimate terms with Rosas, to offer mediation. He was authorised by his Government to do so. But the humiliating terms proffered by Rosas revealed his determination to reject all reasonable accommodation and to chastise his enemies. His recent successes, his ceaseless energy, the exercise of unlimited power and the thirst for vengeance had induced a kind of megalomania, leading him into ambitious schemes which finally prepared his fall, but for a time enhanced his reputation, owing to the ill-considered and ill-contrived joint intervention of France and Great Britain. These Powers made repeated attempts to coerce Rosas into making peace with Uruguay, and failed. The tortuous vacillations of those interventions were due to the changing phases of party politics in Paris and in London and of international relations in Europe. Those matters cannot here be traced: only a brief account of events in the River Plate can find place.

Rosas had never acknowledged Paraguayan independence, and the terms of the Convention with France in 1840 throw considerable doubt on his repeated promises to respect Uruguayan independence. His pursuit of the Uruguayan war, nominally in support of Oribe, indicates an ambition to add to the Argentine system the two provinces which had become independent republics, Paraguay and Uruguay.

In 1841 the Uruguayan Government offered to Great Britain commercial privileges in return for protection: the British Government declined the offer, but communicated it to the French Government and proposed a joint intervention to secure 'Uruguay from further violation . . . and lead . . . to permanent peace'. The joint intervention took place. In December 1842, when Oribe, victorious over Rivera in Entre Ríos, was ready to invade Uruguay, the French and British Ministers in Buenos Aires, who had been led by their Governments to expect naval reinforcements, which never came, issued a formal declaration that the belligerent parties must agree to an armistice. Rosas ignored the intimation. Two months later Oribe, in command of an Argentine army, approached Montevideo. Paz, who was in the city, hastily improvised defences, and Oribe, checked in his advance, began the nine years' siege of Montevideo, 'the modern Troy'. The place was saved from capture by the formation of a 'foreign legion' of French and Italian residents, and by the measures of the British commodore, who, in opposition to the wishes of Mandeville, hindered the Argentine squadron from acting and broke the Argentine blockade of the Uruguayan coast as far as British ships were concerned. But the siege continued. The Uruguayan Government possessed nothing but Montevideo and Maldonado. The intervention had failed.

In August 1843 the Uruguayan Government sent the Argentine Florencio Varela as envoy to England and France to request active intervention. He effected nothing at the time. But the interruption of trade, the closing of the Paraná river, as territorial Argentine waters, to all foreign ships, and a rigorous blockade of Montevideo and Maldonado declared by Rosas in January 1845 produced a second Anglo-French intervention. Rosas' friend Mandeville was recalled, much to his chagrin, together with his French colleague. Ouseley and Baron Deffaudis were sent out in their place, to insist on the cessation of hostilities. They found Rosas uncompromising and withdrew to Montevideo. The allied fleet prevented an assault on Montevideo, seized the Argentine squadron, part of which was added to a defensive flotilla under Garibaldi, captured Colonia and Martín García, and in September declared a blockade of Buenos Aires. In November a joint force, followed by many merchantmen, sailed up the river to open the way to Paraguay and to the Province of Corrientes, which was once more in revolt against Rosas. Batteries erected on the promontory of Obligado and a line of vessels linked by a chain across the river opposed their passage, which was only forced after considerable fighting and loss on both sides. This bold resistance to the naval forces of the two most powerful maritime nations in the world is recorded with just pride in Argentine annals and aroused strong national feeling in support of Rosas. The expedition was disappointing as to commercial results and was disapproved by the British Government.

In July 1846 Hood, formerly British consul in Montevideo and an intimate friend of Oribe, was sent out to negotiate, on behalf of the British and French Governments, a settlement, which was then to be sanctioned by Ouseley and Deffaudis; but they rejected the terms amicably arranged by Hood. In March 1847, Ouseley and Deffaudis were recalled. The joint fleet still blockaded Buenos Aires. Oribe still besieged Montevideo and claimed that the legiti-mate Government of Uruguay was with him, with the Ministers whom he appointed and the Congress which he summoned.

Two months later Lord Howden and Baron Walewski arrived as negotiators. Howden considered the Anglo-French attitude untenable in view of the vehement anti-foreign feeling, the strong position of Rosas and the confusion in Montevideo, which, owing to divisions and desertions, was now only defended by the foreign legion. He found a pretext for dissociating himself from his French colleague, and raised the British blockade in July 1847.

A third mission, that of Gore and Baron Gros, arriving early in 1848, only succeeded in exasperating Rosas by negotiating with Oribe and with Montevideo. But in June 1848, the French in turn raised the blockade of Buenos Aires, only maintaining the blockade of the Uruguayan ports occupied by Oribe.

Finally, through the persuasive and insinuating diplomacy of Henry Southern, sent as British Minister to Buenos Aires, a treaty was signed in November 1849 between Great Britain and the Argentine Confederation, which agreed to withdraw the Argentine troops from Uruguay as soon as the French Government should disarm the foreign legion, evacuate the territory of both republics and conclude a treaty of peace. Great Britain withdrew from Martín García, restored the captured Argentine ships, saluted the Argentine flag and acknowledged the full belligerent rights of the Argentine Republic.

In August 1850, a treaty of peace was concluded with the French, who undertook to disarm the foreign legion as a preliminary to the withdrawal of the Argentine troops from Uruguay: the other terms resemble those of the British treaty. The siege of Montevideo was not raised, although an armistice had been concluded in May 1849 between Oribe and the Montevidean Government.[1]

---

[1] The Anglo-French interventions have been fully narrated by Professor J. F. Cady in *Foreign Interventions in the Río de la Plata*, Philadelphia, 1929.

Throughout these long disputes with France and Great Britain, consular and diplomatic agents from the United States had attempted to strengthen Rosas' hands, but had received no support from the Washington Government, which, fully occupied with Texas and Mexico, kept aloof from affairs in the southern hemisphere. Rosas, unsupported, had successfully maintained a truly American policy of resistance to European interference and had baffled the repeated attempts of two great Powers to dictate to him: and meantime in communications with the Vatican he had vigorously upheld the claim of the Argentine Government to be the inheritor of the ecclesiastical patronage previously possessed by the Spanish kings. A thorough creole, he understood the sentiment of his people; under his leadership the Province of Buenos Aires, with its 140,000 inhabitants, had borne, almost unaided, the burden of long military operations: and in 1848, when the blockade was withdrawn, he appeared to be stronger than ever, dominant in Buenos Aires, predominant among the provincial governors, acclaimed in his capital as the triumphant champion of Argentine independence. He showed his Argentine spirit in another act. In response to an appeal from Ibarra, Governor of Santiago, Rosas, notwithstanding his own financial straits in 1847, sent 30,000 cattle to relieve 'the impoverished Federals' of that province, which was afflicted with a long drought.

In 1849, Rosas offered his resignation. The Legislature declined to accept it, and the principal English residents signed a petition requesting him to retain the government. To them his rule meant order and the pursuit of business undisturbed by revolutions.

But already events were moving towards his fall. The ablest

and strongest of his allies or lieutenants was Urquiza, Governor of Entre Ríos. Urquiza ruled that pastoral province, possessing no considerable towns, with patriarchal autocracy from his estancia near Concordia, in the midst of his vast estates and innumerable herds, surrounded by a guard of gauchos; he kept his executioners busy upon slight occasion and treated the whole province as his personal property. Master of a well-organised gaucho army, he had maintained Rosas' authority during repeated revolts in the Littoral: but in 1846 he made a separate treaty with the Governor of Corrientes, and discussed with him some scheme of federal organisation. Rosas disapproved the treaty as an infringement of the national executive authority committed to himself. The trouble apparently passed: and at the end of 1847 Urquiza by a decisive victory crushed the resistance of Corrientes. But Urquiza, a despot in his own country more autocratic than Rosas himself and the equal of Rosas in vigour and capacity, was not the man to forget the rebuff. The long-standing resentment felt in the provinces at the predominance of Buenos Aires could not be permanently silenced. Moreover the incessant and able propaganda of Rosas' adversaries in Montevideo and in Chile found an echo, in spite of strict censorship, in Buenos Aires itself, whose people were weary of the tyranny and shocked by its excesses, particularly by the tragic fate of Camila O'Gorman, daughter of a prominent Porteño family, who had left her home with a young priest. The guilty lovers were brought back from their distant refuge in Corrientes; and, although Camila was about to bear a child, both were shot by Rosas' command.

In May 1851, Urquiza revoked the powers delegated to Rosas and concluded an offensive and defensive alliance with Paraguay and Brazil. In Buenos Aires there were fervent demonstrations in support of Rosas, and all the provinces except Entre Ríos and Corrientes renewed the delegation of the executive power, with the significant addition in every case that a National Constituent Congress should be summoned. But in October Urquiza, having invaded Uruguay, forced Oribe to capitulate and raised the nine years' siege of Montevideo. In December, supported by a Brazilian fleet, he crossed the Paraná into Santa Fe, unresisted. For Rosas, in his fifty-ninth year, after the exhausting labours of seventeen years, was not the man he had been and met the danger with a strange lassitude. Santa Fe now joined the revolution. Urquiza led towards the capital an army of 24,000 men, the largest force yet assembled in South America, of whom 3000 were Brazilians and 2000 Urugayans. In February 1852 Rosas, deserted by half his troops, fled from the battlefield of Monte Caseros. At midnight he embarked with his daughter on a British war-ship and spent the remaining five and twenty years of his long life farming near Southampton. Once the richest landowner in the province, he left the country a poor man.

A fortnight after the battle, Urquiza, wearing the scarlet federal badge, rode at the head of his troops through the flower-strewn streets of Buenos Aires amid popular acclamations. He had already nominated as Provisional Governor of Buenos Aires, the estimable and generally respected Vicente López, author of the National Anthem and President of the High Court under Rosas. The Provisional Legislature unanimously sanctioned this nomination. Urquiza himself, installed in Rosas' palace of Palermo, assumed the external representation of the nation—an arrangement sanctioned soon afterwards by the Governors of the littoral provinces.

CHAPTER XV

THE EXILES

The darkest period of our political life; the most solid period of our literature.
RICARDO ROJAS

THE literary and intellectual life of Argentina was never more vigorous than during the period of Rosas. That life flourished not under the shadow of the Dictator, but in the hospitable shelter of neighbouring countries, Uruguay, Bolivia, Brazil, Chile. Among the exiles in Uruguay were Echeverría the romantic poet, political idealist and inspirer of youth, founder of the *Asociación de Mayo*, a non-party liberal society; Marmol, poet and novelist, whose historical tale *Amalia* is a vivid picture of the times; the poet Gutiérrez; the veteran classical playwright Juan Cruz Varela and his accomplished brother Florencio, editor of the anti-Rosista paper *El Comercio del Plata*. When Florencio was murdered in the streets of Montevideo in 1848, he was succeeded as editor by the capable and determined Valentín Alsina, a Porteño aristocrat and uncompromising unitario of the school of Rivadavia.

The versatile and cultured Bartolomé Mitre, soldier and scholar, took part in the defence of Montevideo before he emigrated to Bolivia—where he served in the Bolivian army—and thence to Chile, to join a notable group of refugees and to work as a journalist. Being implicated in the Chilian 'Revolution' of 1851, he fled to Peru, and thence returned home from his adventurous peregrination to command a battery at Caseros and to initiate his long public and literary career in Buenos Aires.

Mitre's companion and later antagonist in historical controversy, the vivacious historian López, also worked at Chilian journalism. The pugnacious, indefatigable, impulsive Sarmiento, by turns miner, shopman, journalist, pamphleteer and school master, a man whose strong frame, massive head and firm countenance expressed vigorous energy, threw himself into the task of organising Chilian education, and visited Europe and North America in order to study educational methods. Sarmiento's book *Facundo or Civilisation and Barbarism*, a romantic sketch rather than serious history, which appeared in Valparaiso in 1851, is a telling indictment of the Dictatorship.

The prolific and many-sided writer Alberdi, after four years in Montevideo, travelled to Europe and thence to Chile, where he practised as an advocate. Upon the fall of Rosas he published in Valparaiso his famous book *Bases and starting points for the Political Organisation of the Argentine Republic*, in which he urged that the creation of the nation demanded population, immigration, foreign capital, religious toleration, free navigation of rivers, telegraphs and railways, to link the cities and fill up the wide intervening wastes which impeded union. 'To people is to govern', he exclaimed: 'the enemy of union is not Rosas but distance.' 'To have the capital at twenty days' distance is almost like having it in Spain.' In view of the great distances and diversities between provinces, he argues that a system mainly federal is necessary, with reasonable provision for central authority. Taking as his model the Constitution of the United States, Alberdi added to the second edition, which appeared four months later, a draft or 'Project of Constitution' which was actually used as a basis in drawing up the Constitution of 1853. Thus Alberdi holds high rank among the makers of modern Argentina.

CHAPTER XVI

THE CONSTITUTION, 1852–62.
CEPEDA AND PAVÓN

THE decade following the fall of Rosas (1852–62) is the crucial period of Argentine history. After forty years of trial the country now achieved national organisation—not without much conflict and two pitched battles, before the proud localism of the wealthy port and the jealous regionalism of the scattered provinces could be reconciled. Not only the returning exiles, headed by the uncompromising Alsina, but also many of those who had submitted to Rosas, notably the distinguished jurisconsult, Vélez Sarsfield, who afterwards drew up the Civil Code of Argentina, were full of the unitario tradition and of enmity to any federal scheme which might seem to endanger the predominance of Buenos Aires. Urquiza's task was a difficult one, to allay the apprehensions of the Porteños and at the same time to construct a national system for a Confederation having no cohesion, no Constitution and no Government except the despotism of provincial caudillos.

Urquiza acted promptly. At the village of San Nicolás, near Buenos Aires, he summoned a gathering of provincial Governors. This group of dominant personages, who constituted the only authority existing in the United Provinces, issued the famous *Acuerdo de San Nicolás*. This agreement re-affirmed the Federal Pact of January 1831[1] and ordered that a Constituent Congress should meet, consisting of two deputies from each province without regard to population: meantime Urquiza, as Provisional

[1] See p. 144.

Director of the Confederation, was to conduct Foreign Affairs, regulate river navigation and command all the provincial troops which were maintained by any of the provinces. All such troops were now to be regarded as constituting a national army. Urquiza was also empowered to check hostilities between provinces and to suppress risings within any province.

This agreement was vehemently opposed, as infringing provincial rights, in the Legislature of Buenos Aires and in clamorous street gatherings. The Governor who had signed the obnoxious document resigned his post. Finally Urquiza closed by force the recalcitrant provincial Legislature of Buenos Aires and appointed himself to be Provisional Governor of that Province. The Porteños naturally regarded this closing of their Parliament as an autocratic and unjustifiable *coup d'état*. But Urquiza claimed that it was a constitutional 'intervention' to restore order in the province, an intervention authorised by the recently concluded Agreement of San Nicolás.

As Provisional Director of the Confederation, Urquiza was obliged to leave Buenos Aires in order to organise the Constituent Congress which was to meet in Santa Fe. Accordingly he appointed a Deputy Governor of Buenos Aires to fill his place during his absence. Upon the departure of Urquiza, his nominee at once fell from power; and by the bloodless revolution of September 11, 1852, which was dexterously guided by Valentín Alsina, the Province of Buenos Aires assumed independent sovereignty, seceded from the Confederation, and sent no deputies to the Constituent Congress. The United Provinces, apparently on the point of attaining real union under the guidance of Urquiza, were once more segregated by the secession of the principal member.

But this division into two parts was something quite different from the former dissolution of the provinces under self-appointed autocrats. For seven years after the revolution of September 11 there were two separate organised Governments, the Government of the Confederation and that of the independent Province of Buenos Aires, each of the two Governments having all the machinery of a separate State. Each had a personal Head of the State, a Cabinet or Council of Ministers, a Parliament, and arrangements for dealing with Foreign Affairs.

However, after the revolution of September, the seceding Province of Buenos Aires was not unanimous. An aggrieved soldier, Colonel Lagos, gathering gaucho followers in a war of the Pampa against the city, besieged Buenos Aires (December 1852–July 1853). Urquiza aided the besiegers and sent the national squadron to blockade Buenos Aires. The blockading admiral, a foreigner, sold his ships to the blockaded city, and soon afterwards the siege was raised, and active hostilities were suspended. But the Province of Buenos Aires rejected the Federal Constitution which was sworn in the same month by the other provinces, and drew up her own Constitution as a sovereign republic. An intermittent conflict, warfare of raids and counter-raids, continued between Buenos Aires and the Argentine Confederation.

In this conflict the former parts played by Buenos Aires and by the other provinces seemed to be strangely reversed. Buenos Aires now, at least to outward appearance, represented the spirit of regionalism and of local sentiment. The Porteños professed to be defending provincial rights against a Government which threatened local autonomy. But this was not the view held by Urquiza and those who were aiding him. In their opinion Buenos Aires was fighting for her own predominance.

During these ten years, 1852–61, Buenos Aires was not the centre of national life. The Constituent Congress, which was to give form to the nation, assembled in the little city of Santa Fe in November 1852. A committee, appointed to prepare a scheme, took as their basis Alberdi's famous 'Project' which had just appeared in Valparaiso. The draft so prepared was accepted, with some modifications, by the Congress: and the completed Constitution was promulgated in 1853. It was decided by the Congress that the city of Buenos Aires, the historic capital of the River Plate, should now become the federal capital and should be separated from the province of the same name and formed into a federal district to be controlled by the National Government. This decision was embodied not in the Constitution, but in a separate law. The Legislature of Buenos Aires rejected both the Constitution and this 'Law of Capitalisation'.

The other provincial Legislatures ratified the Constitution, which, with some later modifications, is that of Argentina to-day, resembling in the main that of the United States. There is one notable unitary or centralising provision, that which authorises the President to 'intervene' in any province in order to restore order, under certain conditions. This right has been freely exer-cised, not always with strict regard to the conditions, and tends to give much authority in the provinces to the Federal Executive, that is to say, to the President of the Republic.

In the same month, July 1853, in which this great constitu-tional work was completed, Urquiza took another step of vital economic importance. He concluded identical treaties with France, the United States and Great Britain, whereby the Argen-tine Confederation conceded the navigation of all interior Argentine waters 'to the merchant ships of all nations'. Thus, instead of merely declaring the navigation of the rivers to be open, he imposed upon his country an international obligation, in which three maritime Powers were concerned. In this way he effectively and peacefully achieved his object, and deprived the dissident province of control over the river for ever. Open navigation of the Rivers Paraná and Uruguay was essential to the prosperity of the littoral provinces which bordered those rivers and even to the solvency of the Federal Government. For while Buenos Aires levied customs duties in her frequented port, the Federal Government, having scanty revenues, needed custom houses and open harbours. The growth of Rosario, now the second city and port of the Argentine Republic, a place busy with the export of wheat from an extensive region intersected with railways, dates from this time. Rosario was the chief port and largest city of the Argentine Confederation during the secession of Buenos Aires.

The Constituent Congress, having nominated Urquiza as President of the Republic and having ordered the election of a regular Congress or Parliament of the Republic, Parliamentary elections were duly held in every province except Buenos Aires; and six months later the first Federal Congress, a bicameral Parliament, was opened by President Urquiza in the city of Paraná, which was chosen to be the capital of the Confederation as being conveniently near to Urquiza's estancia of San José, whence he ruled, like a patriarchal potentate, both his native Province of Entre Ríos and the Argentine Confederation, sending out *interventors* to suppress disorders which inevitably broke out in several provinces upon the inauguration of the new system.

Urquiza laboured, with remarkable success, to set up in his little capital the machinery of national administration. But it was found impossible to establish an efficient Federal Tribunal, since the necessary legal experience was only to be found among the lawyers of Buenos Aires. Meantime he did much to further the means of communication which were essential to national union. He granted contracts or subsidies for regular steamboat services on the Rivers Paraná and Uruguay; for carriage of mails to the Andine Provinces; for commercial traffic by mule-trains and caravans of bullock-carts; for tracing the shortest routes from city to city, since made roads were unknown, and, as Darwin says, in that open country direction and road were the same thing. In 1856, Urquiza granted to an optimistic financier, Buschental, a concession for constructing a railway from Rosario to Córdoba. Afterwards the American, William Wheelwright, the true pioneer of railway construction in South America, was associ-ated with Buschental: but the concession, though thrice renewed, fell through until it was granted afresh to Wheelwright, with ad-ditional privileges, by President Mitre in 1863. But to Urquiza belongs the credit of initiating the project. Urquiza also pro-vided funds for a work to which he gave hearty support, the pre-paration and publication of a geographical and statistical de-scription of the whole Republic and its resources by Martin de Moussy, a French physician and man of science.[1] One measure calls for particular remark, as indicating that the sentiment of nationality embraced the Province of Buenos Aires, notwith-standing the political separation: a sum of money was voted by the Congress at Paraná for the ransom of captives in the hands of the Indians in the Province of Buenos Aires.

A treaty of peace and commerce was concluded between

[1] The book was published in Paris, in three bulky volumes, in 1863.

Buenos Aires and the Confederation in January 1855; but it was not observed; and a year later the Federal Congress imposed heavy dues on foreign goods trans-shipped at Buenos Aires for the up-river ports. Buenos Aires retaliated with hostile tariffs; and in October 1859 open war broke out. Bartolomé Mitre led out the Porteño troops, but was defeated at Cepeda by Urquiza, who approached the capital. Negotiations followed and it was agreed that a Convention of the Province of Buenos Aires should examine the Constitution of 1853. This Convention met and proposed some modifications, which were accepted by the Congress at Paraná. The Constitution, thus amended, was declared to be the Constitution of the Confederation; and the Province of Buenos Aires was re-incorporated in the nation amid general rejoicings. But the agreement was short-lived. Sarmiento, now prominent among the politicians of Buenos Aires, was suspected of fomenting an anti-federal outbreak in his native Province of San Juan, where two federal interventors, sent thither by Urquiza as President of the Republic, were murdered in succession. Under a third interventor, a revolutionary leader was shot; and Mitre, now Governor of Buenos Aires, exceeded merely provincial authority by demanding a rigorous investigation into this third homicide. Thus relations were already strained, when the Federal Congress at Paraná refused to admit the deputies from the Province of Buenos Aires, declaring that they had not been legally elected. Buenos Aires thereupon withdrew her stipulated contribution to the Federal Treasury. In consequence war broke out once more between the Province of Buenos Aires and the Confederation. Urquiza, having completed his six years' term as President (1854–60), had been succeeded by Derqui, his Minister of the Interior. This meant divided counsels and diminished strength: but Urquiza, as Federal Commander-in-Chief, led southwards an army gathered from eleven provinces.

In this second conflict the verdict of Cepeda was reversed. In September 1861, Urquiza was defeated at Pavón by Mitre, or perhaps retired from the field, accepting a political defeat. Mitre occupied Rosario, the chief city of the Confederation. The Federal Congress dissolved; Derqui retired, and Mitre, assuming national authority, proceeded to beat down the scattered conflicts in the provinces.

It now fell to Mitre, in his dual character as Governor of Buenos Aires and Head of the Nation, to compose the differences between these rival authorities. A Federal Congress, duly elected, met in Buenos Aires in May 1862. Mitre wished to revive Rivadavia's plan, that is to say, to make Buenos Aires the national capital and federalise the whole province—in reality an anti-federal plan which would have placed under his own immediate authority, as Head of the Nation, the choicest part of the country and one-third of the population. But the Provincial Legislature of Buenos Aires declined to sanction its own extinction or even to choose some other place for its sessions and allow the capital alone to be made into a Federal District in which the National Congress might find a home. Passions rose high and violence was threatened. Finally a compromise was found in the 'Law of Residence', whereby the city of Buenos Aires, while remaining capital of the Province, was to admit the 'co-existence' of the Federal Government as a guest within its precincts, with no territorial authority but with control over customs and ports.

Meantime a Presidential election was held under the constitution of 1853, as amended in 1860; and in October 1862 Mitre entered upon his six years' term as first Constitutional President of the undivided Republic. Disorders stirred up in the west by the caudillo Peñalosa, nicknamed El Chacho, were put down by the national forces.

Mitre was fully aware of the discordant elements in the situation. Observing an opportune moderation and good sense, he did not enquire too nicely into the origin of provincial authorities, provided they gave no trouble; and Urquiza, destroyer of caudillaje, but last of the great caudillos, continued to rule Entre Ríos almost like an independent monarch. Although local tremors, sometimes disastrous enough, still agitated some of the provinces, uneasy as they were through jealousy of Buenos Aires, and not yet immune from the montonera, which in Rioja degenerated into murderous brigandage, yet the great convulsion had passed. Most of the provinces during this decade formed or reformed their Constitutions, generally modelled on that of the Federation. The modern era of Argentine history had opened, although twenty years were to elapse before stable equilibrium was secured by settlement of the 'capital question'.

Notwithstanding the two interruptions to peace, the decade following Caseros was a time of growing economic prosperity in the more settled provinces. Export of wool and hides enriched the estanciero. The Crimean War (1854-5), by closing the Russian tallow market to Western Europe, brought an access of prosperity to the River Plate, where carcasses of sheep were boiled down in quantities. The Provinces of Santa Fe, Entre Ríos and Corrientes initiated the settlement of European peasant cultivators in groups known as *colonias* with state aid. About the middle of the century two English estancieros in the Province of Buenos Aires surrounded their estates with wire fencing, thus preventing their cattle from mingling with neighbouring herds. This startling innovation was slowly spreading, to the great improvement of cattle-rearing. The first railway, six miles long, was opened in 1857—the beginning of a great movement. Both Urquiza and Mitre favoured these economic efforts and laboured also to improve education, which had suffered much under Rosas.

CHAPTER XVII

THE PARAGUAYAN WAR, 1865–70

MANY urgent matters pressed upon Mitre and his Cabinet: to transfer to Buenos Aires, to re-shape and complete, the work of national organisation, initiated by Urquiza at Paraná; to set up anew Federal Tribunals and the whole machinery of national administration; to deal with finance and the National Debt; and to cope with the recurrent and dangerous problem of Indian raids. But perhaps the most pressing necessity was that of providing posts, telegraphs and facilities of communication which might make union a reality. Buenos Aires was already linked by steam navigation with Rosario and the other river ports, but could only communicate with the inland cities across the stoneless Pampa by unmade roads or rather tracks, deep in dust during drought, turned into sloughs by rain and traversing swamps and river-fords. A journey by carriage or horse to Jujuy, 1100 miles distant, might take weeks, and the caravans of crawling bullock-carts, which conveyed merchandise, took months. Thus the final grant in 1863 of a concession to William Wheelwright and through him to a British Company for the construction of a railway from Rosario to Córdoba is a notable event. The concession included the grant of a strip of land six miles wide along the 280 miles of railway—a grant according well with Alberdi's dictum 'To people the land is to govern'.

In order to establish the new system and labour for internal order, Mitre was determined upon peace and upon neutrality in case of any external conflict. There were two dangers to the peace of the River Plate: first the military strength and fantastic imperial ambition of Francisco Solano López, third despot of Paraguay, and secondly a destructive civil war in Uruguay. The successors of Oribe and of the Rosistas, the Blanco party, held the govern-ment in Montevideo: the gaucho leader Flores, successor of Rivera, led the insurgent revolutionary party, the Colorados. The Blancos had aided Urquiza: Flores had fought beside Mitre at Pavón, for Uruguayans were hardly foreigners in Argentina.

Brazilian subjects who had settled in the north of Uruguay suffered murderous outrages during this civil war, which also infected the contiguous Brazilian Province of Rio Grande do Sul. The protests, the demands and finally the menaces of the Brazilian Government in consequence of these outrages drove the Uruguayan Government to seek the support of the Para-guayan Dictator: and here a brief retrospect is necessary.

During the sombre despotism of Francia (1811–40) the little sub-tropical state of Paraguay, largely inhabited by Indian peasants speaking the Guaraní language, had been sealed up from contact with the outer world and, at the cost of ignorance and stagnation, immune from the civil wars of the neighbouring provinces. She was also, thanks to the geographical position, immune from any royalist attempt at counter-revolution. She took no part in the War of Independence, but sat still and secure while Argentine arms achieved independence for the whole River Plate. The second despot, Carlos Antonio López (1840–62),[1] shrank from active hostilities, but his suspicious dislike of foreigners and his petulant meddling self-assertion did not con-

---

[1] López only became President in 1844; but his predominance may be dated from the death of Francia in 1840.

duce to amicable relations. The Paraguayan alliance with the dissident province of Corrientes in 1841, an alliance which was renewed in 1845, was an affront to the Argentine Confederation. In the latter year, López' son, Francisco Solano, aged eighteen, Commander-in-Chief of the Paraguayan army, led 5000 men into Corrientes and marched them home again. Rosas in reply closed the river, which was the only road into Paraguay. Indeed Rosas vainly claimed that Paraguay, independent in fact since the treaty of 1811 with the Junta of Buenos Aires,[1] was an Argentine province. But the Paraguayan Republic was recognised in 1844 by Brazil, by the Argentine Confederation under Urquiza in 1852, by Great Britain, France, Sardinia and the United States in 1853, and by Buenos Aires in 1859. In that year, after the battle of Cepeda, Urquiza and Mitre accepted Paraguayan mediation; but this incident has little historic significance.

López was no fighting man; but he carried on a protracted dispute with Brazil concerning the navigation of the River Paraguay. That river provided the only practicable route whereby the Brazilians could travel from the Atlantic coast to their interior province of Matto Grosso. López attempted to claim the course of the river as interior Paraguayan waters and to exclude foreign ships from the navigation above Asunción. Finally he was obliged to give way and to permit the passage of Brazilian ships northwards past his capital. Resenting this intrusion, as he regarded it, he constructed the fortress of Humaitá, to form a southern river-gate to his territory, and, in addition to this, he increased his army and accumulated munitions, largely under the influence of his son, who having been spoilt and flattered from childhood, returned home from a European mission filled with

[1] See p. 78.

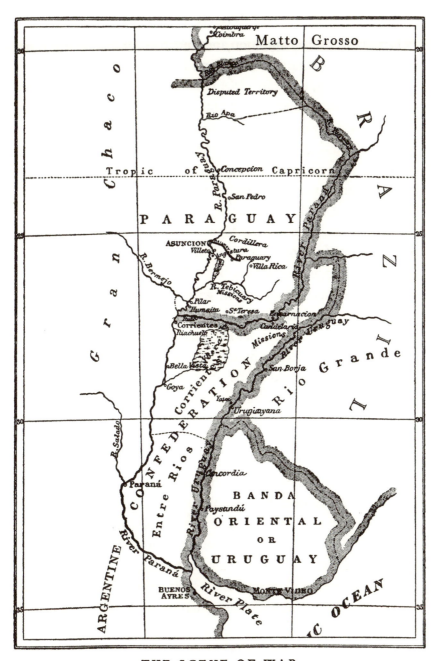

THE SCENE OF WAR

self-conceit, military ambition and imitative admiration of Louis Napoleon's Crimean adventure and Parisian Court.

López I at his death in 1862, the year in which Mitre became President, bequeathed to his son Francisco Solano the most formidable army in South America and also an autocracy which placed at his disposal the property, persons and lives of all his subjects. This corpulent voluptuary, López II, clad in a gorgeous uniform, surrounded by barefooted Indian soldiers, obsequious ministers and ready executioners, in a sham court presided over by his mistress, the notorious Madam Lynch, might seem to have stepped out of a comic opera, but that he was the protagonist of a horrifying tragedy. Paraguay had a frontier question with Brazil in the north, and also questions with Argentina about the Missions east of the Paraná, and about the Chaco, the little-known forest region west of the River Paraguay. The best policy for Paraguay would have been to make every effort to settle peaceably the questions with Argentina; for Argentine amity was essential to Paraguay both in her economic expansion and in her resistance to any Brazilian encroachment. Had López II been reasonable, he had a strong position. For Argentina, like Paraguay, had a frontier question with Brazil, and inherited the secular rivalry between Spain and Portugal in the New World. Indeed in 1863 President Mitre, soon after his own accession to the Argentine Presidency and that of López to the Paraguayan dictatorship, proposed to López that a joint commission should examine the boundary questions between Argentina and Paraguay, that the two countries should co-operate in their territorial disputes with Brazil, and should abstain from intervention in the Uruguayan civil war.

López declined this valuable overture, and, instead of avoiding a conflict, proceeded to provoke one. He found his opportunity in the appeal which had been made to him by the Uruguayan Government for aid against Brazilian aggression. López, as he said himself, meant 'to make his voice heard in the affairs of the River Plate'. He made that voice heard by addressing to Brazil in August 1864 a note which implied that any occupation of Uruguayan territory by Brazilian forces would be regarded as a *casus belli* by Paraguay. Such an occasion soon arose: a few days after the dispatch of López' menacing note to the Brazilian Government, a Brazilian admiral attempted to seize a Uruguayan ship in the River Uruguay, and Brazilian forces entered Uruguay to claim reparation for injuries suffered by Brazilians during the civil disorders in that country.

Two months later a Brazilian ship, in the course of her regular service, steamed up the Paraguay conveying the Governor of Matto Grosso to that province. López seized the ship and imprisoned the Governor. The Brazilian Minister at Asunción thereupon demanded his passports. War had begun. López sent a force which invaded Matto Grosso, took and sacked several places, carried off much military stores and cattle, and occupied a great part of that Brazilian province.

In February 1865, López requested permission of Mitre to send Paraguayan troops through Corrientes to invade the Brazilian Province of Rio Grande. Mitre, determined upon neutrality, rightly refused permission. Two months later five Paraguayan war-ships, without declaration of war, appeared off Corrientes, seized two Argentine gunboats and landed a force which occupied the city. This insolent aggression roused the Argentine nation in support of their soldier-President Mitre. Urquiza, who, hating the Brazilians, had been in communication with López,

KA   12 visited Mitre, offered cordial support and helped to conclude the secret tripartite treaty with Brazil and also, strange to say, with Uruguay, the country on whose behalf López had ostensibly gone to war, but which now joined his enemies. For a Uruguay-an Revolution, aided by Brazil, had upset López' friends the Blanco Government, and thrown the Uruguayan Republic into alliance with Brazil. The treaty provided that the allies should fight until the overthrow of López and should never negotiate separately. The independence and territorial integrity of Paraguay were guaranteed. Paraguay was to pay all the expenses of the war and to be completely disarmed. Argentina and Brazil were to acquire the boundaries which they claimed.

The odds were not so unequal as might appear; for the whole resources and population of Paraguay were organised for war: every man, on pain of torture and death, was blindly obedient to the inflexible will of the Dictator; and the difficult entrance to the country was fortified, and was held by a strong army. López had 60,000 troops—some say 90,000—under arms. The Argen-tine regular army numbered 6000 men, scattered through the provinces.[1]

The war-fleet was supplied and commanded by Brazilians. Mitre commanded the land forces, since the first task of the allies was to expel the invaders, who held great part of the Province of Corrientes, carrying off cattle, horses and other property. In seven months, before December 1865, they had been thrust back into Paraguay. López had also thrown away 12,000 men in an unsupported and isolated expedition against Rio Grande, and had lost several ships in an attack on the Brazilian fleet anchored

[1] These preliminary matters are treated in full detail by Dr P. H. Box in *The Origins of the Paraguayan War*, published by the University of Illinois, 1927.

near Corrientes. Argentine territory having been cleared of the enemy, there was a movement in Argentina towards peace: but the Brazilian Government insisted upon the terms of the treaty both on this occasion and later when protests were raised in Argentina against an apparently needless invasion of Paraguay. There was reason for these protests. While the forces of the nation were engaged in foreign war, Indian raiders on the southern frontier were killing, robbing and destroying within 120 miles of the city of Rosario.

In April 1866, a year after the attack on Corrientes, the allies crossed the Paraná, to enter a region of jungle and swamp, where difficulties of transport and of supply caused long delays and where the defenders had every advantage. López was wasteful of the valour of his troops in repeated onslaughts, which, without winning victory, checked the allied advance. In September 1866 the allies took the fortified position of Curuzú, but upon attacking a stronger place, Carapaity, they met with a reverse, followed by months of inaction, while cholera swept both armies. In July 1867 an important advance towards Humaitá was made, but four months later the Paraguayans stormed and pillaged the allied camp, a success which, however, was not followed up.

Twice President Mitre was obliged to relinquish the command for a time in order to suppress revolts, first in Mendoza and then in Córdoba, which were partly movements of protest against the war: and in January 1868 the death of the Argentine VicePresident compelled him to return home, resigning the command into Brazilian hands. A month later the Brazilian fleet steamed past the batteries of Humaitá, losing one ship which was taken by thirty Paraguayan canoes. Thereupon López sent a fleet of canoes covered with foliage so as to resemble floating islands, with orders to attack the Brazilian fleet: his men actually boarded one ship, but were swept away by fire, and cannon-shot sank the canoes.

In August 1868 Humaitá surrendered, and López retreated to Angostura. In December he suffered crushing defeat and Angostura fell. Yet the fighting dragged on for fifteen months longer, López being beaten back from post to post, driving before him the starving and diminishing remnant of his people, forcing children of ten and twelve years into the army, torturing and executing many men whom he accused of treason or conspiracy. In his last flight he was caught in a quagmire and fell, refusing to surrender (March 1870). His death ended the war.

The Missions east of the Paraná remained in Argentine hands; and after long negotiation the River Pilcomayo was fixed as the boundary in the Chaco by the arbitration of President Hayes in 1878. The five years' war threw a heavy financial burden upon Argentina; for although a war indemnity was required from Paraguay by the treaty of peace, it was impossible to exact this indemnity from a republic where all the wealth of the country had perished, together with two-thirds at least of the population and all the able-bodied men.

Although recruiting had been difficult in the northern Argentine provinces, where the names Asunción, López, Humaitá, signified something remote and of little concern, and although provincial discontent had flamed out in two serious revolts, yet the challenge to the nation and the national effort to meet that challenge did much to weld together the newly organised Confederation.

CHAPTER XVIII

UNSTABLE EQUILIBRIUM, 1862–80

MITRE and his two successors had a difficult task—to hold the balance of an incomplete Constitution, admittedly a temporary compromise, yet prolonged for eighteen years. The city of Buenos Aires contained two Governments, that of the nation and that of the most populous and powerful province: within the same city there sat two Cabinets and two Parliaments. The Government of the Province of Buenos Aires, with its long tradition of national activity and its recent independence, inevitably concerned itself with national politics and became a watchful rival of the National Government which was a guest within its territory, possessing in theory no more authority in Buenos Aires than in Mendoza or Salta. Mitre, although opposed to the provincial 'autonomists', was himself a thorough Porteño: his Cabinet consisted mainly of Porteños, prominent provincial politicians. Thus provincial politics and parties overflowed into the National Cabinet and Parliament. Both Governments, that of the nation and that of the province, particularly the latter, incurred the jealousy of the other provinces, and a League of Provincial Governors came into being, headed by Córdoba, which aimed at controlling elections, combating Porteño influence and maintaining the all-powerful oligarchies of great land-owning families, who—more peaceful but not less autocratic successors of armed caudillaje—dominated most of the provinces, monopolised all official posts and nominated the members of the provincial Legislative Chambers who, according to constitutional theory, were supposed to be elected by the votes of the people.

The election of Presidents has always mattered far more than that of Parliaments, and the personality of a President matters more than his supposed political creed or party. An epidemic of cholera, which swept through Buenos Aires in 1868 and left the city half deserted, weakened the activities of the Porteños and thus facilitated the election of the provincial Sarmiento, a native of San Juan and the self-taught son of a muleteer. His election might seem to be a victory for the provinces and even in some sort for democracy. But the self-willed imperious Sarmiento was not much of a democrat, except in his zeal for popular education: and he had long been identified with the Porteño politicians. As Governor of San Juan (1862–4) and then as Argentine Minister in Peru and in Washington he had cordially supported President Mitre. But, knowing that Mitre had not favoured his candidature, he excluded Mitre and his friends from the Cabinet, thereby exposing himself to vehement parliamentary opposition, which he met with characteristic stubborn vehemence, aided by a convenient deafness. He was no party man and sought support from no party. He fought for his own hand. Sarmiento continued the work of Mitre, promoting immigration, public works, foundation of schools and teachers' training colleges, construction of railways. To aid in the work which he valued most, the furtherance of popular education, the President chose a man of proved zeal and capacity to be Minister of Education: this was a young Tucumano, Nicolás Avellaneda. In 1870, Sarmiento concluded the treaty of peace with Paraguay, and also presided at the opening of the railway from Rosario to Córdoba—two legacies from the previous administration. The completion of the Córdoba-Rosario railway, the first of the great lines which bring distant cities close together, is a notable historical event, which may be almost said to mark the opening of a fresh phase in the life of the Republic.

The same year, 1870, brought a tragedy. Urquiza, the old chieftain of Entre Ríos, was murdered in his estancia house, in his daughter's presence, by the partisans of López Jordán, a rival caudillo, who was elected Governor of Entre Ríos by the provincial Legislature. Sarmiento, rejecting the easy solution of recognising the new Entrerriano Government, decreed 'intervention', and sent into Entre Ríos an army which had been destined for the Indian frontier—which in consequence was left exposed to destructive raids, as always in time of civil war. López Jordán was expelled, but invaded Entre Ríos twice during the following six years.

Another tragic event brought to public notice a want which had not yet been supplied in the system of public administration. In 1871, Buenos Aires was swept by an epidemic of yellow fever, in which a great part of the population perished, while numbers fled from the city. At that time no really representative municipal system existed which might cope with the visitation. After the first days of terror or agitation, volunteer societies took in hand the work of organising methods of giving aid to the stricken and dying and of maintaining order, and physicians were found who voluntarily devoted themselves to combating the plague.

In 1873 a law was passed by the Legislature of Buenos Aires for the establishment of representative municipalities in the province: but it was long before municipal elections became truly representative in character.

During the latter part of Sarmiento's Presidency the provinces, as distinct from Buenos Aires, gained ground in the Parliament and in the Cabinet. Rival candidates for the election of 1874 were the polished and cultured 'Nationalist' ex-President Mitre, victor at Pavón, leader in Paraguay, and the 'autonomist' Adolfo Alsina, son of Valentín Alsina, who had been the champion of the autonomy and even of the independence of the Province of Buenos Aires in the Revolution of September 11, 1852. Now the son was the champion of that autonomy; but, following the change of times, he differed from his father in the motives of that action. Valentín Alsina, an aristocratic Porteño of the old school, had held that the cultured capital and the province which con- tained it had a kind of natural claim to primacy. But it was as a convinced liberal that the son, Adolfo Alsina, defended pro- vincial autonomy and local institutions, seeing in them an anti- dote to any autocratic tendencies in the National Government. An unkempt beard and a certain carelessness in exterior appear- ance marked out Adolfo Alsina as a man of the people, a liberal leader, the predecessor of Leandro Alem and of Hipólito Irigoyen.

Adolfo Alsina, a man of high character, able and energetic, had won a notable reputation as Governor of Buenos Aires (1866-8) and as Vice-President of the Republic under Sar- miento;[1] and he was a likely candidate for the Presidency in 1874. Then a third candidate came forward, the Tucumano, Nicolás Avellaneda. His candidature made such way in the provinces that Alsina retired in his favour, aided his election and served in his Cabinet. A caricature of the time represented Avellaneda as a child led by a stalwart mentor, Alsina. Nothing could be more

[1] At the Presidential Election of 1868, it had fallen to Valentín Alsina, as Presi- dent of the Senate, to read out the names of the newly elected President and Vice- President of the Republic. He read out the name of Sarmiento, elected as President, and then emotion checked his utterance. The person elected as Vice-President was his son, Adolfo Alsina.

unjust. The new President, a man of diminutive stature and feeble frame, with odd peculiarities of speech, dress and gait, was a notable orator in a country where oratory was even a greater power than in the contemporary British arena of Gladstone, Disraeli and Bright: he was also a man of vigorous determination, who surrounded himself with able ministers—four of them future or past Presidents. He began and ended his Presidency by suppressing armed revolts, settled the Paraguayan frontier question, disposed of López Jordán in Entre Ríos, conducted with sagacity delicate frontier negotiations with Chile, dealt with a serious financial crisis due to speculation in land—rapidly increasing and even multiplying in value with railway construction—and solved the two crucial problems which agitated the life of the nation, the Indian question and the 'capital' question.

In 1874 Mitre, the unsuccessful candidate, alleging fraud and undue influence in the recent election, headed an armed revolt—a proceeding difficult to justify, since everyone was aware that a genuine uncontrolled election was a thing unknown and that many of Mitre's own supporters in Santiago and San Juan had voted to order. The revolt collapsed. A more serious outbreak near Mendoza was suppressed with little bloodshed through an ingenious strategical movement by Colonel Julián Roca,[1] a young Tucumano, commander of the Indian frontier in Córdoba, who as a youth had fought at Cepeda in Urquiza's army against Buenos Aires and had later distinguished himself in the Paraguayan War. Mitre was made prisoner and exiled, but was soon pardoned by Avellaneda; and two years later, when fresh trouble

[1] The story goes that Roca, after disposing his troops so that the enemy could not escape, made his way to the quarters of the insurgent commander, General Arredondo, who greeted him with the words, 'You are my prisoner'. 'Pardon me, General,' replied Roca, '*you* are the prisoner.' And so it proved.

threatened, Mitre exerted his influence for peace. Avellaneda himself brought Mitre and Alsina together and effected a reconciliation, sealed by an embrace.

In 1877, Adolfo Alsina, Minister of War, who had been attempting to solve the Indian problem by extending and strengthening the traditional method of defensive lines and garrisons, died, aged forty-eight, at the moment of a destructive Indian incursion. He was actually visiting the frontier line of blockhouses and organising defence against the savages when his fatal illness overtook him and he returned home to die. His successor at the Ministry of War, Julián Roca, now promoted General, who knew the Indian frontier as a practical soldier, induced Avellaneda to settle the question once for all by thrusting the Indians beyond the Río Negro, and so winning for white settlement the extensive region lying to the north of that river. Roca himself took command, and in 1878-9, by a sweeping military operation, accomplished the main part of the work. The habitable limits of the Republic were pushed southwards to the Río Negro, and the sight of captive Indian chiefs in Buenos Aires convinced the incredulous capital that the age-long terror was indeed laid. Nearly 500 Christians, captives among the Indians, were restored to their homes. Much of the cleared land was sold with careless rapidity, and townsmen in wild speculation were buying and selling unknown tracts of desert and imaginary pastures.

This 'Conquest of the Desert', by establishing security, greatly increased the value of extensive lands already occupied, and prepared the way for the spread of sheep-farming through Patagonia and Tierra del Fuego during the following generation, a movement which was largely the work of British settlers.

The growing tension between Buenos Aires and the National

Government was increased by a dispute concerning the newly acquired lands, which had been conquered by national forces and were now claimed by the province. Eventually the province of Buenos Aires received a large slice; the rest became a Federal Territory entitled *Gobernación de La Pampa Central.*

General Roca, as candidate for the Presidency in 1880, was favoured by the President, and by twelve provinces; for Corrientes supported Buenos Aires. The Porteño candidate was Carlos Tejedor, Governor of Buenos Aires, who had won high repute by a blameless public life and by his work as author or compiler of the Penal Code of the Republic. He was now involved in very different scenes. Preparation within the city for the Presidential Election took the form of rifle practice, drilling and gun-running. A boat belonging to the National Navy, on attempting to impede these proceedings, was seized by the gun-runners of Buenos Aires. Volunteer civic battalions, marching daily through the streets, rifle on shoulder, to the parade-ground, raised provocative cries—*Viva Buenos Aires*; *Viva Tejedor*—as they passed under the windows of the President of the Republic. Tejedor even called out the National Guard of the Province of Buenos Aires. On the other hand President Avellaneda brought troops of the regular army near the city.

Two Governments which 'co-existed' in the capital were arming against each other. The heads of those two Governments, namely the President of the Nation and the Governor of the Province of Buenos Aires, met in consultation in hopes of finding some mode of accommodation, but without result. Elections for the renewal of half the Chamber of Deputies were held amid intense excitement. Avellaneda was no fighting man; but he decided that the National Government could no longer reside as a guest in an armed and hostile city. Accompanied by the Ministers, the Senate and half of an incompleted Chamber of Deputies, he withdrew to Belgrano, four miles outside the city; and from this temporary suburban capital he decreed the 'intervention' of the Province of Buenos Aires.

This meant a fight. Party lines were obliterated and most of the Porteños, including the 'nationalists', fought for their city. The conflict was between the Federal Government and Buenos Aires, and at the same time between Buenos Aires and twelve provinces, headed by Córdoba. The National troops approached the city, which was defended by trenches. In three combats they lost 1000 killed and wounded, but inflicted twice as many casualties on the defenders. The civic battalions finally gave way before the trained troops. The National fleet blockaded the port. In order to stop the carnage, the Diplomatic Corps offered mediation. Tejedor resigned the Governorship; and Mitre, now averse from civil strife, accepted command in the city with a view to a settlement.

That settlement was a drastic one. The National Congress and the Legislature of Buenos Aires were both dissolved. A newly elected National Congress decreed that the city of Buenos Aires, separated from the province, should be the federal capital. A newly elected Legislature of the province assembled to accept that decree. Acceptance was inevitable; yet to the last one vigorous voice protested, that of Leandro Alem, who had succeeded the 'autonomist' Adolfo Alsina as tribune of the people, to become ten years later founder and apostle of the radical party and to bequeath his spirit to his nephew, Hipólito Irigoyen. Harsh, vehement, nervous, melancholy, Alem was a striking figure, with his tall lean frame, his patriarchal beard and his passionate utter-

ance. When he was a child aged nine years, his father, a hench-
man of Rosas, had been executed after Caseros for his share in the
tyranny. The young Leandro had a struggle with poverty in
achieving a modest education; and he spent his life in a restless
struggle as champion of democracy and enemy of all autocratic
and arbitrary rule: at the same time he represented the more popular side of the Rosista tradition, the creole sentiment, the feeling
of the illiterate and inarticulate masses.

His protest availed nothing. The Legislature of Buenos Aires
accepted the decree of the National Congress. Thus the city of
Buenos Aires, with its immediate neighbourhood, became a
federal district, not connected with any province but belonging
to the nation, that is to say, to the Confederation of Fourteen
Provinces.

Two years later the city of La Plata was founded, as capital of
the Province of Buenos Aires. The work of national organisation,
begun in 1853 and modified in 1860, was thus completed in form,
to find general acceptance and reach a working arrangement
during the succeeding generation. Avellaneda handed over the
Government to his collaborator and successor, Roca, and died
five years later, aged forty-eight.

Since the year 1880 marks an epoch in the political life of
Argentina and may be also regarded approximately as the beginning of a new economic era, that of the export of grain, it is
well here to emphasise two points which have already been indicated by the way. In the first place, in Argentina, as in Canada,
real national union was only rendered possible by the construction of railways. Accordingly the political movements which
are traced in these chapters were accompanied and aided by the

continual addition of fresh links in the iron chains which brought the provinces together. In the second place the great annual event which most affects the life of the Republic has little to do with Cabinets or Congresses. That annual event is the harvest. The disasters which are most felt are a drought or a visitation of locusts or rain in harvest time: and the happiest of events is an abundant and well saved harvest. These matters can hardly be narrated in detail, but they must be continually borne in mind by anyone who wishes to understand the story of the growth of Argentina.

Nor does this consideration in any way lessen the need of tracing the political growth of the country. It was only when gaucho cavalry ceased to gallop over the land, when statesmen had succeeded in establishing some kind of order, when the Indian problem had been settled, that the farmer was able to go about his business in peace and pursue the work upon which the progress of the country depends. Political order and the cessation of internal strife were obviously an indispensable preliminary to steady economic progress. And in turn that economic progress has had a steadying influence on the further development of the political life of the nation. The two movements, political and economic, are complementary to each other and cannot be separated.

CHAPTER XIX

THE CREOLE

Our incomparable Gaucho. RICARDO ROJAS

BEFORE the crucial year 1880, a railway had reached Tucumán, penetrating the sugar region, drawing the whole north-west nearer to the Littoral and providing a material link to the Federation. A branch line, owned by the State, had been pushed from Villa María, a half-way station on the Córdoba-Rosario Railway, through the Province of Córdoba to Villa Mercedes in San Luis, bringing all the west nearer. Several lines now radiated from the capital through the Province of Buenos Aires, to grow later into the great systems of to-day.

Wherever the railway went, the face of the land changed; settlement grew; tillage encroached upon pasture; the pastoral industry itself was transformed by the more general use of wire fencing and by improved methods of stock-raising, which dispensed with the lasso. In 1880 the country was still mainly pastoral, exporting wool and hides and growing not enough grain for home consumption: but already the change had begun which transformed rural life during the following twenty years. The gaucho survived in remoter parts well into the twentieth century and may be still found in Salta: but when Roca completed his campaigns, the range of gaucho life was shrinking. The 'son of the soil' (*hijo del país*), however much he might affect to despise the *gringo*, could not rival the industry of thrifty Italian and Basque immigrants.

Thus, while the antagonism between the capital and the provinces was finding political and economic solution, these

new conditions were lessening the gulf between urban life and
the primitive life of the Pampa—a gulf partly corresponding to
that which divided Buenos Aires from the other provinces but
by no means identical with it: for nowhere was the contrast between urban and rural life more marked than in the Province of
Buenos Aires, although the very existence of the city depended on
rural industry. It is true that the great estancieros, living in
patriarchal fashion and exercising a generous hospitality in a
rambling homestead, the centre of a vast pastoral estate, 'patrons'
of troops of peons—every peon the owner of half-a-dozen horses—
were often political as well as territorial magnates, forming an
aristocratic oligarchy which might guide or check a 'revolution',
manage elections and influence public finance or policy. They
usually spent part of the year in a town house, and some of their
names recur throughout the four generations of independent
Argentina.

But in general the division between rural and city life was more
marked than in other parts of the world. The latter, which is a
continuation of European life, is rather the subject of formal
histories: but the former is the product of the soil, of the vast level
plain: it is thoroughly native, thoroughly creole (*criollo*). The
contrast is illustrated by two notable documents. The first of these
is a petition presented in 1853 by a number of farmers in the
Province of Buenos Aires to the provincial Legislature, asking
that some kind of representative local government might be
granted to them. 'We poor shepherds and farmers', they say,
'when we decided to abandon the tyrant Rosas, had the simplicity to believe that Caseros was to be the end of our servitude.
But ... we are daily torn from our homes or hunted on the
plains like ostriches; and if we fall into the hands of some local

magistrate (*teniente alcalde*) he makes us serve, at his arbitrary will, as militia-man or servant or soldier. . . . We are forced to work without pay in the service of Government. . . . We solicit some kind of parochial or municipal institutions. We beg that decisive measures be taken to put a stop to cattle-stealing.'[1]

The second document is the famous narrative poem in the gaucho dialect by José Hernández, published in 1872, *El Gaucho Martín Fierro,* a fictitious story which vividly represents reality. In six years, 30,000 copies were sold, and the popularity of this thoroughly creole and characteristic work has never waned. It is the story of a countryman, pressed into an infantry frontier battalion, who deserts under ill-treatment, becomes a wanderer and outlaw, fights and vanquishes the squad of police sent to take him, lives for a time among the Indians, has the 'misfortune' to kill in fair fight (*en buena ley*) two bullies at the gatherings round the *pulpería* on feast-days, and distinguishes himself as a *payador,* a minstrel improvising *coplas* to the guitar, sometimes in competition with a rival singer—a competition apt to end in the clash of knives.

In 1872 there also appeared *Santos Vega,* by Ascasubi, a miscellany in verse, wherein a legendary payador, sitting over the camp-fire, is made to describe various scenes of Pampa life, the patriarchal estancia with its troops of peons, the Indian invasion, the *rodeo* when the cattle were thrown with the lasso and branded, the pursuit of the malefactor by the *rastreador,* the tracker who unerringly follows the criminal's trail.

Any account of Argentina must dwell upon this characteristic pastoral life, which was the basis of early prosperity and strength.

---

[1] This petition is printed in *Descripción amena de la República Argentina* by C. A. Zeballos, Buenos Aires, 1883–4.

The modern Argentine, at least in his more imaginative moments, loves to recall, as typifying the spirit of his country, the figure of the horseman, clad in poncho and chiripá, who herded the cattle on the great estates, or drove them hundreds of miles to market, or ranged over the public lands, or worked, sometimes on very insecure tenure, a plot of ground about his mud hut: a being independent of all the world with the lasso coiled behind his saddle, the boleadora slung round his waist, and—stuck through the belt across his back—the long knife which served him to kill an ox, to carve his meat, or on occasion, with poncho rolled round his left arm as guard, to fight some provocative rival at the Sunday gathering about the pulpería: a virile figure, regardless of tempest, frost or scorching sun, accustomed to face the disasters of drought, locusts, or prairie fire, enduring pain, wounds, and fatigue with Indian insensibility, although his bearded countenance—for the Indian was beardless—denoted an ancestry mainly European.

The gaucho life was well described by the Spanish traveller, Azara, in 1808. The English reader may gather some impression of the vast level spaces of the Pampa and of the riders upon it from the writings of Sir Francis Head, Darwin, W. H. Hudson and Cunninghame Graham, whose sketch, entitled *San José*, descriptive of Urquiza and his surroundings, throws a vivid sidelight on Argentine history. The gaucho gradually yielded to the change of times. But the creole tradition which he represented survived and had a marked influence on the political developments of the past half-century. His manners were those of a Spanish hidalgo. His food was beef and maté or sometimes for long periods beef and water alone. On a campaign against the Indians, the gaucho cavalry lived, like their savage enemy, on the flesh of mares driven before them as they rode. 'What other troops in the world', exclaims Darwin, 'are so independent? With the sun for their guide, mare's flesh for food, their saddle-cloths for beds, as long as there is a little water, these men would penetrate to the end of the world.'

CHAPTER XX

VICISSITUDES OF PROGRESS, 1880–1910

THE astute, somewhat frigid and scrutinising glance of Roca, the new President, was tempered by easy sociable manners and a pleasant smile. A man of vigorous resolution, shrewd, tactful and conciliatory, having personal knowledge of all parts of the Republic, he did much to tranquillise the uneasy capital, which was now directly subject to the Presidential authority of a provincial, and he strengthened the Confederation by quietly upholding that authority without arrogance or undue interference in the provinces, winning the support of the provincial Governors for the Federal Executive. He encouraged immigration and railway construction—mainly the work of British capital and Italian labour—and he strove to forward, by means of public works, the economic movement which was improving the pastoral industry, was spreading tillage and was turning the country into an exporter of grain. These public works involved heavy expenditure and increase of the National Debt both at this time and in the later course of economic expansion. The President was much aided in this work, particularly in raising a loan in London, by a minister of marked ability and energy, Pellegrini, who as Minister of War under Avellaneda, had organised, in co-operation with Roca, the military movement of 1880. Pellegrini, founder of the Argentine Jockey Club, son of a French father and an English mother, had been educated at Harrow. He was a thorough Argentine, yet a representative of the cosmopolitan element which was beginning to modify the character of the community.

Provinces and Territories
of
ARGENTINA

Territories are underlined

Roca's Presidency (1880–6) was a time of unprecedented peace and also of unprecedented growth in the national wealth. The railways doubled their length; and the railway, wherever it went, multiplied the value of land, sometimes tenfold or more. The 'Conquest of the Desert' was rounded off by subjecting the few remaining savages; and wider tracts of the southern plains were thus opened out first to pasture and later to tillage. British capital poured into the country. Improved steam navigation brought Europe nearer. Year by year export of grain increased, and the first essays were made towards export of meat, to become later a great industry. Every year numbers of Italian peasants, nick-named *golondrinas* ('swallows') from their annual migration, travelled 6000 miles from Italy to reap the Argentine harvest, returning with a bag full of gold coins to spend the Italian summer at home.

These migratory harvesters had no strong inducement to re-main in the country, owing to the difficulty of acquiring land, a difficulty which runs through the whole of Argentine agricul-tural history and has no special connexion with Roca's term of office. The great landowners clung tenaciously to their *latifundia*, and usually would only let land for a term of years. Fiscal lands had been sold or granted in large slices measured by the square league, without regard to the small cultivator. On the great estates, although married men occupied outlying shepherds' huts (*puestos*), most of the peons were lodged in sheds about the es-tanciero's homestead, living a kind of barrack life in celibacy: an arrangement not conducive to the peopling of the country or to wholesome domestic life. It is true that many Italians and Basques saved money and bought land. But these were sporadic unaided efforts. The settlement of some Italian or Swiss 'colony' was an isolated episode. A country, whose immense arable lands called for cultivators, has had no system such as the Canadian method of inviting immigrants to acquire moderate-sized farms on easy terms. Partly in consequence of this, there has been a considerable annual emigration which to some extent cancels the figures of immigration.

Notwithstanding this omission, for which some partial reme-dies have lately been introduced, the prosperity of the 'eighties rested on a sound foundation, that of the soil itself. But this rapidly rising tide of prosperity, and especially the sudden access of wealth bestowed upon landowners by railway construction, produced one of those outbreaks of speculation which seem to punctuate the growth of all young nations. Towards the end of his term, Roca, after a first indignant refusal, was finally per-suaded to declare the notes issued by certain banks to be incon-vertible into gold—a disastrous precedent for the succeeding administration.

The wave of speculation reached its height under Roca's successor, Juárez Celman (1886–90), a connexion of his own by marriage, Governor of Córdoba and the most prominent member of the Córdoba League, which procured his election. Men who in normal times were accustomed to act with sobriety and prudence were dazzled now by the phantasm of rapid opu-lence, and plunged into the rush of buying and selling. But the Executive, the Congress and all the public departments were the worst offenders.

The growing prosperity and economic expansion of the country were checked and shaken by wasteful extravagance, by favouritism or carelessness in the granting of public lands, of monopolies and of concessions—which to the holders were objects of traffic and sale—by reckless inflation of the falling paper currency, by scandal in public finance, and excessive public borrowing, for which British financiers and British investors or speculators were partly to blame. Immense sums were spent on public works, particularly in the improvement and embellish- ment of the capital, things excellent in themselves, but pushed on with needless and lavish haste. Provincial Governments caught the infection of wasteful borrowing and spending. The President, who, according to some, was too facile in acquiescence and care- less in supervision rather than over-precipitate in action, uttered some warnings of impending disaster; but he effected no econo- mies; and a Head of the State who demands, as Celman did, 'unconditional' adherence, must be held responsible.

This financial orgy, together with interference in the provinces and a strange effort at absolutism, provoked widespread in- dignation and meetings of protest in the latter part of 1889. Early in 1890 ten thousand people met in the tennis court of Buenos Aires. A 'Civic Union' took form which issued a manifesto denouncing not only the faults of the Government in power but also more fundamental abuses—'suppression of the suffrage'— 'personal and arbitrary authority both in the provinces and in the National Government'—'an ominous and intrusive oligarchy'.

Moderate men desired the resignation of the President, a change of persons and of policy. But a radical party, headed by the vehement democrat Alem, sprang into being which aimed at destroying the whole system which had made Celman's Govern- ment possible. They held that constitutional methods were denied to them, that force was therefore justifiable, and that armed revolt should sweep away the whole Presidential and Parliamentary system and should set up a Provisional Government until a

genuine uncontrolled election—a thing so far unknown—could
be held. A Revolutionary Committee was formed to organise
revolt. They won over the fleet and part of the garrison: they
seized the artillery arsenal and seemed to be on the point of cap-
turing Government House and mastering the city. But the
officer commanding the insurgents was dilatory or half-hearted,
or out of touch with the Revolutionary Committee: ammunition
ran short or was said to be short; and after two days of sanguinary
fighting, while cannon and rifle fire swept the streets and squares
of the city and 1100 men fell killed or wounded, Alem and his
companions capitulated and accepted an amnesty.

The movement of 1890 was summed up in the phrase: 'The
Revolution was beaten, but the Government was killed'.[1] Celman
resigned, and the Vice-President Pellegrini took his place, to deal
with a sensational financial crisis—the failure of the London
House of Baring, deeply concerned in Argentine finance, the
closing of one bank after another in the capital, the menace of
national bankruptcy. People who had been spending wildly
were now unable to get money or credit. The collapse of spending
power meant diminution of imports and of customs duties, which
were the main source of public revenue.

Pellegrini, although he made fresh issues of paper money, perhaps unavoidably, in order to meet the public obligations, strove
vigorously to retrieve the disaster. He stopped the construction of
public works, imposed economy upon the administration, saved
salaries by dismissing superfluous officials, and resumed into

[1] The revolution of 1890 illustrates the fact that the Constitution of the Republic,
although it contains cumbrous and unpractical machinery for the impeachment of
a President, provides no really practicable means of peacefully putting an end to an
unsatisfactory administration. A summary of the Constitution is given in the
Appendix.

State possession much public land which had been filched away or alienated without authority. An emissary[1] was dispatched to London to make terms with British financiers. The amortisation of the public debt was suspended. The foundation of the Banco de la Nación, which proved to be a sound institution, did much to restore credit.

The country took nearly ten years to recover from the crash of 1889–91, as the falling-off in immigration shows. But as the Argentine historian Vera y González remarks, Pellegrini had two potent allies in his work of recovery, the railway and the plough. And the distinguished economist Bunge declares that the thirty years from 1878 to 1908 were the great period of economic growth and does not dwell upon this temporary depression, since the business of agriculture was steadily proceeding throughout the time of trouble.

In 1891 Mitre, now seventy years of age, the historian and first citizen of the Republic, received an enthusiastic ovation upon landing from Europe in Buenos Aires, to be a candidate for the Presidency as a 'National solution'. He met Roca, and their embrace was an attempted embrace of Provincials and Porteños. But it soon appeared that the Córdoba League and the Provincials would not back up their leader in supporting the historic leader of the Porteños. Talk of admitting a radical Vice-President fell through, and the radicals were irreconcilable. Mitre's candidature proved to be no 'National solution' and was withdrawn. Mitre, Roca and Pellegrini, the three heads of parties, came to an understanding and joined in a kind of loose triumvirate, known as the *Acuerdo*. By way of finding a solution to all rivalries, the

[1] The emissary was Victorino de la Plaza, who twenty-three years later, as President of the Republic, was himself to deal with another financial crisis.

three leaders agreed to promote the candidature of an estimable citizen, removed from all party, a judge of the Federal Court, Luis Saenz Peña.[1]

Meantime the Civic Union had split into two parts, the extremists breaking away to form the 'Radical Civic Union', which aimed at overthrowing by force, if no other method would serve, the system which they denounced as 'el Régimen' (the Régime), 'Officialism', 'the Electoral Machine'. In their view the *Acuerdo* was part of this immoral system and hardly less odious than Celman's Government. In every province a branch of the Radical Civic Union carried on a vehement agitation for electoral freedom, particularly in those provinces where the Governors defied the Constitution by maintaining troops to support their authority.

The other and more conservative section of the Civic Union called itself the 'National Civic Union' and generally adhered to Mitre, but without any clear guiding principle. There were frequent secessions, fractions, re-groupings, among its members. The current use of the terms Mitristas, Roquistas, Pellegrinistas, indicates that parties in official circles were more concerned with persons than with policies or principles, but were loosely held together by a common interest in resisting any violent change.

Before the Presidential Election of 1892 Pellegrini, to prevent any disturbance, proclaimed a state of siege and arrested Alem and his friends, who were kept in confinement for some weeks and then exiled. Luis Saenz Peña became President.

Being no party man, the new President had no following; he even failed to retain the undivided support of the *Acuerdo* through

[1] Don Luis was father of a more famous son, Roque Saenz Peña, who was also a candidate for the Presidency in 1892 but withdrew in favour of his father. Eighteen years later, Don Roque entered upon a historic Presidency.

omitting to back up the Roquistas in certain provincial disturbances. Thus he soon found the difficulties of the time too much
for him, complicated as they were by a grave frontier dispute with
Chile and by renewed revolutionary attempts of the Radical Civic
Union in several provinces, notably in Santa Fe. Here Alem,
now returned from exile, commanded 6000 armed men in 1893
and was greeted in Rosario as President of the Republic, but
yielded upon the approach of Roca at the head of national forces.
After a rapid succession of colourless or coalition Ministries,
Saenz Peña summoned a prominent radical, Aristóbulo del
Valle, to form a Ministry. Del Valle, a handsome, cultured and
attractive person and an effective orator, who used to harangue
the people from the balcony of his house, was regarded as the
brain of the radical party. His acceptance of office under Saenz
Peña showed that he had more balance, more faculty of adjust-
ment than the nervous agitator Alem, who, with his adherents,
maintained uncompromising opposition to all officialism. But
for del Valle's premature death in 1895, the radical party might
perhaps have pursued a less violent and more effective course by
offering to the country some constructive plan of legislation, instead of treating electoral reform as an end in itself.

Del Valle, as Minister under Saenz Peña, gave support, by
means of 'intervention', to a movement which overthrew in the
Province of Buenos Aires an autocratic Governor who had
maintained his authority by armed force. But del Valle's Ministry was short-lived; and the President, after several ministerial
experiments, finding himself unsupported by Parliament, resigned his uneasy post in 1895.

In the following year, Leandro Alem committed suicide. His
nephew, Hipólito Irigoyen, became leader of the Radical Party.

In his agitation for electoral reform, Irigoyen was joined by several members of aristocratic Argentine families, among them Marcelo Alvear, bearer of a historic name, and Honorio Pueyrredón, grand-nephew of the Supreme Director of 1816–19.

Upon the resignation of Saenz Peña, the Vice-President, José Evaristo Uriburu (1895–8), took his place. Uriburu belonged to a notable family of Salta and was son-in-law of General Arenales, the Salteño warrior of Independence. A sagacious and able man, having the support and the counsel of Roca and Mitre, Uriburu guided the country through a period of economic recovery, signalised by the resumption of the full debt service early in 1897. A frontier dispute with Brazil concerning Misiones was settled by the arbitration of President Cleveland, whose decision, favourable to Brazilian claims, was loyally accepted by Argentina. Much more serious was the acrimonious and long-drawn-out frontier dispute with Chile. Public sentiment, always excitable upon such questions in Latin America, was fiery; and much money, which could ill be spared, was spent on military preparations. Common sense prevailed and the tension relaxed, only to be renewed three years later; but Uriburu, partly influenced by the advice of Roca, finally agreed to the Chilian demand that the question should be submitted to arbitration.

Yet the possibility of war with Chile—for relations were still strained—was one of the motives which induced Mitre and Pellegrini to throw their decisive influence in favour of the candidature of Roca, an experienced soldier, yet a cautious and sagacious man of peace, who had exercised a moderating influence under Uriburu and was the leader best qualified to deal with the activities of the Radical Civic Union and to smooth away the linger-

ing jealousies between the capital and the provinces. The candidature of *El viejo zorro*, 'the old fox', as Roca was nicknamed,
was a godsend to the caricaturists of *Caras y Caretas* ('Faces and
Masks'), the Argentine *Punch*.

The institution of two new Ministries, of Agriculture and of
Public Works, on the eve of Roca's election, points to the most
prominent path of recent Argentine history, the spread of tillage
and scientific stock-farming and the accompanying provision of
transport, harbour facilities and the varied needs of modern life.
Roca strove to aid these movements, and particularly to provide
transport on the remote steppes of Patagonia, which, partly owing
to his own 'Conquest of the Desert' in 1878–9, were now becoming a vast sheep-farm.

Roca stabilised the currency by fixing the paper dollar at
44 centavos of the gold dollar. He maintained internal peace,
cultivated amicable relations with Brazil by an official visit to
Rio de Janeiro, and was escorted by an Argentine squadron to
meet the Chilian President, Errazuriz, in the Chilian town of
Punta Arenas on the shore of Magellan Strait. The two Presidents agreed to moderate the Argentino-Chilian race of arma-
ments: and although bellicose sentiments and mutual suspicion
recurred, Roca finally had the satisfaction of seeing the frontier
dispute finally settled.

And here a retrospect is necessary. Before the middle of the
nineteenth century, that is to say before the southward spread of
population, the frontier question was not prominent. The foundation of a Chilian settlement in 1847 on the shore of Magellan
Strait roused some apprehension: but until the close of the Paraguayan War in 1870 Argentina was not in a position to provoke

trouble abroad. Then came ten years of growing acrimony in dispute. In 1881 Roca concluded a treaty which granted to Chile both shores of Magellan Strait, the control of which passage is, in Chilian opinion, essential to the national security of Chile. This same treaty declared that northwards from latitude 52° the boundary should 'pass along the highest crests of the Cordillera which divide the waters'. As joint exploration of these vast mountains proceeded, this agreement proved to be mere confusion, since the watershed does not coincide with the highest peaks. Chile claimed the watershed, which in Patagonia lies far east of the peaks. Argentina claimed the highest peaks, some of which stand upon Pacific islands.

After ten years of exploration and argument, the two Republics were on the verge of war in 1895. Again, in 1898, war was imminent owing to a third question, concerning the boundary in the plateau of Atacama. But the moderation of the two Presidents, Roca and Errazuriz, led to a settlement. The Atacama question was settled by a tribunal sitting in Buenos Aires, consisting of a Chilian, an Argentine, and Buchanan, United States Minister in Buenos Aires. Buchanan solved the difficulty promptly by dividing the disputed line into sections, proposing that a vote should be taken on each section and then ensuring a majority upon each section by his own vote. The main question, concerning the long boundary line along the Cordillera of the Andes, was submitted to the arbitration of the sovereign of Great Britain; but as the arbitration tribunal in London was concluding its labours in 1901, both republics resumed warlike preparations. British diplomacy strove to calm animosity. The award was given in 1902 and was peaceably accepted.

Thus the preliminary settlement of 1881, as well as the accept-

ance of arbitration in 1898 and the successful issue of that arbitration in 1902, were all in great part due, upon the Argentine
side, to Roca, who deserved much credit for the quiet dignity and
tact with which he treated the question throughout.

The year 1902 also brought a rich harvest and pastoral prosperity. The country had recovered from the decade of depression
which followed the crisis of 1889–91.

As the date of the Presidential Election (1904) approached,
most of the leading politicians and office-holders met in convention. The Pellegrinistas were absent, for their chief, who hitherto
had been Roca's financial adviser, was now in opposition. Pellegrini, a man of stalwart physical strength, on twenty successive
evenings pronounced as many harangues attacking Roca's administration and advocating electoral reform. A scheme, which
Pellegrini had shaped for the unification of the public debt, had
been adopted by Roca and then, in face of determined popular
opposition, had been dropped, to the bitter mortification of its
author. Pellegrini was perhaps also aggrieved at not being
adopted as official candidate for the Presidency. But it is fair to
suppose that, with his cosmopolitan outlook and his long experience of public life, he thought the time had come for admitting
a genuine republican and representative system. Electoral reform
was in the air: it had been often on the lips of public men: and
when it came eight years later, it was by no means solely the result
of radical agitation.

In 1904 the Convention unanimously adopted the candidature of Quintana, a prominent lawyer and public man, who, as
a matter of course, became President. A few months after his
accession to office, a radical Junta, headed by Hipólito Irigoyen,

attempted to seize the arsenal and master the city by force (February 1905). The Government was forewarned and the attempt was crushed at once. Simultaneous revolts in four of the provinces also collapsed. A recent historian of the radical party,[1] himself a fervent radical, who claims that the majority of the people were opposed to the 'Régimen' and radicals at heart, frankly declares that public opinion condemned these outbreaks, preferring to await the course which President Quintana might take.

It would be truer to say that no one now wanted any fighting. The country was in the full tide of prosperity and had recovered both its financial credit and its general reputation abroad. Capital and immigration were flowing in, and, whatever political discontent might exist, people wanted to go quietly about their business and not to allow property to be destroyed, business to be interrupted and immigrants to be frightened away by the sight of Argentine citizens killing one another. As long as Government was peaceful, fairly efficient and not oppressive, people did not care to enquire too nicely into its origin. It must be remembered that the constitutional education of the Argentine people was, naturally and reasonably, a gradual process. Indirect election and parliamentary methods were exotic importations. To the native tradition, whether creole or Spanish, personal government was more customary and more intelligible.

Accordingly the administration of Quintana was simply a quiet continuation of the 'Régimen' in times which were prosperous and tranquil, except for labour troubles, which, as in other parts of the world, also recurred during the succeeding period—a common symptom of economic change. The fact that

[1] *Bosquejo de una Historia y Doctrina de la Unión Cívica Radical*, by A. M. Etkin. Buenos Aires, 1928.

a rise in the cost of living was not accompanied by fully propor-tionate increase of wages caused natural discontent, which was fanned and exploited by organisers of strikes, mostly new-comers from Europe.

In 1906 Bartolomé Mitre died at the age of eighty-five, having preserved to the last his faculties and active interests. His funeral was a national demonstration. He had long been a familiar and much-respected figure as he walked the streets in his soft wide-awake and loose frock-coat, the living embodiment of sixty years of history. His historico-legendary fame, as Groussac calls it, has been preserved by the newspaper, *La Nación*, which he founded in 1870, partly in order to provide funds—for he was not a rich man—for the book-collecting which was his one luxury. His house in the centre of the city, with the library contained in it, is now the property of the nation. Surrounded by lofty blocks of building, its low façade and open patio provide a valuable monu-ment of the mode of living in earlier and less crowded times.

The same year brought the death of Pellegrini and of President Quintana. The Vice-President Alcorta, a clear-sighted and re-solute man, who thus became President until 1910, prepared the way for reform. He had some interviews with the radical leader, Irigoyen: and he sought, with much astuteness, to undermine the power of the land-owning oligarchies in the provinces by means of 'interventions', following local revolts. The humorous term, 'revolutions from above', was popularly applied to some of these revolts, suggesting that they had the support or connivance of the Federal Executive, in order to provide ground for 'interventions'. When a recalcitrant Parliament refused to vote the budget,

Alcorta sent the city firemen, who used to act as emergency armed police, to close the Chamber; and he himself decreed, of his own authority, the continuance of the previous budget. Later he had amicable dealings with the re-assembled and now tractable Deputies. The incident, which provoked popular satirical comment rather than indignation, illustrates the unreality of these non-representative Parliaments and the disposition of the people to ignore theory and acquiesce in any established executive which works with efficiency and common sense.

It may be remarked here by way of a general observation, not merely applicable to this instance, that the Constitution of the Argentine Confederation grants very large powers to the President. When that office is held by men endowed with strength of will and discretion in its exercise—qualities which have been possessed in marked degree by most of the Presidents—then still larger powers are tacitly conceded to the Head of the State by general acquiescence and by custom—a custom which is not confined to Argentina but is characteristic of the Spanish-speaking world in general. It must also be remembered that the Federal District, which comprises the capital and contains one-fifth part of the population of the country, is under the direct control of the National Executive, except in purely municipal matters; and that the territories (*gobernaciones*) which cover three-sevenths of the total area of the Republic are administered by the same central authority.[1]

---

[1] In the more remote and sparsely populated parts of these territories, for example in the southern parts of Patagonia, the executive authority is, by the force of circumstances, in great part delegated. In those regions the local magistrates exercise a good deal of initiative and sometimes, by virtue of a custom which it is not easy to dispute, they assume a certain degree of discretionary power in the administration of the law.

Furthermore, in the present century the telegraph and the railway have facilitated a tendency towards centralisation which
strengthens the hands of the Federal Executive, that is to say of
the President and of the Ministers who are nominated and controlled by him—for the President is his own Prime Minister. In
former days an interventor, after long journeyings from the capital
to the scene of his activities, might find that his authority was repudiated and that conditions had completely changed since he
received his instructions in the federal capital. To-day the President's emissary can reach the capitals of the farthest provinces
within forty-eight hours; and his authority is less likely to be
challenged when it is known that means of enforcing it are within
reach, and that messages and orders from Government House can
be flashed in a few minutes to the most distant parts of the country.

Alberdi in his famous *Bases*, which are mentioned in Chapter xv, pointed out that a federal system was unavoidable owing
to the slowness of communication over the wide spaces which
separated the centres of population. But at the same time he dwelt
upon certain characteristics of the people and of the country which
were favourable to unitary methods. Those unitary elements have
gained ground since the distance between the provinces has been
shortened by steam. The tendency towards centralisation has also
become stronger through the attraction which in every part of the
country is exercised by the federal capital, owing to its favoured
position, its contact with the outside world, its commercial movement, its intellectual activities and the varied occupations or recreations which are to be found in a great city.

Englishmen have long been aware that in their own country
there is a marked distinction between the theory and the practice
of the Constitution, and that the actual working of the Consti-

tution undergoes constant modifications and adaptations. In Argentina, notwithstanding the apparent rigidity of a written Constitution, the gap between theory and practice is at least as wide. The practice of the Constitution varies somewhat with the character of the President. But on the whole it may be said that in the Argentine Confederation a working compromise has been evolved between the two theories of government which divided the nation a century ago. If a federal and an unitario of the 'twenties of the last century were to come to life to-day, each might find something to criticise at first, but each might find, upon further observation, equal ground for a reasonable satisfaction.

CHAPTER XXI

MOVEMENTS OF DEMOCRACY

THE year 1910 is a notable landmark in Argentine history. In that year the Centenary of the Republic was celebrated with an enthusiasm which was fully justified by the tranquillity, prosperity and growing wealth of the country. A pleasant compliment was paid to Argentina in the fact that the fourth Pan-American Congress, held under the auspices of Washington, met in Buenos Aires in that year. But the great event of the year was the Presidential Election. The seat of First Magistrate in Argentina has been occupied by a series of romantic figures: Mitre and Sarmiento, who had passed years of adventurous exile and had fought their way through the stormy period which followed Caseros; Avellaneda, puny in frame but vigorous in speech and action; Roca, the soldier of Cepeda and of Paraguay, the cunning strategist of 1874, who came to the Presidential chair fresh from the conquest of the desert; Pellegrini, sportsman, Harrovian, aristocrat, who yet carried to an extreme the easy and outwardly democratic informality of giving audience in an atmosphere of general conversation and cigarette-smoking and ended his career an advocate of democracy.

But not the least romantic figure is that of Roque Saenz Peña. Born in 1851, he was President of the Chamber of Deputies at the age of five-and-twenty. Three years later, upon the outbreak of war between Chile and Peru, he offered his sword to Peru. When the Peruvian commander Bolognesi and then the other officers fell one after another on the Promontory of Arica, exposed to the fire of the Chilian war-ships, this Argentine volunteer found himself in command of the surviving remnant of Peruvian soldiers, was wounded and made prisoner by the Chilians, and returned to his native country with the rank of a Peruvian general: a Quixotic figure, but perhaps Argentina needed a Quixote as ruler.

For twenty years the Radical Civic Union had been urging electoral reform and, on occasion, fighting for it. Many politicians had talked of it; Alcorta, as President, had pointed towards it. And now Roque Saenz Peña, although owing his appointment to the Régimen, had the courage and self-abnegation to introduce a measure which meant the abdication of the powerful caste to which he himself belonged.

The President had an interview with Irigoyen, whose insistent demand was 'Open the voting urns'. In a public letter to the Governor of Córdoba, Saenz Peña argued that, in view of the large foreign element in the population,[1] the privilege of citizenship should be made a reality and its value made manifest. In 1911 he recommended to the Congress the law of the secret, compulsory and universal vote: the ballot was to secure freedom of voting, and in addition every citizen was to perform the public duty of voting under penalty of a fine. This law, which was to effect a peaceful revolution, or rather to add a chapter to the Revolution initiated on May 25, 1810, was debated in the Congress with much eloquence; but its acceptance was a foregone conclusion.

In the Parliamentary Election which was held in 1912 for the renewal of half the Chamber of Deputies, a number of radical

[1] The census of 1914 showed 2,350,935 foreigners out of a total population of 7,836,615. By Argentine law everyone born in Argentina, whatever his parentage, is of Argentine nationality.

candidates were returned, having been elected by the ballot under the new law. But the author of that law was obliged by ill-health to hand over his functions to the Vice-President, Victorino de la Plaza, and did not live to see the notable result of his action in the Presidential Election of 1916, which by the eclipse of the Régimen and the election of a radical President was to open a new phase in Argentine history. However, two years before that election a more epoch-making event, the beginning of the Great War, was to agitate the current of that history.

In August 1914 the outbreak of the World War fell like a bomb in the midst of a financial depression in Argentina, which was due partly to two successive bad harvests, partly to trouble in the Balkans, which affected the European money market, partly to a certain profuse optimism in Argentine public finance. The shock, which reverberated through the world and struck upon all the shores of all the oceans, fell upon Argentina with peculiar intensity owing to her intimate economic connexion with the belligerent Powers and with all Western Europe. The outbreak of war meant a sudden interruption in the normal course of things, a bewildering uncertainty as to the future, the menace of a financial crash. The President and his Finance Minister took prompt action. A seven days' Bank Holiday was proclaimed. For some time public works, railway construction and private building were at a standstill.

But it soon appeared that the alarm was exaggerated. Imports from Europe, it is true, fell to almost nothing. But before long the needs of the allied armies sent up the prices of grain and chilled meat to record heights. Notwithstanding difficulties in obtaining labour, agriculture and pasture earned surprising profits. Thus the loss of revenue due to diminution of customs was made good

by new imposts, an internal tax and a tax on exports. Exchange
rose, and although English goods were scarce, English sovereigns
were plentiful in Buenos Aires. Capital was forthcoming from
the United States, which henceforth acquired a growing
economic connexion with Argentina.

With some notable exceptions, public opinion whole-heartedly
favoured the allies. German experts, it is true, had rendered acceptable service to the country in the training of troops and also
in educational and scientific work. But the long-standing and
affectionate admiration of France was deep-rooted. Successive
generations of Argentine historians and politicians had expressed
their debt to French political theory and example. To the Argentines, essentially a Latin people, Paris is the capital of civilisation.
French influence in literature, in art and in the graces of life was
prevalent. Great Britain, again, had done much to build up the
economic structure of the national life; and the British community,
though not numerous, was respected, and was prominent in sport,
in country life and in business. Six thousand young men, sons of
British families, departed for war service in Europe. The Italians in
Argentina numbered nearly a million, and Argentine citizens of
Italian parentage were yet more numerous. Thus the entry of Italy
into the war on the side of the allies swelled the tide of anti-German
sentiment, already deeply stirred by the violation of Belgian neutrality and by the sufferings of the occupied regions of France.

But the political and diplomatic aspect of the war only became
prominent after the election of 1916. That election was surrounded
with much excitement: the citizens of Argentina for the first time
freely chose in every province electors who should nominate the
President. The radical leader, Dr Irigoyen, obtained a narrow

majority and was carried shoulder-high to Government House by an enthusiastic crowd.

The new President was something of a mystery. He lived modestly and alone. Since 1890 he had abstained from parlia-mentary life, like his fellow-radicals; but by ceaseless propaganda and sometimes by open fighting had opposed the Régimen. He gave away in charity the salary which he had received as a teacher in State schools until he was dismissed from Government em-ployment after his armed revolt in 1905. He was no orator, and the language of his written pronouncements was involved and obscure. Born and educated in the city, he knew also the life of the Pampa, had sat with cowboys and peons round the camp-fire, and was everywhere welcome as the friend of the working-man. Moreover, his unbending determination and the stubborn stalwart vigour inherited from his Basque ancestry inspired confidence.

Irigoyen was the most powerful of Argentine rulers since Rosas. He was appointed by the authority of the people for six years, bound by no mandate, not committed by any definite promises. From the beginning he showed himself determined to exercise his own will, permitted little initiative to his ministers and expected unquestioning loyalty from his followers. He out-did most of his predecessors in the number of interventions in the provinces. Everywhere, in the Provincial Governments and in the municipalities, all possible influence was brought to bear in order to place power in the hands of members of the Radical Party, supporters of the President.

On assuming the Presidential scarf, Irigoyen was faced with two difficult tasks: to justify by his domestic policy, at a time of much unrest and labour agitation, the rise to power of new men and a new party, untried in public life, and at the same time to deal with the diplomatic problems arising from the war.

These war problems became urgent five months after his accession to office, when in February 1917 Germany notified to Argentina, as to all neutral countries, the establishment round the coasts of Great Britain, France and Italy of a zone from which neutral ships were barred on pain of destruction by German submarines. The Argentine Government replied to the German note by simply expressing adherence to the rules of international law. In the following April an Argentine vessel was sunk by a German submarine, and in July two others were sunk. In two cases the Argentine Government demanded apology and reparation. The German Government, rather than risk a rupture with the most powerful of Spanish-American countries and the most important for German trade, gave way in each case. It was in the eyes of the world a singular triumph for Argentina, a complete vindication of her national dignity and the recognition by Germany of the high international status of the Republic.[1]

In May 1917 and again in July, Count Luxburg, German Minister in Buenos Aires, wrote to Berlin advising that Argentine ships should be spared if possible or else 'sunk without a trace'. These despatches, intercepted by the United States Government, were published in September. The German Minister at once received his passports from Irigoyen's Government with an order to leave the country. But this dismissal was notified to the

[1] Professor P. A. Martin, in his book *Latin America and the War* (Baltimore, 1925), suggests a possible inference that, while Germany promised to spare Argentine ships, President Irigoyen entered into a secret understanding with Germany that Argentine ships should not enter the zone barred by Germany.

German Government in a conciliatory note by Honorio Pueyrredón, Irigoyen's Minister for Foreign Affairs.

Both Houses of the Argentine Federal Congress now passed resolutions demanding the rupture of diplomatic relations with Germany; and excited mass meetings, assembling in the open spaces of the capital, indignantly clamoured for rupture. But in Argentina, as elsewhere in Latin-America, it is the President who rules. After the declaration of war against Germany by the United States, Brazil also declared war; and Uruguay broke off relations with Germany and opened her ports to the war-ships of the Allied Powers. But the Argentine Government, satisfied with its diplomatic victory and with the concession of all its claims, maintained amicable relations with Germany throughout. Herein the President was perhaps partly actuated by a certain stubborn caution which preferred a negative or waiting attitude, a disposition which also showed itself in his slowness to act during the labour troubles and in his later refusal, during his second Presidency, to sign the Kellogg Pact. But his main motive was his firm belief that neutrality was best for his country. 'The foreign policy of Irigoyen was neither pro-German nor pro-Ally, but simply pro-Argentine'.[1]

For Irigoyen was no pro-German. He maintained relations of increasing cordiality with the Allied Powers. A United States fleet which visited Buenos Aires in 1917 and the British Diplomatic Mission of Sir Maurice de Bunsen in the following year received not only an enthusiastic popular ovation but also a warm official welcome. But the most striking disproof of pro-Germanism was the agreement whereby at the end of 1917 the Argentine Government granted to the Governments of Great Britain and

[1] *Latin America and the War*, by P. A. Martin.

France a loan or credit of forty million pounds sterling for the purchase of Argentine cereals and other produce. Within a year 4,358,340 tons were purchased of wheat, flour, maize, oats and linseed; and large purchases, chiefly by Great Britain, continued during the following two years. Indeed Argentina gave the best help possible to the cause of the allies by the supply of grain and meat to provide the needs of their armies in the field.

Argentina joined the League of Nations in 1919: but when the Assembly of the League met in the following year, the Argentine delegate, Pueyrredón, under peremptory orders from Irigoyen, demanded the admission of Germany to the League, and also equal status in the constitution and counsels of the League for all nations which might become members of it. When these demands were rejected, Pueyrredón withdrew from the Assembly. Irigoyen held that the League was vitiated by the circumstances of its origin and that, if any nation were excluded, it was no true League of Nations. The withdrawal was an assertion, on a singularly public stage, of the vigorously independent attitude of Argentina. This action was probably inspired in part by a desire to avoid all external engagements, to accept no guidance from abroad and to have no foreign policy except the interests of Argentina.

Herein Irigoyen was following the Argentine tradition of all parties, of Rivadavia as well as of Rosas and Urquiza, a tradition partly due to the long trouble with Brazil concerning the Banda Oriental in the early years of the Republic. Bolívar's great schemes of union found no favour with Rivadavia and his generation. The anti-foreign attitude of Rosas was notorious. Urquiza, as President of the Argentine Confederation, declined in 1854 an invitation to join an alliance of Chile, Peru and Ecuador, which was an essay towards a definite system of *Americanismo*. The invasion of Paraguay in 1866, reluctantly undertaken in continuation of an unavoidable war, was an exception. A Treaty of Alliance, known as 'the A.B.C. Treaty', which was negotiated in 1915 between Argentina, Brazil and Chile, was ratified by the other two Republics but not by Argentina, perhaps partly because the projected alliance roused some apprehensions in other South American republics. With regard to all such matters the Argentine asks, 'What good will it do to my country?' His attitude is essentially national: the central point of his political outlook is the enthusiastic cult of *La Patria*.

On the other hand, Irigoyen fully shared with his countrymen the sentiment of *Americanismo*, the feeling that the Ibero-American peoples form a group or constellation of nations distinct from all others, and united among themselves by similarity, if not complete identity, of origin, language, customs, interests and outlook upon life. This sentiment, which is summed up in the current phrase *Nuestra América* (Our America), was signally manifested by Irigoyen when he offered to Uruguay unstinted Argentine aid in case of any invasion of Uruguay by the Germans of southern Brazil: and he showed a similar sentiment in two curious and abortive attempts to assemble in Buenos Aires a Conference of neutral Latin-American Republics, and, when this failed, a Conference of all the Latin-American Republics. On the other hand it may be questioned whether Irigoyen fully interpreted the expediencies of the time in his suspicious aloofness from that Pan-American movement which met a response in Uruguay and Brazil. Possibly, with his characteristic caution in all external matters, the President did not entirely dissociate Pan-

Americanism from the Monroe Doctrine and its later re-state-
ments or from United States activities in the Caribbean region.
The Monroe Doctrine, which gave no help to Argentina in the
question of the Falkland Islands or in the Anglo-French interventions of the 'forties, has been generally viewed by Argentines
either as a remote and indifferent matter or as a series of unilateral
statements of policy by a Foreign Power.

In domestic affairs, Irigoyen introduced no radical constitutional changes and no comprehensive system of state socialism
such as that which had been adopted in Uruguay. But he justified his reputation as friend of the working-man by proposing
and, so far as he obtained parliamentary sanction, carrying out
legislation concerning wages, hours of labour, contributions by
employers towards pensions, sanitation, protection of children,
arbitration in industrial disputes and reform of the Penal Code
concerning strikes.

In 1917, after Germany had announced unrestricted submarine
warfare, there was a general railway strike, accompanied by
much disorder and destruction of property; and some accused
the President of bias and of laxity in repressing criminal
violence.

The last two years of Irigoyen's term were a difficult time. The
accidental prosperity of the later war years fallaciously outlasted
the war for a short time. Those who had made money went on
spending lavishly, confident in a continuance of their gains.
Argentine importing houses sent large orders for European goods.
Then came disillusionment. Exports diminished in volume and
in value. The prices of grain and of meat suffered disconcerting
oscillations and then went down, while the cost of production

remained at post-war level. There was a glut of imported goods, while more were on the way upon the high seas or already ordered in Europe. The importing houses could not meet their obligations. In the midst of the economic trouble, labour disturbances broke out again.

'When Dr Irigoyen took office in 1916', wrote the correspondent of *The Times* in Buenos Aires, 'Argentina was on the crest of war prosperity. Four years later exports had been blotted out in the post-war slump, the peso had dropped into an abyss, businesses were bankrupt and unemployment stalked the cities. Strikes multiplied, the leaders confiding in the sympathy of the President. But when at long last, after months of struggle, the whole work of the port of Buenos Aires remained paralysed, Dr Irigoyen took a resolution. "The strike will be over in 24 hours", he announced, and he utilized the strong arm of the military. The lesson was sharp, sanguinary, and successful, and when Dr Irigoyen went out of office a few months later his popularity had suffered no decline.'

The Constitution forbids immediate re-election of a President. Accordingly the radical leaders arranged that their candidate in 1922 should be Dr Marcelo Alvear, Ambassador in Paris, a genial and cultivated man of the world, bearing a historic name, who belonged to the moderate wing of the Radical Party. The new President, a man of fine presence, carried out with quiet dignity both the administrative business and the outward functions of his high office, an office enhanced in status by the international position acquired by Argentina during the war. That international position received signal acknowledgment in two official visits, that of the Italian Crown Prince and that of the Prince of Wales. The brilliant entertainment of these royal guests by Presi-

dent Alvear fully satisfied the national pride and the growing
sense of national greatness.

The six years' term, 1922–8, was a time of tranquillity and of
gradual recovery from the depression caused by the post-war fall
in prices, a time during which political and social theories were
of minor importance. The President's position was not quite easy.
A man of notable personality and not a vehement partisan, his
independent attitude displeased the advanced radicals. There was
much heart-burning among the Irigoyenistas or 'Personalistas'; for
attachment to the person of Dr Irigoyen was regarded as the test of
true radicalism. A coolness also showed itself between Executive
and Parliament. To the English mind it is strange to find the
President, who was assiduous in the daily performance of duty,
reproaching Congress for inactivity in legislation, particularly
concerning public works in aid of agriculture. The Executive
was active in giving aid to the farmer, and also concluded an
agreement with the railway companies that these companies
should colonise lands adjacent to their lines by the settlement of
working farmers on moderate-sized holdings with fixed tenure
and ultimate ownership. This agreement aimed at remedying in
part a defect or grievance which, as was pointed out in the previous
chapter, had been an obstacle to the peopling of the country,
namely the difficulty of acquiring moderate plots of land with
secure tenure.

The election of 1928 was a strange one. The candidature of
Dr Irigoyen was announced a week before the election, and was
everywhere received with acclamation. He made no speeches,
wrote no address, never appeared in public. He was returned by
an overwhelming majority on a very large poll, and re-entered
Government House an autocrat by the popular will, having

issued no programme, but expected by his supporters to initiate a prolific period of progress and constructive liberalism.

These hopes were not realised. Hipólito Irigoyen, when he took upon himself for the second time the heavy burden of presidential office, was an old man and shaken in health. After two years, in September 1930 he was obliged by a *coup d'état* to resign the Presidency and to give place to a Provisional Government. The causes which led up to that event and the event itself are too recent for historical treatment.

CHAPTER XXII

THE ARGENTINE PEOPLE

THIS book may conclude by repeating the remark with which it began, that this country is destined by nature to be the seat of a great civilisation, mainly European in character. That destiny has been in great part fulfilled and is in process of further fulfilment. It has in its favour the enthusiastic belief and pride in the country felt by every Argentine born and by thousands of Europeans who have made their homes in the country. The traveller, landing in Buenos Aires after twenty days at sea, hardly feels that he has left the Old World. The atmosphere—with a difference, it is true—is European: and it is an atmosphere of movement, of confidence, of alert intelligence.

According to the Argentine economist, Bunge, Argentina in the middle of the nineteenth century contained about a million inhabitants, with much mixture of Indian and negro blood, except in a governing class of European origin who governed with difficulty. Dr Bunge declares that in 1927 there were ten million inhabitants of pure European origin, including at least two million immigrants born in Europe, and less than half a million showing traces of Indian or negro blood. Nearly five million persons entered the country by sea between 1857 and 1913. Dr Bunge, after deducting emigrants, reckons that 3,371,000 immigrants made their homes in the country during that time. Most of these came from Italy and Spain, people in great part akin to the Spanish creole, speaking similar languages and easily assimilated. Their children, many of them born of

15-2

Argentine mothers, are enthusiastic Argentines, true sons of the soil, heirs of the tradition which is represented by the statue of San Martín and by the anniversary celebrations of May 25 and July 9.

The monuments presented to the Argentine nation by the various 'colonies' of foreign nations to celebrate the centenary of independence in 1910 symbolise the contribution made by each of these groups to the growth and character of the community. For even the least numerous groups have contributed something, not only to material advance but also to the character and habits of the people. For example, the introduction of football, now universally popular even in the remotest villages, has not only provided wholesome physical training, but has done much to accustom the young citizen to habits of fair play, voluntary discipline in co-operation and good humour in defeat. Again, the Boy Scout movement has taken root, holding up a high standard of honour, truthfulness and conduct.

North American influence demands mention, since the Argentine Constitution is derived thence, although modified in use by French theory and by native methods of action which are Spanish rather than French or Anglo-Saxon in character. The 'colony' from the United States—a country occupied until recent years in the development of her own resources—is naturally recent and not numerous. But the influence of North American character and methods is visible and is growing. Conditions during and after the war brought about greatly increasing commerce with the United States, and increasing investment of North American capital in Argentina—matters which inevitably exercise a social and cultural effect; and this influence is fostered by the warm welcome given to Argentines in the United States, by scholarships granted to Argentines in United States Universities, by scientific and educational missions to Argentina, and by the various activities of the Pan-American Union, which has its headquarters in Washington. In addition to the Pan-American Congress which meets every fourth year, there are frequent Pan-American or Inter-American Conferences on matters of common interest, such as finance, transport, hygiene, education. There has been in the past some hesitation in Argentina concerning full participation in the movement which takes form in the gathering of these various assemblies. But the trend of events favours in-timate and cordial relations with all the peoples of both Ameri-can continents. Argentina still faces towards Europe, as she has always done: but she welcomes every wholesome and progressive outside influence.

Recent immigration from central Europe has not been suffici-ently numerous to affect in marked degree the evolution of the nation: most of these immigrants have been of a good physical type. On the other hand, arrivals from Syria have introduced an alien element which resists assimilation. But the authorities are fully alive to the dangers of indiscriminate immigration and have taken measures accordingly.

The complete elimination of negro blood is remarkable. The population of Argentina, as has been seen, was from the be-ginning and throughout mainly European in origin; but negro slavery prevailed at the period of emancipation and was only gradually extinguished. Battalions were formed of black men, most of whom perished in the War of Independence. To-day, in watching the troops march past on the national anniversary, one seems to be watching a European army: only here and there in the moving columns there appears some grizzled old *moreno* sergeant, whose weathered and humorous countenance recalls the bivouacs of Indian warfare.

And while the negro has disappeared, the Indian has been for the most part eliminated or absorbed. In the central provinces, from Buenos Aires to Tucumán and to the borders of Corrientes, there is little trace of Indian blood. Further north some descend-ants of the sedentary village Indians, who at the time of the con-quest cultivated the ground, still survive, speaking native tongues, and have left their mark on a half-caste peasantry in those remoter parts. Indeed, a certain native sentiment among many Argen-tines seeks to preserve this influence as part of the creole heritage and of Argentine culture. Dr Ricardo Rojas in his *History of Argentine Literature* gives expression to this sentiment.

Notwithstanding the cosmopolitan aspect of the capital—for the capital is not Argentina—there has grown up in the country a community generally of Latin character, where the prevailing influences have been Spanish, Italian and French, with contri-butions from other countries—the whole modified by local con-ditions and by the creole tradition. In a country which might support many times more than its present population, obviously the process is not complete: but that process is producing a distinctly Argentine national type.

Argentines acknowledge a particular indebtedness to French thought and culture. And this influence is assiduously cultivated both by the visits of eminent Frenchmen to Argentina and also by the hospitable and sympathetic activities of Frenchmen in France, particularly in the work of the Comité France-Amérique. But in the unstudied and the unpremeditated habits and views of life, the original unconscious Spanish influence counts for much, as must be already obvious to those who have read the preceding chapters. The student of Spanish history finds himself quite at home in tracing the course of Argentine history. A common language means much; and some familiarity with *cosas de España* will help to interpret Argentine affairs. Lovers of Spain will find in Argentina much of that which has attracted them in Spanish life.

Moreover, in the notable and prolific literary movement of recent years, French influence is not everywhere predominant. There is a considerable literature, particularly in the novel and the drama, which deals with the life of the country and has a distinctly creole or Argentine flavour not only in subject but also in character. So far as this literature owes anything to Europe, it is Spanish rather than French in inspiration. The most famous of Argentine novels, *La Gloria de Don Ramiro,* by Larreta, deals with life in Spain and in Peru in the time of Philip II; the book has won a recognised place in Spanish literature. And although most Argentine travellers turn to Paris rather than to Madrid, the Argentine novelist Manuel Gálvez in his book *El solar de la Raza* —'The Ancestral Home'—has expressed in moving language the feelings which stirred him on visiting the ancient cities of Spain. In Argentina, as in Spain and in all the Spanish-American lands, October 12th, the anniversary of Columbus' landing in America, is celebrated as a public holiday. And this *Fiesta de la Raza* or 'Racial Festival' has a real significance. The easy and natural intercourse between Argentina and the mother country is also kept alive by the frequent journeys to Argentina of Spanish professors and lecturers who address the people in their own tongue, and by the visits of dramatic companies from the Peninsula whose speech is the familiar Castilian.

It has been already pointed out that the Great War opened a new era for Argentina. So far, the country had acquiesced in economic dependence upon Europe. European immigration, Government loans raised in Europe, European capital for public enterprises, importation of almost all manufactured articles from abroad—these had been the accepted conditions of life. The country had been content to export raw materials and to import manufactured goods. The outbreak of war upset this economic equilibrium. The stream of European capital dried up; so also the stream of immigration. The supply of labour dropped after Italy joined the allies. Argentines were thrown upon their own resources: they had to manage their own finances and provide their own labour: they were obliged to find for themselves the things hitherto imported from Europe.

The shock was a wholesome one. It put a check upon profuse borrowing and profuse spending. It compelled the people to rely upon themselves, to restrict extravagance and to push forward the industrial development of their own resources in order to satisfy the needs hitherto supplied by importation. The economic re-covery which followed the first shock, the urgent demand of the allies for foodstuffs and raw materials, the increase in the value of exports and the consequent increase of wealth in the country, favoured this industrial movement. The whole effort of self-reliance, of domestic development, furthered national self-con-sciousness, national consolidation, the sense of national dignity.

The moral effect of the war in the political field has been already indicated. Argentina found herself the object of assiduous court-ship on the part of the belligerents on both sides. Her decision was awaited with anxiety as a matter of international concern. Her diplomatic dealings with Germany were signally successful.

She took her place distinctly among the family of nations. Moreover the contrast between her own domestic progress and the
destructive turmoil of the nations of the Old World gave fresh
significance to her confidence in her own character and destiny.

In Argentina, although the country is entirely dependent on
the products of the soil, the population, as in other parts of the
world or perhaps more than in other parts of the world, crowds
into the towns. Some estancieros make real homes for themselves
and their families among their fields, somewhat after the English
fashion, diversifying the face of the Pampa by the plantation of
woods and orchards, and surrounding themselves with all the
amenities of country life. Others inhabit their estancia houses
rather owing to business necessities than from choice or preference. But no general sentiment prevails that it is in any way in-
cumbent upon a landed proprietor to live upon his estates as a
matter of social obligation and as a service which may be reasonably expected of him by the community. The capital contains
over two million people, one-fifth of the whole population of the
country.

Some have observed in this urban life a materialistic tone, an
excessive esteem for wealth. Commercial intercourse with Europe
has not always brought the best that Europe can offer, and there is
perhaps a tendency to regard the modern conveniences and ad-
juncts of civilisation—things borrowed from Europe and the
United States—as constituting civilisation itself. 'Nowhere in
the world,' says Lord Bryce, speaking of Buenos Aires, 'does one
get a stronger impression of exuberant wealth and extravagance.'
But he finds an antidote to this spirit in the ideal of patriotism
which everywhere prevails among the citizens of the Argentine

Republic. Moreover this light-hearted lavishness is obviously confined to a class: and, as Lord Bryce himself points out, it is the result of the rapid enrichment of great landowners through the increase in value of land. This is an exceptional phase which must gradually be modified through the operation of the law which divides an inheritance among the children of the owner.

Again, it must be remembered that Buenos Aires is not Argentina: the whole nation is not to be judged by the costly luxury of Mar del Plata or by the large magnificence of palaces built by opulent Porteños. In the cities of the interior a very different atmosphere prevails. Moreover in the capital itself a more just view is gained by a visit to the University, to the National Library, to the Museums, to the booksellers' shops, or even by a perusal of the great daily newspapers, which devote more space than any English newspaper to thoughtful and scholarly articles on historical subjects. In view of the excellence of these journals, in view of the many publications on every branch of human activity and thought, in view of an abundant and varied literature, it cannot be said that modern Argentina neglects the things of the mind. Indeed, nothing is more remarkable in the recent growth of the country than the great expansion of University studies and the large sums assigned by the State to the maintenance of these studies.

To conclude, the prosperity of the country rests on the soundest and least precarious of all foundations, that of the soil itself. Argentina has had a picturesque past and offers a present of absorbing interest. And there is abundant reason for a firm belief in the capacity of the people to guide the country through the great future to which they look forward with just confidence.

CHIEF TOWNS AND RAILWAYS IN 1914

SUMMARY OF GOVERNMENTS OF THE RIVER PLATE

(a) ROYAL GOVERNORS, 1536–1776

FROM the beginning of settlement in Paraguay in 1536 down to 1776, the River Plate formed part of the Vice-royalty of Peru. From 1563—except for a short interval—the Audiencia of Charcas was the Supreme Tribunal of the whole region and also exercised administrative authority superior to that of the Governors. From 1536 to 1620, the capital of the riverine region was Asunción, but during the latter part of that period the royal Governor often resided in Buenos Aires. In 1620 Buenos Aires, Corrientes and Santa Fe were separated from Paraguay, were formed into the Government of Buenos Aires and were placed under a Governor nominated by the King and resident in Buenos Aires.

The interior region, containing the cities of Jujuy, Salta, Santiago del Estero, Tucumán, La Rioja and Córdoba, formed a separate Government, whose Governor, nominated by the King, resided at first in Santiago, afterwards in Córdoba. The region of Cuyo, comprising Mendoza, San Juan and San Luis, formed part of Chile down to 1776.

In 1776, all these provinces, together with Paraguay and Upper Peru, were united to form the Viceroyalty of the River Plate or of Buenos Aires.

(b) VICEROYS OF THE RIVER PLATE OR OF BUENOS AIRES

1. Pedro de Ceballos, 1776–8.
2. Juan José de Vertiz y Salcedo, 1778–84.
3. Nicolás del Campo, Marqués de Loreto, 1784–9.
4. Nicolás de Arredondo, 1789–95.
5. Pedro Melo de Portugal y Villena, 1795–7.

Melo died in office at Montevideo in 1797 and was buried in Buenos Aires. The Audiencia ruled for a fortnight and then handed over the Government to an officer holding subordinate command in the River Plate, who had been designated by the King to succeed in case of vacancy, viz.:

6. Antonio Olaguer Feliú, 1797–9.
7. Gabriel de Avilés y del Fierro, 1799–1801.
8. Joaquín de Pino, 1801–4.
9. Rafael Sobremonte, Marqués de Sobremonte, 1804–6.
10. Santiago Liniers, 1806–9.
11. Baltasar Hidalgo Cisneros y la Torre, July 1809–May 25, 1810.

(c) POST-REVOLUTION GOVERNMENTS

Governing Junta, May 25, 1810–September 23, 1811.
Triumvirates, September 1811–January 1814.
These were succeeded by the following six Supreme Directors:
Gervasio Posadas, January 1814–January 1815.
Carlos María de Alvear, January–April 1815.
José Rondeau, April 1815–April 1816.

Antonío González Balcarce, April–July 1816.

Juan Martín de Pueyrredón, 1816–19.

José Rondeau, June 1819–February 1820.

From 1820 to 1824 the United Provinces had no national Government. The Constitutional Congress, which met in Buenos Aires in December 1824 and sat until August 1827, assumed in some degree the functions of a national Government and nomin-ated, as first President of the Republic,

Bernardino de Rivadavia, February 1826–July 1827.

A National Convention, which assembled in September 1828 at Santa Fe, entrusted the conduct of War and of Foreign Affairs to the Governor of the Province of Buenos Aires,

Manuel Dorrego, August 1827–December 1828.

Juan Lavalle, December 1828–August 1829.

In his brief and precarious tenure of the Government, Lavalle made some attempt to represent the nation.

Juan Manuel Rosas, Governor of Buenos Aires, 1829–32.

Rosas received the charge of Foreign Affairs in 1831 from the Littoral Provinces and, after the defeat and capture of Paz, from the other provinces also. The same charge was undertaken by the following, who were Governors of Buenos Aires:

Juan Ramón Balcarce, December 1832–November 1833.

Juan J. Viamonte (Governor *ad interim*), November 1833–October 1834.

Manuel V. de Maza (Governor *ad interim*), October 1834–April 1835.

Juan Manuel de Rosas, April 1835–February 1852.

(d) CONSTITUTIONAL PRESIDENTS OF THE ARGENTINE CONFEDERATION

Justo José Urquiza, 1854–60.

Santiago Derqui, 1860–2.

Bartolomé Mitre, 1862–8.

Domingo Faustino Sarmiento, 1868–74.

Nicolás Avellaneda, 1874–80.

Julio Argentino Roca, 1880–6.

Miguel Juárez Celman, 1886–90.

Carlos Pellegrini, 1890–2.

Luis Saenz Peña, 1892–5.

José Evaristo Uriburu, 1895–8.

Julio Argentino Roca, 1898–1904.

Manuel Quintana, 1904–6.

Figueroa Alcorta, 1906–10.

Roque Saenz Peña, 1910–13.

Victorino de la Plaza, 1913–16.

Hipólito Irigoyen, 1916–22.

Marcelo T. de Alvear, 1922–8.

Hipólito Irigoyen, 1928–30.

Provisional Government, 1930.

DECLARATION OF INDEPENDENCE
TRANSLATION

'WE, the representatives of the United Provinces in South America, being assembled in General Congress; invoking the Eternal who governs the Universe, in the name and with the authority of the peoples (*pueblos*) which we represent; asserting to Heaven, to all the nations and inhabitants of the globe the justice which guides our votes; do declare solemnly in the face of the world that it is the unanimous and undoubted will of these Provinces to break the forcible bonds (*los violentos vínculos*) which linked them to the sovereigns of Spain; to recover the rights of which they were deprived and to invest themselves with the lofty character of a nation free and independent of the King Ferdinand VII, of his successors, of the mother country and of any other foreign domination; accordingly these Provinces now possess *de facto* and *de jure* full and ample power to shape for themselves the constitutional forms which justice may demand and which their present circumstances require. All and every one of these Provinces thus publish, declare and ratify the fact, undertaking, through us their representatives, that they will accomplish and sustain this their determination under the security and the guarantee of their lives, their property and their reputation. Let this Act be communicated to all whom it may concern in order that it may be publicly known and that due respect be paid to the nations of the world; and let a manifesto be issued in order to set forth the grave and fundamental reasons which are the basis of this "solemn declaration".'

Twenty-eight signatures follow. There were no deputies from the Banda Oriental, Santa Fe, Corrientes and Entre Ríos.

OUTLINE OF THE CONSTITUTION OF THE ARGENTINE NATION

THE written Constitution of the Argentine Confederation is an admirably clear document. It is divided into three parts, with the following headings:

1. Declarations, Rights and Guarantees.
2. The Authorities of the Nation.
3. The Judiciary.

The Third Part need not here be examined. The First Part, after declaring that the form of Government is Representative, Republican, Federal and that the Federal Government supports the Catholic Apostolic Roman religion, goes on to define briefly the relations between the Federal Government and the provinces; the relations of the provinces with one another; the rights and duties of citizens; the rights of resident foreigners, who are treated with great liberality; and the conditions of naturalisation.

The Second Part, headed 'The Authorities of the Nation', contains the working provisions which are the gist of the document and demand brief analysis. It is divided into two sections: (*a*) the Legislature, (*b*) the Executive Power, that is to say the President.

The Chamber of Deputies or Lower House consists of 158 members. These are elected by direct universal suffrage for a term of four years, and are re-eligible. Every two years an election is held for the renewal of half the Chamber. Thus every Deputy is irremoveable for four years. The Chamber is never dissolved, but has a continuous life, although half of the members retire or offer themselves for re-election every two years.

The Senate or Upper House contains thirty members, that is to say two Senators from each province, elected by the provincial Legislatures, and two from the federal capital, who are elected by a body of electors. Every Senator holds his seat for nine years, and is re-eligible; but an election is held every three years for the renewal of one-third of the Senate. Thus every Senator is irremoveable for nine years. The Chamber is never dissolved, but every three years one-third of the members retire or offer themselves for re-election.

The President and Vice-President of the Nation must belong to the Roman Catholic Church. They are elected at the same time for a period of six years and cannot be re-elected except after an interval of six years. They are appointed by indirect election in the following manner. In every province and also in the capital a Junta of Electors is chosen by universal suffrage, the number of electors in every province being double the number of Deputies and Senators who represent that province. The President and Vice-President are chosen by these electors by means of signed voting papers.

The President, who holds the Executive Power of the Nation, nominates the eight Ministers who constitute his Cabinet.

Thus it will be seen that the President, the Vice-President, every Senator and every Deputy hold their posts for a fixed number of years. The Senate and the Chamber of Deputies are never dissolved, so that there is no such thing as a general election for Parliament, although there are frequent partial elections.

There is a cumbrous method theoretically provided by the Constitution for the removal of a President by means of impeachment, the House of Deputies acting as accuser and the Senate acting as Tribunal. In such a case the President of the Supreme Federal Court is to preside in the Senate, while that body is acting as judge. But this theoretical provision can hardly be regarded as a working part of the Constitution. The office of President is far the most powerful part of the Government, and is not likely to provoke such vehement and united opposition in the Congress as to lead to impeachment. Thus, as was pointed out in the footnote on p. 201, the Constitution provides no really practicable means of peacefully putting an end to an unsatis-factory administration.

The clause concerning intervention runs thus: 'The federal Government may intervene in the territory of the provinces in order to guarantee the republican form of government or repel foreign invasion; and—upon request from the constituted authorities of a province—in order to support or restore these, if they should have been deposed by sedition or by invasion from another province'.

The last clause of the Constitution runs thus: 'The Provincial Governors are agents of the federal Government in order to carry out the Constitution and the Laws of the Nation'.

Since the capital, with its immediate surroundings, was formed into a Federal District in 1880, it was necessary to make special provision for the government of the capital. This was done by means of 'The Organic Municipal Law for the Capital', a law which may be regarded as complementary to the National Constitution.

APPENDIX IV

THE FALKLAND ISLANDS

(See pages 36 and 143)

EARLY in the year 1811, Montevideo being the only part of the River Plate still under Spanish authority, the royal Governor of Montevideo withdrew 'the remaining part of the detachment of the Falkland Islands'. During the previous five-and-thirty years whalers and seal-fishers of various nations had visited the group, undeterred by the existence, on one spot in the islands, of the small Spanish settlement of Soledad, which in 1784 had eighty-two inhabitants, including twenty-eight convicts. A Spanish ship sometimes cruised among the islands and warned off the interlopers, who retired for a time. In 1787 three English ships were thus warned. Six years later a Spanish brig-of-war cruising among the islands found seven American ships and one French. During the years of war with Great Britain (1796–1802 and 1804–8) foreign ships among the islands can have suffered little disturbance; and later American claims suggest that Americans, who were the most numerous and active among these visitors, already regarded their fishing and seal-hunting as legitimate enterprise. After the abandonment by Spain in 1811, many foreign ships resorted to the islands to kill seals on the coasts and to provide themselves with water and fresh meat, hunting the cattle descended from those introduced by the Spaniards.

In November, 1820—the 'terrible year', when the United Provinces were in a state of dissolution—an Argentine armed vessel arrived commanded by one Jewitt, who found about thirty American and British ships—or fifty, according to one account—warned them that their fishing was illegal, hoisted and saluted the Argentine flag, and sailed away. The Buenos Aires Government confirmed Jewitt's action.

Three years later the Buenos Aires Government appointed a Governor of the islands, and soon afterwards granted concessions of land, cattle and fisheries to two applicants. One of these, Louis Vernet by name, a Frenchman by birth, but reputed to be German owing to long residence in Hamburg, pushed forward his enterprise in spite of losses and failures. In 1828 he received from the Buenos Aires Government a larger concession, including a monopoly of the seal fisheries for twenty years on condition that he should establish a colony. This he did, recruiting colonists in Europe and North America. But finding that the principal part of his concession, the seal fishery, was threatened with extinction by the activities of American vessels, he applied for a war-ship. The Buenos Aires Government, distracted by civil strife, was unable to accede: but on June 10, 1829, during the brief and precarious government of Lavalle, his deputy Rodríguez published an edict which affirmed Argentine sovereignty over the Falklands through inheritance from Spain and announced the intention of appointing a civil and military Governor. That post was conferred on Vernet, and munitions were sent to him. In November, Woodbine Parish, British Chargé d'Affaires in Buenos Aires, under instructions from his Government, protested against the edict, declaring that the islands belonged to Great Britain. His note of protest was acknowledged, but never received a reply.

Vernet, now endowed with authority, warned American ships against fishing and seal-hunting. His warnings were dis-

regarded; and in July and August 1831, he seized three American vessels, *Harriet*, *Breakwater* and *Superior*, placing the captains
and crews under arrest. The *Breakwater* escaped; Vernet concluded a contract with his prisoner the captain of the *Superior*,
that the latter should sail to the Pacific to fish for seals, on Vernet's
account if the *Superior* should be condemned by the Buenos
Aires courts, on the owners' account if she should not be condemned. Vernet afterwards declared that this was a free contract
and denied the charge of 'operating on the fears' of his prisoners
and of using 'his military and civil powers to extort a written
obligation' of endeavouring 'to seduce American seamen from
their flag...by the promise of extravagant wages'. But Vernet,
by his own showing, used his official authority in order to send
an American ship, arrested in the name of the Government, upon
a private venture for his own profit. In his memorial to the
Government, a very able document, he writes, 'The title of
Governor, which relates to public business, did not divest me of
that of Director of the Colony, which is relative to my private
and mercantile undertaking. I could legally perform private acts
of commerce, for the benefit of my colony'. To the charge that he
only arrested American ships and took no notice of a British ship
which was equally trespassing, Vernet gave the not very convincing reply that the British ship was fishing outside his jurisdiction: it is difficult to avoid the inference that Vernet wished
to stand well with the British in case of certain eventualities. It
was unfortunate for the dignity and the claims of the United
Provinces that the Argentine Governor was a cosmopolitan immigrant, a man of energy and capacity, it is true, but one whose
object was to make his fortune rather than to uphold the credit of
the Argentine nation. It was a greater misfortune that, during the

greater part of the troublous years 1820–31, the United Provinces had no national Government and no organised Foreign Office, although the frequently changing Governments of Buenos Aires conducted Foreign Affairs, partly by prescription, partly by consent.

The *Superior* having been dispatched on her sealing expedition, the *Harriet* arrived at Buenos Aires in November 1831 as a prize, with Vernet on board. Davison, the American captain of the *Harriet*, and Vernet each had a story to tell. Rosas was now in power and in charge of Foreign Affairs. The United States Chargé d'Affaires in Buenos Aires had died five months earlier: the consul, George Washington Slacum, a man without tact or diplomatic experience, assumed his functions and in the course of an intemperate correspondence with Anchorena, Rosas' Minister, asserted the 'undoubted right' of the citizens of the United States to the use of the fisheries. Anchorena denied this right and pointed out that Slacum had no diplomatic character.

Captain Duncan of the U.S.S. *Lexington* now intervened, demanding that 'Louis Vernet, having been guilty of piracy and robbery, be delivered up to the United States to be tried or that he be arrested and punished by the laws of Buenos Aires'. This was not done: Duncan sailed to the Falklands, spiked the guns, burnt the powder, sacked the dwellings, seized some seal skins, arrested most of the inhabitants, handcuffed seven of them and carried them prisoners to Buenos Aires.

In June 1832 Francis Baylies reached Buenos Aires as United States Chargé d'Affaires. In notes presented to the Buenos Aires Government he accused Vernet of robbery and violence, asserted the right of Americans to the fisheries, demanded reparation and indemnity for the seizure and—as he alleged—the pillage of the *Harriet* and disputed the claim that the United Provinces had inherited from Spain the sovereignty of the Falklands. Failing to get satisfaction, he asked for his passports, but was persuaded to meet Maza, Anchorena's successor, in conference. The conference led to nothing and Baylies departed in September 1832.[1]

Meantime no reply had been given to Parish's protest against the decree of June 10, 1829. In January 1833 H.M.S. *Clio* appeared off Port Louis (formerly Soledad). The Governor, Vernet's successor or deputy, had just been murdered in a mutiny. The Argentine schooner *Sarandí* which had brought him was anchored in the roads. Onslow, captain of the *Clio*, requested Pinedo, captain of the *Sarandí*, to lower the Argentine flag on shore, announcing that he had come to take possession in the name of His Britannic Majesty. Upon Pinedo's refusal, Onslow landed a party, which struck the Argentine flag and hoisted the British flag. This action was ultimately followed by a formal occupation by a naval detachment.

Wellington took the view that the British Government had no clear title to the *whole* of the islands. But he thought the old Spanish claim no better than the British. Sovereignty, he felt, had not been determined; so he wished to prevent settlement either by Great Britain or from Buenos Aires.[2] John Backhouse, the Permanent Under-Secretary for Foreign Affairs, considered that 'whatever right we possessed then (in 1774) we have still'. In other words he claimed that our abandonment of the islands did not abrogate the British claim to that part which she had then held (i.e. Port Egmont). Other opinions on the British side seem to have been more definite as to the British claims over the islands as a whole.

[1] The whole correspondence is given in *Brit. and For. State Papers*, 1832–3, vol. xx, pp. 311–441.

[2] *Despatches, Correspondence and Memoranda of the Duke of Wellington*, London, 1877, vol. vi, pp. 41 and 48–9.

In the end there was an exchange of notes between Don Manuel Moreno, the Argentine Minister in London, and Lord Palmerston,[1] the Foreign Secretary. The former emphasised the points of prior discovery by Spain and France, effective Spanish occupation during 1764–74, and the Argentine claim to inherit the rights of Spain. Palmerston did not reply in detail but rested his case on the ground that 'the British Government would not permit any other State to exercise a right as derived from Spain, which Great Britain had denied to Spain herself'. In the end the islands remained in British occupation.

The demands repeatedly presented by the Argentine Government to the Government at Washington for reparation and indemnity for the *Lexington* raid were equally ineffectual. In December 1841 Webster, as Secretary of State, informed the Argentine Government that he could not concede their demands so long as their claim to jurisdiction over the Falkland Isles was contested by another power. In 1885 President Cleveland in his message to Congress spoke of 'the action of the commander of the sloop of war *Lexington* in breaking up a piratical colony on those islands in 1831', and in the following year Bayard as Secretary of State, replying to Vicente G. Quesada, Argentine Minister in Washington, repeated the substance of Webster's argument and added that, even if it could be shown that the Argentine Government possessed sovereignty over the islands, there were ample grounds on which Duncan's conduct could be defended. The Argentine view is that there is ground for both claims, on Great Britain and on the United States.

---

[1] *Brit. and For. State Papers*, 1833–4, vol. XXII, pp. 1366–94. The question of the 'Secret Promise' of 1771 was emphasised by Moreno and strongly denied by Palmerston. This need not be discussed here, as it is mentioned on p. 36.

INDEX

For EU product safety concerns, contact us at Calle de José Abascal, 56–1°,
28003 Madrid, Spain or eugpsr@cambridge.org.

www.ingramcontent.com/pod-product-compliance
Ingram Content Group UK Ltd.
Pitfield, Milton Keynes, MK11 3LW, UK
UKHW010049140625
459647UK00012BB/1712

* 9 7 8 1 1 0 7 4 5 5 6 1 0 *